Perkin Warbeck's Notebook

Perkin Warbeck's Notebook

Or, Redeeming Jacob—A Parson's Tale

Duke T. Gray

RESOURCE *Publications* · Eugene, Oregon

PERKIN WARBECK'S NOTEBOOK
Or, Redeeming Jacob—A Parson's Tale

Copyright © 2022 Duke T. Gray. All rights reserved. Except for brief quotations in critical publications or reviews, no part of this book may be reproduced in any manner without prior written permission from the publisher. Write: Permissions, Wipf and Stock Publishers, 199 W. 8th Ave., Suite 3, Eugene, OR 97401.

Resource Publications
An Imprint of Wipf and Stock Publishers
199 W. 8th Ave., Suite 3
Eugene, OR 97401

www.wipfandstock.com

PAPERBACK ISBN: 978-1-6667-3741-7
HARDCOVER ISBN: 978-1-6667-9683-4
EBOOK ISBN: 978-1-6667-9684-1

11/03/22

Scripture quotations are taken from the New Revised Standard Version Bible, copyright © 1989 the Division of Christian Education of the National Council of the Churches of Christ in the United States of America. Used by permission. All rights reserved.

Prayerbook quotations are from the Book of Common Prayer (*BCP*), 1979

*For the beloved next generations
who will shape the world to come:*
Ted, Julia, Arthur, Cynthia,
Eleana, Lillian, Emalyn, Thomas, Aaric

And especially for:
Gloria, encouraging cheerleader,
and spiritual mother to thousands.

Grateful thanks to Maria Klatecki for serving
as Personal Secretary during the
publication process.

With grateful thanks to:
Joe Bassett, Scott Axford, and Kelly Babson
for their invaluable comments as advance readers
of the first draft, enabling the necessary rewrite.

Contents

Preface | ix
Introduction | xi
Warning | xiii

Part One: Seedtime
One	How Old Is Ann? | 3
Two	Formation | 13
Three	Assertion | 39
Four	Confusion | 66
Five	Conversion | 83

Part Two: Harvest
Six	Darkness | 113
Seven	Forgiveness | 149
Eight	Blessing | 177
Nine	Perkin Revisited | 208

Postscript | 239
About the Author | 241

Preface

The unexamined life is not worth living...
—SOCRATES, *according to Plato's Apology*

THIS IS A BOOK about growing up. More than that, it is a book about growing, which does not necessarily follow. Some grow in wisdom; some grow in foolishness. Some only grow old, without much else.

The story it tells touches three centuries: the 19th, the 20th, and the 21st. All this is an extended prayer of confession, with the hope that you might find a blessing here to cheer your journey through this mortal life.

This is a personal narrative about growing in faith, but it is not only for Christians. This is for anyone seeking to make sense out of being human in a confused society.

This is about spiritual struggle, whatever your faith or lack of it. It is about believing—what you believe and what you do not; what you believe now and what you come to believe later.

This is a parson's tale, but it is not only for pastors. Your path in life may be that of a soccer mom or a senator, a chef or a college professor, a plumber or a basketball coach. If you have issues, either you master them, or they will enslave you.

If the *unexamined life* is not worth living, as said Socrates, then what about the *examined life*? Where does that lead?

At his trial before Pontius Pilate, Jesus said that he *came into the world to testify to the truth*. In reply, Pilate asked him (*John 18:38*), "*What is truth?*"

Truth is the first casualty in a culture war. If you believe in nothing, you'll fall for anything. And if everything is permitted, then nothing is true.

—*Duke T. Gray*

Names are changed to protect the innocent

Introduction

Thus says the Lord, he who created you, O Jacob, he who formed you, O Israel: Do not fear, for I have redeemed you; I have called you by name, you are mine.

—ISAIAH 43:1

THE REDEEMING OF JACOB was a long process. It occupies more than eight chapters in the *Book of Genesis*. Jacob was a tough customer. Noah, Abraham, and Mary, the mother of our Lord, each responded readily to the summons of God. So did many others in scripture.

But not Jacob. He was bullheaded and devious. It took an all night wrestling match with God to bring him around. As a result, his hip was put out of joint as a perpetual reminder.

Jacob has been a template for my own life. More important than my personal narrative, he is a template for modern culture. We live in a world deeply in need of renewal, revival, and redemption. It will not be easy.

Some 15 years ago Joe Bassett invited me to lunch at the Stockyard Restaurant in Brighton. He suggested I write a book. So I wrote this. Or better, as the drama unfolded, it wrote itself. What began as a family saga quickly became an adventure story of promise and peril, darkness and threat, survival and blessing. Along the way it becomes a conversion testimony about the power of God to intervene and to save.

Introduction

This is a chronicle about growing up in twentieth century America. The tale begins with the colorful character of Perkin Warbeck, born in 1866. His specter remains a hidden but potent presence throughout the substrata of the entire work until he emerges from the shadows once again in the final chapter. In this way, what follows spans 150 years and touches three centuries.

My calling as a pastor (and his) unfolds with struggles over things that matter and things that don't, with some questions answered but just as often not. It all takes place at the intersection of faith and culture, piety and politics, personal formation and pressures to conform.

The structure of the book begins with family roots and the forces that shape us. It moves forward in time from then to now. At the end, Chapter 9 returns to revisit and re—examine those beginnings and values from Chapters 1 to 3 that provided both personal development and cultural formation in the first place. In between there are many turns in the road, as with any of our lives.

The twentieth century was a time of unspeakable evil and unprecedented promise. Promise derives from either destiny or fantasy. It can drive us to fulfill a great future, or it can be the offal of blissful speculation and vain imagination. The 1920's and more especially the 1960's were decades of unbridled optimism where it seemed that everything was permitted and anything was possible. Neither ended well.

As we grow into our life's work and calling, we face false starts, uncertain pathways, unfounded hope and, too often, the pain of betrayal. My life has been a pilgrimage with many adventures, missteps, heartaches, and victories. I have seen a lot over the years—some of it edifying, some of it terrifying, some of it mortifying, some of it gratifying. Life has much to lure us or disappoint us, derail us or exalt us.

Sometimes we are cast into the pit by the malice of others. In some cases we fall into the pit by walking in darkness. Then there are times when we stumble into the pit by our own bad choices. I have known all three. Yet the Lord has used these things to bless me. Take this as a message of hope, whatever your circumstances.

We each have a tale to tell. I encourage you to recount yours. It has taken me a lifetime to ponder where my own journey has led—and I am not done yet. We are never too old to learn something new.

—Duke T. Gray,
Easter season 2019

Warning

If you want to grow, be wary and beware. Consider this:

*Be sober, be watchful. Your adversary the devil
prowls around like a roaring lion, seeking someone
to devour. Resist him, firm in your faith.*
—*I PETER 5:8–9a—BCP translation,
Office of Compline, page 132*

Part One

Seedtime

The kingdom of God is as if someone would scatter seed on the ground, and the seed would sprout and grow, he does not know how.

MARK 4:26–27

One

How Old Is Ann?

The Sphinx had a riddle, and the monster devoured all who could not answer it. Only Oedipus was successful. As a result, the Sphinx committed suicide.

Newark, New Jersey, 1903

ON APRIL 21, 1903, the following riddle appeared in the Tuesday edition of the *Newark Evening News*:

> Mary is 24.
> Mary is twice as old as Ann was
>   when Mary was as old as Ann is now.
> How old is Ann?

The readers went wild. No one seemed able to answer this teasing question. As the conundrum spread, more and more people were baffled. The pandemonium went on for months. People demanded an answer to this confounding enigma. Some said it was a trick. Some said it was a hoax—that it had no answer. More than that, they demanded to know who had perpetrated such a vexing question.

Finally the culprit was exposed. It was none other than an editor for the paper itself: *Perkin Warbeck*. He was both vilified and idolized. Pressmen who had put the edition together had spent the entire night in a fruitless effort to solve this inscrutable puzzle. Exasperated, they plastered signs all over the newspaper office the next morning aimed at the author, saying: *Put him out . . .* and, *Hang him . . .*

The controversy quieted down for a while until other papers around the country picked it up, and the entire nation became enthralled. The Philadelphia *North American* devoted an editorial page to it and received 18,000 letters to the editor within the next two weeks. Then it moved to their front page. The whole nation seemed in a frenzy. Papers in Chicago, St. Louis, San Francisco, and elsewhere continued the drumbeat until the *Newark Evening News* published an exposé more than six months later in its Sunday edition of November 15.

[CAP] *A summary of Perkin Warbeck's sensational conundrum* [/CAP]

Letters to the editors of various papers ranged from their own humor to fury over being duped. Answers given stretched from *She ain't born yet* to giving Ann the fanciful and improbable age of 99 years and six months.

One paper ran a feature article called *The Five Ages of Ann Rival the Seven Ages of Man*. All this notoriety served to catapult Perkin into the public spotlight and win him a place as President of the *American Press Humorists' Association* in 1905.

The same year he became editor of *Judge*, a celebrated New York humor magazine, and a year later he became editor of its companion publication, *Leslie's Weekly*. Then in 1907 he became President of the *Judge Company*.

During his time at *Judge*, Perkin signed on with the *J. B. Pond Lyceum Bureau* of New York as a public lecturer. His promotional brochure listed such available subjects as *An Evening at The North Pole*, *In Funny Old New York*, and others, describing his presentation as *refined and high—class humor, with a delightful personality that gives a promise of a notable platform success*. His brochure also provides the following disclosure: *Hiring committees need not hesitate in making a selection for fear they will not choose my best lecture, for they are all the same lecture. I only change the titles to please the public . . .*

Perkin Warbeck in 1905 as *Editor of* Judge *magazine, a popular and celebrated humor weekly.*

Riddles and humor, however, were not to become his larger calling. As he moved on in life, he increasingly saw himself as a social reformer and champion of the downtrodden and oppressed. In 1908, he left *Judge* to purchase a controlling interest in the *Scranton Morning Tribune*. There, he began to engage circumstances that were decidedly unfunny, and his life took on a new direction.

Where did this colorful character come from, and how did he get to this notable position?

Harpers Ferry, West Virginia, 1870

Perkin Warbeck was born Robert Duke Towne in Warren, Ohio, in 1866. He soon was orphaned at the age of four when his mother died. Following her death, Perkin was sent to live with his mother's brother at the family homestead in Harpers Ferry, West Virginia, where she had grown up.

Perkin's father, mother, and uncle had all been swayed by the abolitionist movement and Horace Greeley's *Tribune*. As a result, his Uncle Robert had freed his slaves seven years before Abraham Lincoln's *Emancipation Proclamation*.

It is not clear whether the activities of John Brown and his party at Harpers Ferry had played any part in his uncle's action, but Perkin, along with his brother Frank, were brought up in what was clearly an unconventional environment for its place and time. His uncle had given his former slaves the option to remain in their cabins on the farm, rent free, and work for wages. Many did, and as a child, Perkin grew up with the children of these former slaves as his playmates and with their parents as his mentors.

However redeeming this new milieu might have been, not all was halcyon for the young orphan from Ohio, a footloose youngster in the 1870's South. When Perkin was fourteen, his uncle died. He missed him deeply, and began to discover that farm work was not his calling. His aunt gave him permission to find work in a neighboring town. He shortly moved on to join his brother Frank who had resettled in Baltimore. After a while, he was moved by fond memories of the stories his uncle had told him about the "glamour" city of Philadelphia, so he moved on again to find new opportunities there.

He started out as a general errand boy at the University of Pennsylvania medical school. Several of the doctors took note of him and offered him the opportunity to study medicine. He declined, with a strong sense that this was not his calling. He moved on through a series of odd jobs—furniture factory, tailor shop, grocery store—until the allure of the big city lost its charm. Its enthralling aura was replaced by poverty and anxiety, and it was time for something new.

He and another boy finally boarded a freight train as stowaways in a boxcar. Perkin ended up in Poughkeepsie, New York, for the next chapter in his young life.

Poughkeepsie, New York

Having mastered being a railway stowaway, Perkin found work in a Poughkeepsie flour mill. With a few coins in his pocket, he purchased his first book from his meager wage. It was *Progress and Poverty* by Henry George. He later recalled, *I didn't know much about "progress," but the word "poverty" made an instant hit.*

His spiritual curiosity also led him into a local church that seemed more promising than the hard line religion he had known in Harpers Ferry. This new contact provided a cordial community of hospitality and encouragement, which offered him a welcome relief from his labor at the mill. He was attentive and engaging, and people in the parish saw him as attractive and talented. It happened that one of the active members was the owner of the flour mill where Perkin worked. This businessman, along with the Pastor and other supporting parishioners, were impressed enough with young Perkin's gifts that they decided to sponsor him to study for the ministry. They provided the means to send him off to theological school at St. Lawrence University in upstate New York. This would launch Perkin on a new and unforeseen career in the world.

Today, theological seminary usually means a 3–4 year graduate degree following the completion of college, including field work and/or internships. In Perkin's time, the seminary he attended did not provide a degree. Upon graduation, he was granted a diploma. It is an elegant and impressive parchment, larger than any I would later receive. I keep it over my desk at home as a memento of a bygone era. It reads, in sprawling script:

> *The Faculty of the Theological School certify that*
> *Robert Duke Towne has completed the Course of Study*
> *and the Examinations prescribed by them; and that*
> *his character and deportment have been such as*
> *to warrant them in commending him to the church*
> *as worthy to enter the Christian Ministry.*
> *In witness whereof they award this Diploma: June 26, 1888.*

It is signed by the faculty and affixed with a ribbon and the seal of the university.

After graduation, he soon married and served churches in Sherman, New York; Marlborough, New Hampshire; and Lewiston, Maine. It was in Lewiston that his life would take another new and adventurous turn into uncharted waters, with great bravado and success.

Lewiston, Maine

Perkin served ten years in the parish ministry. After six years in Lewiston, the people of his church were so impressed with his preaching on social reform that they pooled their resources and bought him the local newspaper, *The Lewiston Sun*, with the exhortation that he *go out and preach to a larger congregation.*

This striking turn of events launched the editorial and publishing career that would dominate the rest of his life. However, it took him only a year to discover that he was in over his head in matters of administration, management, and corporation finance. So he sold his new paper and took an editorial position with the *Philadelphia Call* to learn the newspaper business from the ground up. From there, he moved to New Jersey to accept a position as editor of the *Burlington Enterprise*.

Moving On, and Moving Up

During this time, he had been developing his creative writing skills by submitting columns to various newspapers around the country. His name and popularity increased as he became a syndicated columnist avidly read by many.

In 1902 he became telegraph editor of the *Newark Evening News*, and his columns ran regularly there as well as in other papers far and wide. After the sensation of *How Old Is Ann?* new successes came rapidly—as editor of *Judge, Leslie's Weekly*, then President of the *Judge Company* itself.

While President of Judge, a contributing artist submitted some cartoon sketches of little monkeys. Perkin had been a staunch supporter of Theodore Roosevelt and suggested to the artist that they be turned into Teddy Bears. Perkin wrote the dialogue to go with them, and the *Teddy Bear* book was born. Teddy Roosevelt was riding high in the public limelight and *Johnny and the Teddy Bears* was published in 1907 as a children's book to catch the wave of the times.

Everything was moving upward with an inexorable force that spelled progress toward vistas undreamed of in Perkin's lowly beginnings. Life felt driven by a relentless power toward a destiny shining with promise. Or so it seemed.

Scranton, Pennsylvania

In 1908, Perkin resigned from the Judge Company and moved to Scranton, Pennsylvania, to purchase his own paper. The move to Scranton beckoned toward glory. It was there that a prophetic mantle began to replace the entertaining banter of the humorist. It also was there that the romantic glory began to unravel.

His first paper was the *Scranton Morning Tribune*. When he purchased the paper for $3000, it had a circulation of less than 5000. Theodore Roosevelt advised him to *do something for the coal miners in that region*. So Perkin began to publish articles and editorials that highlighted a variety of mine abuses. Within a year his paper made a giant leap in circulation and a move toward a solid financial foundation.

He used his newspaper as a platform to advocate for coal miners and for other average folk who reported sensational stories of leaving for work in the morning, only to arrive home in the evening to find that their house had disappeared into a pit when an abandoned coal mine had collapsed without warning to swallow it up.

In those years, coal was king in Pennsylvania, and Scranton was home to the anthracite industry. Perkin, the crusading newspaper publisher and social reformer, battled what he saw as the menacing threat of corporate coal mining interests. He perceived these forces to be ruthless toward the condition of coal miners and blind to the plight of ordinary citizens whose homes were in constant and unpredictable peril.

During his second year in Scranton, his *Tribune Publishing Company* purchased the *Scranton Republican*, a morning competitor, and then the *Scranton Truth*, an afternoon daily. Miners, merchants, and ordinary people now had both a morning and an evening paper which he saw as representing their interests. Perkin made his position clear throughout his editorial writing, a perspective no doubt shaped by both his pastoral career and his advocacy of Henry George's economics. Perkin declared:: *I believe in both capital and labor. They are the two legs, the two feet, the two arms and the two hands—and the one brain—by which civilization walks and works. Capitalism includes labor—IS labor.*

At the same time. he seemed not to be troubled by the possible thought that his corporate monopoly over the local newspapers could be viewed as a one—sided constraint on public expression. That was a day in which newspapers were virtually the only media. Radio was barely on the horizon and television was unheard of. The newspapers were it, and they were his.

It Began to Unravel

Perkin had been a delegate from Pennsylvania to the Republican National Convention in 1912. When the party split over Theodore Roosevelt's bid to run for President again, and renominated President William Howard Taft instead, Perkin became a founding operative in the formation of Teddy Roosevelt's *Progressive Party*, nicknamed the *Bull Moose Party*. When that endeavor came to naught, Perkin finally became a supporter of Woodrow Wilson and his vision of a new world order under the aegis of the League of Nations. Along the way, Perkin remained a steady advocate of Henry George and his Single Tax movement, designed to rescue all from poverty and usher in a new age of unparalleled prosperity.

In Scranton, Perkin made enemies as well as friends. Formidable powers and dark money were arrayed against him. Scranton saw a lot of strife between newspapers and banks, with remorseless mining interests in the shadows behind the lines. In 1913, hostile forces found a surreptitious way to take control of the Tribune Company. Perkin was forced out of his own paper. So he walked across the street with his entire workforce loyally following him, and started a new paper, the *Scranton Daily News*. It had an immediate success, as dramatic as the original turnaround of the *Tribune* five years before.

On the first page of the first edition of his new paper, Perkin published his mission statement:

*A good newspaper tells the news
as faithfully and truthfully as it can,
without fear and without favor,
and comments on it
with the best intelligence it can command.*

The Scranton Board of Trade began a new campaign with the slogan, *Watch Scranton Grow*, and growing it was, with enthusiasm and civic pride. The new *Daily News* was at the heart of this renascence, and the people of the city were ebullient with hope. Not only was the circulation of the paper growing, but local investors—ordinary people—were buying stock in it to support it.

The forces of darkness, however, do not surrender easily. Industrial powers that did not call Scranton home took no interest in the city's issues. They were bitterly opposed to this upstart newspaper crusader. In 1915, when the new *Daily News* was barely two years old, malignant adversaries again managed to find a way to move against the new paper with stealth, this time with an overnight coup. During the night an agent working on behalf of Perkin's enemies managed to acquire a controlling interest in the paper, and when the workers reported to the newsroom the next day, the paper was no longer there. Strangers were already in the office, and an edition was published with the death notice for the paper in a neat little box on page one.

It was all over for Perkin in Scranton.

In 1916 he began publishing his own magazine to be circulated as far and wide as interest would permit. He called it *The Areopagitica*, taking his title from the *Areopagus* in ancient Athens where the classic Greek philosophers and others would gather to debate the great ideas of the time. It advocated the Single Tax principles of Henry George, whose book he had purchased as a youngster in Poughkeepsie, along with other social and political issues.

Philadelphia, Pennsylvania

By 1918 Perkin had relocated to Philadelphia where he wrote for the Philadelphia *North American* and later for the Philadelphia *Public Ledger*. The Ledger was a daily paper that was part of the large *Curtis Publishing Company*, a dominant influence in American culture whose publications included the *Ladies' Home Journal*, the *Saturday Evening Post*, *Jack & Jill*, *Country Gentleman*, and others. Additional Curtis Publishing ventures later came to include the *Philadelphia Inquirer* and the *New York Evening Post* newspapers.

Perkin continued as a columnist with the Public Ledger until 1927, while in 1926 he became President of the *Gazette Publishing Company*, which circulated a variety of suburban weeklies. In 1928 he became Treasurer of the *Charles H. Ingersoll Dollar Pen Company* until his retirement. In 1929, he also served for a year as a Federal Receiver in northern New Jersey. He was active in various ventures during these years, but none matched the impact on the nation of his first splash in Newark or the glory days of contest and conflict in Scranton.

Perkin Warbeck embodied the American dream. He came from humble beginnings, worked hard and attained what were unthinkable heights for a child of such rude and unseemly origins. But not all good dreams end well. He rose like a bright shining star, but like a Roman Candle at a 4th of July fireworks, he burst forth in a flashing display of dazzling light only to fizzle out just as quickly as a burnt cinder of ash. He rose from poverty to fame and plenty, but descended into an indigent degradation.

Perkin Warbeck was my grandfather. I knew him only at the end of his life when I was a small child. He lived with my Aunt Marian, my mother's older sister, in a small apartment on the floor above us. I was in and out of their flat daily, as if it were our own. He and my aunt often indulged my childhood whims. I once took apart his old Smith Corona typewriter, strewing bolts and screws all over their living room floor. I was playing exploratory mechanic. We did manage to put it back together again, to everyone's relief.

Grandfather Perkin was placid though winsome in his declining years, but his final state was a sad and demeaning end. His life had displayed all the hopes and dreams that romantic expectation can garner, but also is a telling commentary on the darkness that ensues in the wake of romantic collapse. I knew him mostly as an invalid, confined to a large wing chair, unable to walk, afflicted with a urine bag on a tube from a hole in his stomach from failed prostate surgery, and surviving on only the barest subsistence from public welfare.

It was not nice. Yet he was a joy to me as a child, despite his debilitated state. I thank the Lord for the life he was given, and the life he passed along to me. Without him, I would not exist.

I remember the night he died. My mother wept. It was evening. I was 13. I had not faced death before. I crawled into my bed. He lay upstairs in the apartment above me until the undertakers came.

Two

Formation

*Now the man knew his wife Eve, and she conceived and bore
Cain, saying, "I have produced a man with the help of the Lord."*
—GENESIS 4:1

How It Starts

NONE OF US PLANS to be born. We arrive into this mortal life without a clue about what is going on or of the forces that have given us shape. We slowly wake up to the fact that we are here. Only later can we begin to ask questions about where and why. It all starts with conception by parents of whom we are oblivious, and over whose action we have no control. We are given shape and form by blood and genes, sounds and silence, the nurture of the aboriginal womb and finally we see daylight. After that, relationships, language, and cultural formation come into play.

Through it all, the Lord is at work. We are not without guidance. Cain had no idea where he came from or why. Circumstances early on led to conflict with his younger brother Abel. So the Lord said to Cain (*Genesis 4:6–7*):

> *"Why are you angry, and why has your countenance fallen? If you do well, will you not be accepted? And if you do not do well, sin is lurking at the door; its desire is for you, but you must master it."*

Sage advice—from the Lord himself. As we know, Cain did not do well, and that is a warning to us. God loved Cain. That is why he warned him. He saw trouble down the road. God likewise loves you too, as he also loves me. He warns us because he cares for us. Take heed.

There is a further fundamental fact in this: No one is born a Christian. Your parents may have been faithful church members for seven generations, but that does not count. You still are born of the flesh, a carnal creature spiritually unformed. Even if the hand of the Lord is upon you, you must grow into your calling if God is to have any claim on your life. You can always run the other way. Try running. See what happens.

Origins, 1892 and 1896

My father, John Gray, was born in 1892. He remembers seeing Queen Victoria in a parade during her final years. He would also tell me about the first electric streetcars in Glasgow and what a marvel they were as a replacement for the horse drawn trolley.

My mother, Bertha Towne, was born in 1896. Her childhood was very different. Yet both my parents were vivid story tellers. As a result, much of their childhood years seems almost like my own. I marvel at the fact that I carry within my own memory bank an oral history that touches three centuries.

There is an old psychological development theory bouncing around somewhere that says we inherit our calling in life from our mother, but inherit the manner in which we carry it out from our father.

I do not know how valid this theory is generally, but it certainly rings true for my own life. My mother was a pastor's daughter and a woman of the church. My earliest spiritual formation came at my mother's knee, listening to stories of scripture and faith. My father was a symphony musician and I grew up in the Greenroom of the *Academy of Music* in Philadelphia, a magnificent hall that replicates *La Scala* opera house in Milan. As a small child I had no idea what I might be doing in life. In the larger sweep of things, I too turned out to become a person of the church like my mother, but the manner in which I express it resembles a musician's attention to form as the foundation for content, although I am not a musician myself.

Glasgow, Scotland

My father was born in Hawick, Scotland, a small woolen mill town near the English border. That said, a primary fact of his identity was that he was *not English*. Don't ever confuse the English with the Scots. When Dad spoke the name of his birthplace, he would render it as a one syllable word vaguely similar to *Hawk*. But when he pronounced it, it sounded more like the clearing of your throat with a bad case of post–nasal drip when need to expectorate. By contrast, English friends I have met insisted on the crisp and clear two syllable pronunciation of *Hah—wicke*, which Dad would never have recognized, much less tolerated.

My Dad and me in the Greenroom at the Academy of Music—1954

When he was young the family moved to Glasgow, a grimy industrial city in what was then thought to be the poorest country in Europe. He would describe to me in detail, many times over as I was growing up, what it was like to survive in poverty. He would tell me these stories without much trace of outward bitterness, because he would couch his narrative against the background of American opportunity in which he would easily rejoice—as did so many immigrants to this country in the opening decades of the twentieth century.

But the bitterness was there, buried and hidden. He never wanted to go back, and he would never speak of "*the Auld Sod,*" or "the old country," outside the house. Like so many immigrants of that era, he wanted to pretend and prove that he was a 200% American. But his accent always gave him away. As soon as he would open his mouth, the inevitable Broad Scots dialect was there. For him, his origins were like a dark and shameful past, never to be spoken of in public. His purpose in relating them to me was more to serve as a warning than to be edifying, in hope that I would seek a new life as he did.

The Return

In 1949, after World War II, he did have the opportunity to go back and he didn't want to go. But it was inevitable that he should, because the State Department sponsored a British tour for the Philadelphia Orchestra as America's first cultural ambassador to war–torn Britain. He came back amazed at the English for their stubborn perseverance in recovery. He related an incident with communications that left him almost speechless. As the Orchestra was checking out of their hotel in London to go to Birmingham, he mentioned to the desk clerk a concern he had about his reservation at the new hotel where they were heading. The clerk said, *Well, I'll post them a letter and it will be taken care of.* "A letter?" he though to himself, "That will never get there before we do." The clerk put the letter into the morning mail. When they got to the new hotel in Birmingham later that same day, the letter had already been delivered in the afternoon mail and was waiting for them.

Those were the days before the internet. Britain had more than one mail delivery a day. We too had morning and afternoon delivery in the United States, but rarely did we expect an item to go from one city to another without taking an overnight.

The Orchestra played to rave reviews with sold out houses. A headline in the London Daily Mail for the music critic's review blazoned the message: *Philadelphia's Lesson in Orchestral Perfection.* Another review in the Birmingham Mail reads in part:

> *It is doubtful whether Birmingham has ever heard such orchestral playing as that of the Philadelphia Orchestra at the Town Hall last night. The most significant thing about it all was that the glorious tone and the unflagging exhilaration were not due, as might have been supposed to weight of numbers, but to each individual player, who gave unremittingly of his best. In other words it was the detail of each performance that was so remarkable . . . There must be tremendous discipline within its ranks . . .*

I remember Dad's comment that whenever there was a turnover in personnel and a new member joined the 'cello section, it would take up to two years for the newcomer to blend in with the precision ensemble playing and not stick out like a sore thumb. That spells *teamwork*.

This is a parable for the church, the Body of Christ on earth. The church is held to this same high standard of ensemble teamwork. The issue here is ego—the musician, the choir singer, the church member, even the pastor, who enjoys parading himself above others. St. Peter tells us this as we await the coming of the Lord *(II Peter 3:14b)*:

> *. . . strive to be found by him at peace, without spot or blemish . . .*

Sadly, too many churches fall short of this sublime expectation. For example, St. Paul had his hands full with the church at Corinth. He writes to them *(I Corinthians 1:10a,12–13a)*:

> *Now I appeal to you, brothers and sisters, by the grace of our Lord Jesus Christ, that all of you be in agreement and that there be no divisions among you . . . What I mean is that each of you says, "I belong to Paul," or "I belong to Apolos," or "I belong to Cephas," or "I belong to Christ." Has Christ been divided? Was Paul crucified for you?*

The Philadelphia Orchestra was at the top of the chart in reputation at the time, so they expected the effusive accolades, but were nonetheless elated to receive them. After all, anything can go wrong without warning to mar the performance, even by a top flight ensemble. What the musicians were not prepared for, however, was to open the newspaper and see that the same night they had played in London, five other local orchestras had also played to sold out houses: The London Symphony, the London Philharmonic, the Royal Philharmonic, the Philharmonia Orchestra, and the BBC Symphony. No city in America had such a lineup.

When they got to Glasgow, the demeanor of his report changed. His major comment was that when he went to the city park he found the same old tin cup on a chain at the water fountain that had been there when he left, 40 years earlier. The bitterness was clearly showing.

Grim, but Edifying

Dad's family tradition was that of the archetypical Scottish peasant—urban or rural—who spent his days laboring in the field or in the factory, but who would then spend his evenings reading Shakespeare. As an expression of this, when I was a youngster my father would often take me to the Philadelphia Museum of Art, just as his father had taken him to the art gallery in Glasgow.

The museum in Philadelphia had on display the Het Scheepje room from the early seventeenth century that had been imported from the Netherlands and reconstructed. That was always a major stop on our museum tours, because Dad said that in dimensions and layout it was an almost perfect replica of the flat in Glasgow where he had grown up—despite one major difference that was highly instructive: the room at the museum was part of a lavish townhouse owned by a wealthy Dutch ship captain, Dirk Dirick, who lived there in 1612. It was opulent, with a stylish decor of polished hard wood paneling along with an enormous fireplace whose mantel was finished with intricate porcelain tiles.

By contrast, my father's childhood home was a complete living space for a family of eight, all in one room. Two parents with six small children—five boys and a girl, each almost exactly two years apart in age—occupied a very small space. However, Dad identified with the room at the museum because of the fireplace on one wall and a sleeping bed built into another wall.

The entire apartment in Glasgow was smaller than the 16x24 foot size of the sea captain's room in Haarlem, Netherlands. On one wall at the family home was a fireplace for cooking and heat. There was barely room for a table and a few chairs. On the opposite wall was a sleeping alcove. The parents had a mattress on a shelf about waist high in the alcove, and underneath was a drawer where the children slept.

At night the drawer was pulled out and the six children slept head to toe to maximize space—three in one direction and three in the opposite, as in a can of sardines. In the daytime the drawer was pushed closed to make space to walk around the room, cook, and sit to eat. The Dutch room at the museum in Philadelphia seemed to him an uncanny reproduction of his childhood home, even despite the universe of difference between the wealthy decor of the one and the abject poverty of the other.

Hard Work

Dad's childhood day began early. He would rise up about 4:00 AM and make his way to the local dairy where he had a job delivering milk. The milk was placed into pint and quart tin cans, each with a large shoulder hoop attached. His task depended on needing to memorize the orders for each customer on the route—*the size*: pint or quart—*the product*: milk, cream, or buttermilk—and the number of items for each household. He would then arrange the cans in proper order with the hoops over his right shoulder. He would make his way down the street, stopping at each address with the correct cans in their prearranged sequence, there to slip the hoops gently down his right arm and off his fingertips to make the delivery. Then on his left arm, he would gather up the empties by their hoops to be returned to the dairy for washing. When work was over he would return home by six o'clock for breakfast, and then be off to school.

The diet was simple: oatmeal for breakfast, sometimes with orange marmalade and toast. Supper was mostly potatoes, sometimes with finnan haddie or other smoked fish. An occasional breakfast delicacy, if there was time on the weekend, was to make potato scones from a previous night's mashed potatoes.

There was little protein. The result was that he and all his family were short in stature. By contrast, I and my brother were each over six feet, and my sister nearly so. Many immigrant families from poor cultures show the same effect when their children, born here, grow up on an American diet.

The school day was long—until after four. There was a short time to play before supper, homework, and bed. Play usually meant kickball in the street. Since there was no money to buy a soccer ball, a ball was made from bunched up old newspapers taped or wired together and sometimes swatted with a tree branch when not kicked.

Each child had one pair of shoes, which were worn until they no longer fit. Then they were passed down to the next younger brother. Shoes were limited to October through April. The other five months it was bare feet only—in the house, on the street, and in school. You would plead with the weather to cooperate at the colder ends of the summer season. When the sole of a shoe wore a hole through to the street, it was patched by cutting a thick piece of cardboard to make an insole to spare you from the sidewalk and the snow. The weather in Scotland was not tropical.

Obligatory public school was required only through age 14. Dad always lamented that because of his April birthday, he was not permitted to complete the eighth grade by remaining in school until June. Why? Because he had to go to work to help support the family. Even so, he had managed to maintain a record of perfect attendance for his seven years and seven months, so the school awarded him a small thick book of 330 pages for his achievement. It was one of his prized possessions and I still keep it on my bookshelf as a memento.

The book is titled *The Romance of the Animal World*, by Edmund Selous—and subtitled *Interesting Descriptions of the Strange and Curious in Natural History*, published by Seeley and Company Limited, 38 Great Russell Street, London. Its binding is tattered and crumbling with age, but the faded bookplate in the front cover is still readable. It says: *U. C. F. Normal School, Glasgow—session 1904–1905, T. M. Morrison, MA, Rector. Advanced Department, Junior Class—Prize for Perfect Attendance, Seventh Consecutive Year*. His perfect attendance record was possible, despite the fact that Dad suffered an eye infection in his middle years and had his eyes bandaged closed and could not read. His brother led him by the hand each morning until the bandages came off and he could see once more. This was so that he could arrive in class in order to raise his hand for attendance when his name was called and then be led home again.

He never explained what medical help he had for this, but affording a doctor would have been a daunting challenge. He did speak of the time his father had ripped his arm on a rusty nail while painting a house and developed blood poisoning. His remedy was to apply an oatmeal poultice with nearly boiling water until the long red streaks on his arm went away.

Moonlighting

Dad always referred to his father, my Scots grandfather, as *"the auld mon."* *The auld mon* was a house painter by trade and worked a six day week from 7 AM to 7 PM. For his last three years in Scotland he added a moonlight job from 9 PM until midnight to earn extra money to emigrate the family to the United States.

His second job was playing 'cello in a vaudeville house orchestra. The vaudeville theatre had no greenroom to change clothes, so he came home from painting houses every day, scrubbed the paint out from underneath his fingernails, had supper, then put on a tuxedo and went to the theatre to play for the evening.

During this time, he also took on the task of teaching music to his children so that they might have a better life in America than painting houses. He would set up a music stand at the supper table and have one of the boys at his elbow playing his music lesson while he had his meal.

He taught the five brothers in turn, one each evening. For the strings, he taught them as a traditional quartet—two violins, viola, and 'cello. The string instruments were similar enough that he could teach them all. But the task for the youngest brother was more difficult. He taught him piano, but did not play the piano himself. So he wrote away to a correspondence school that sent him piano lessons in the mail, and learned enough to teach his son by keeping one week ahead of him for his own lessons.

These long days went on for three years until *the auld mon* had saved enough money for his own passage to the United States. Then he came to this country by himself for another three years in order to earn the higher American wages that would enable him to bring over the rest of the family those three years after.

Streets of Gold

The whole family arrived to join my grandfather in 1907 when Dad was 15. Unlike so many immigrants of the day who arrived at Ellis Island in New York, they arrived at the Port of Boston and settled in Cranston, Rhode Island. I never learned why.

Dad began his own musical career at age 12 in Scotland while he was still in school, where as a small child in short pants he took his father's place for those last three years playing 'cello in the vaudeville house orchestra.

The New World seemed brimming over with opportunity. My father and his brothers passed along a standard immigrant joke about the fellow who stepped off the boat and saw a blind man sitting on the street with a tin cup. Right next to him on the sidewalk was a gold coin. So the new arrival took pity on him because he could not see, and picked up the coin and dropped it into the blind man's cup. This was because he had heard that the streets in America were paved with gold, so he expected to find his own gold coin just around the corner.

At 15 Dad and his twin, my Uncle Alex, found their first jobs setting type in a printing shop. This required reading—and sometimes memorizing—the manuscript being set up for printing and then picking up the loose letters, scrambled in a box, with tweezers and placing them into the letterpress. This meant learning to spell backwards and to place the type as rapidly as possible if you wanted to keep your job. They quickly became proficient to survive.

Dad's first job in the printing shop paid a nickel an hour for a 60 hour week, which at $3 a week seemed like a handsome sum. But there was a hitch. The owner of the shop held back 50¢ a week *in escrow* as an incentive to stay on the job at his shop for a period of seven years, at the end of which time your accumulated escrow would be returned as a reward for being loyal. This seemed OK at first, until Dad found another printing shop down the street paying $4 a week. This led to another, and another, until after two years he had worked his way up to $7 a week, which certainly made the forfeit of the escrow worthwhile.

The Next Break

At age 17 Dad found his break into the music business. He interviewed with the Head Waiter at the Crown Hotel in Providence, RI, to play in a string trio at the hotel dining room for lunch and afternoon tea. He landed this job at $17 a week—so life at the printing shop was done. It also gave him the opportunity to begin playing in vaudeville orchestras in the evening after tea was over at the hotel. But the whole program began with a difficult stumbling block: He needed a tuxedo to start his job at the hotel, which he could not afford until he got paid. So he went down to a flea market on the Providence waterfront and purchased a used tuxedo for $5. All seemed well until he got home. Then he discovered that the suit had been custom tailored for the previous owner, and the label on the inside of the jacket named the Head Waiter at the hotel dining room who had just hired him as the one for whom the suit had been made. He swallowed his pride and wore the suit to work in fear and shame. The maitre d' never said a word, and Dad never knew whether his boss had actually recognized his old suit or not and perhaps had said nothing out of politeness.

This new career not only provided more money. It also was musical heaven. He was tired of playing popular music for vaudeville and wanted to play serious music. His musical companions at the hotel shared this desire, so they set about making their own trio transcriptions of entire Beethoven Symphonies and other major works to play at the hotel dining room. Life was very good, even though he had to continue playing vaudeville at night for the money since he was soon to be married at a young age and would have a family to support.

One customer who was impressed was a wealthy older man who lived at the hotel. He arranged for Dad to visit one morning, with room service for breakfast, so that they could talk about music at leisure. When the breakfast trolley arrived, Dad discovered that one of the items was a half grapefruit. He had never seen a grapefruit before and had no idea how to eat it. In the old country he had never seen fresh fruit. The only citrus he had ever known was orange marmalade. So he stumbled through this embarrassment, feeling like the uncouth barbarian peasant whose past he had tried to bury. This dark shadow would haunt his spirit for his entire life, a demonic message of shame and unworthiness, no matter what accomplishments he would in fact achieve.

He pressed on in the music industry, playing vaudeville and in summer pop orchestras on the Fall River Line ferry from Narragansett Pier to New York. On one occasion there was a small fire on board ship, so the orchestra was ordered to play without stopping to calm down the crowd. He said that he played *Alexander's Rag Time Band* until his thumbs were sore—and he had had enough of pop music.

He also hated bagpipes because they were always out of tune. He remembers his father (*the auld mon*) telling him once that "*Sandy Mac-Tavish cam o'er the oth'r night ta tak about music—an' he brought 'is pipes w' 'im—so I throo 'im oot th' hoose.*" Now a highlander might dismiss this as a typical lowlander bias, but I know better. *The auld mon* had a sharp ear, as did my father. The issue was not culture, but tuning. My Scots grandfather also told the story about once being given a ticket to attend an unusual concert where the entire ensemble was harps. If you have watched at any symphony concert, the harp player is constantly tuning and retuning her instrument, quietly, when she is not playing. (The same is true for the tympanist). Both the harp and the tympani are constantly going out of tune with every mild breeze that goes by. So *the auld mon* returned from the harp concert, dismayed, with the terse comment: *There wer' a hundred harps onstage, and every bloody one of th'm was out a' tune.*

The Big Step Up

Relief came soon. In 1926 Dad traveled to Philadelphia for the Sesquicentennial World's Fair. While there, he decided to look for work. He landed a job playing for the *Fox Theatre Orchestra*, a major vaudeville and movie house. Celebrities he played on stage were George Burns, Jack Benny, and George M. Cohan. Cohan, dancing and singing *I'm a Yankee Doodle Dandy* while waving an American flag, made an unforgettable impression, although with deep and complex sub—texts. On one hand, Dad had tired of pop music—if he ever had given it any credence at all. On the other, Cohan's persona validated Dad's sense that in America, *anything was possible* if you applied yourself—even for a poor and untutored immigrant Scotsman.

Dad often told me that in "the old country" if your father was a carpenter, it was because his father had been a carpenter, as had been his father before him. As a result, this meant that you too were destined to become a carpenter. But in America it was different, he said. Here, you can become anything you want to be, no matter what your father had been. This immigrant perspective drove him.

Having obtained a paying job in Philadelphia that seemed a secure musical position, he could have rested on his laurels and called it a day—or a lifetime. Instead, he applied to the new *Curtis Institute of Music* and became its first 'cello graduate. He reported feeling somewhat of an oddity since he was half a generation older than most of his classmates.

An early Stokowski extravaganza in 1916

The Curtis Institute was established in 1924 under the inspirational vision of Leopold Stokowski, Music Director of the Philadelphia Orchestra, along with the esteemed pianist Josef Hofmann.

In a fortuitous circumstance, which the secular mind would call *chance*, but the faithful would deem *the action of the Holy Spirit*, the

Curtis Institute of Music had been established by the same Curtis family in Philadelphia that had given my other grandfather Perkin Warbeck his last opportunity for an editorial career in the 1920's at various Curtis Publishing enterprises.

And Then the Glory

In 1927 came the momentous move that would define the rest of Dad's life. He interviewed with Leopold Stokowski, and was given a position with the Philadelphia Orchestra, where he would be for the next 32 years. His twin, my Uncle Alex, joined him in the viola section.

This move also carried another event that would dog his days for the rest of his life. Dad resigned his position as *First Chair* at the Fox Theatre Orchestra to take a rear desk position in the Philadelphia Orchestra, for less money. At the same time, the person he replaced took his former position as *First Chair* at the Fox, for more money.

Then, a year later, Dad watched in horror as 800 musician friends in Philadelphia, playing in vaudeville/movie theaters like the Fox and the Mastbaum, were laid off without warning one summer with the advent of sound movies that replaced the old silent films. Most of those musicians never worked again in the music industry.

Dad's job was safe and he could rejoice at playing the kind of music he had always longed for, but this episode stirred up all of the old fear of poverty that he had known as a child and the bitterness that went with it.

This impacted my life too. As I was growing up, Dad said that I could do anything in life except become a musician. The very thought of it filled him with rage. He did not want me ever to suffer the financial stress and unremitting threat of poverty that he came to believe was his lot in life. It was just as well, because I learned on my own, struggling to play trombone in the high school band, that I did not have his musical aptitude.

Becoming Myself

So what have I done in life? I became *a pastor in the church*—hardly a lucrative calling for the parson with a typical pastoral charge. But I do not serve the Lord for money or glory or the promise of fame. St. Paul tells us in *II Corinthians 10:17*:

> *Let the one who boasts, boast in the Lord.*

I am glad to be a foot soldier in the army of the Lord—which is the basic summons given to every Christian.

And how did I come to be on this mortal earth, anyway? My mother and father came from totally different backgrounds and were hardly a compatible pair. She came from money and he came from poverty. Her family roots stretched back to the first English settlers of Salem, Massachusetts, in the 1630's. His family roots were shrouded in the shame and anonymity of nameless generations of Scottish peasants who knew nothing but a slavish struggle to survive.

Even at an early age I began to figure out that aside from my mother's gentle surface cheerfulness, she harbored a deep and hidden belittlement of my father as a vulgar immigrant barely one step above a barbarian. He, on the other hand, harbored his own deep sense of unworthiness in the face of her family's accomplishments, which was fueled by a kind of reverential awe at a world to which he could never belong, and could only enter by mingling with the wealthy above him who were enthralled enough with his musician status to want to invite him to dinner.

It is one thing to speculate on the psychodynamics of such matters, which secular minds can do at length. It is quite a different perspective to see them from the eyes of faith. The Lord tells us that all of us are on the same level playing field. As the Book of Proverbs has it *(Proverbs 22:2)*:

> *The rich and the poor have this in common:*
> *the Lord is the Maker of them all.*

And St. Paul declares *(Romans 10:12b)*:

> *The same Lord is Lord of all*
> *and is generous to all who call on him.*

All of us are sinners, yet all of us are *creatures of infinite worth* in the eyes of the God who created us. He cancels every shred of our own unworthiness by his abiding love and grace. The Lord has done that for me.

We do not choose our parents. They procreate us. We simply wake up one day, and here we are. Our lives unfold in unexpected ways. We can give our thanks to the Lord for life and breath, and for the particular gifts and talents and idiosyncrasies that mark off who we are. Or instead we can choose to "*Curse God, and die,*" which was the advice given to Job by his wife *(Job 2:9)*. Many of us also struggle, as I did, to forgive our parents for their imperfections—knowing that we each are likewise imperfect—and we therefore honor them for being God's conduits who granted life to us, as *Exodus 20:12* instructs us to do.

Lewiston

My mother was born in the Parsonage in Lewiston where grandfather Perkin was Pastor of an established church in town. Years later, when I had an Interim Pastor appointment in Maine, I went to Lewiston to find Perkin's old church. It had merged with a local Methodist Church many years before, and all that remained of it was a brass plaque on the outside of the Methodist building, marking an existence now gone.

The Gray twins at the orchestra

Mom was the youngest of three. Her older sister, my Aunt Marian, became a second mother to me. The oldest sibling was her brother, Duke Towne, the uncle for whom I was named. He died in his early 20's at a sanitarium in White River Junction, Vermont, from tuberculosis. His death was a family trauma that later played itself out in my own childhood development—although I had no inkling of it at the time.

Only the passing of years and some very particular help from a spiritual director led me later to comprehend the very difficult dynamic that had cast a dark shadow over my own growing up years.

That dynamic was like a scissors on my life. My grandfather Perkin's failed visions of social reform—which my mother expected me to fulfill—was one side of the scissors.

The other blade came from my father's perception of the world as a brutal place to be conquered by cunning and good fortune. I was like a piece of meat ready to be sliced by the shears. We will come to that later.

Newark and Scranton

My mother was only six when the family moved to Newark in 1902, when grandfather Perkin became an editor for the *Newark Evening News*. I learned little about those years except for his sensational splash with *How Old Is Ann?* This propelled him on to the next stage of his newspaper career when he moved to Scranton, Pennsylvania, to become editor and publisher of the *Morning Tribune*. By this time Mom was twelve.

The Scranton years were my mother's glory days. Those were her teen years before World War I, leading to her young adult years in the Roaring Twenties.

The car in Scranton

Mom would describe to me in great detail the family car that made them the talk of the town at the dawn of the automobile age. She spoke of it as a *Matheson Super Six*. To run it and maintain it required that you have your own private chauffeur as well as mechanic—amenities that were available only to such persons as Perkin, the local newspaper magnate. It was particularly adept at negotiating the legendary hills of Scranton—like those of San Francisco—which typically would defeat a vehicle of lesser fortitude. At the same time, it required regular attention to its fickle constitution. The family mechanic would routinely dismantle the entire engine so that you could see all the parts strewn about the floor of the commodious garage. Costly, but nice—if you could afford to have your own mechanic and his machine shop as part of your sprawling estate. But no matter—it's only money, so long as the money does not run out.

In due time the money did run out. The assault of corporate and political enemies took its toll on the Tribune Company. To what extent Perkin's own managerial skills—or possible lack thereof—might also have led to the unravelling of his life we do not know. But it did unravel. Even so, the die had been cast to fashion the lives of father and daughters with the expectation that there would always be money—even when there was none—and denial can sometimes carry you further than you might expect.

Philadelphia

By 1918, the family settled in the fashionable Philadelphia neighborhood of Germantown, a comfortable residential community not too far from Center City, but far enough to maintain a quiet life of its own.

I have old family photos of my mother in the close—cropped bell shaped hats common for flappers at the time, where she cut a dashing figure. Other photos from those years show her as a slim and handsome young woman. The Roaring Twenties were the decades—something like the 1960's—where everything seemed possible and nothing was ever imagined to be out of reach for those who saw themselves invincible.

The hazy glow of nineteenth century Romanticism had not yet begun to dim, although its underpinnings had already been dealt a body blow by the mustard gas and trench warfare of what was called *The Great War*, and the *War to End All Wars*. The Great Depression and the Holocaust had not yet reared their ugly heads.

Music had been a regular feature of family life from early on. My Aunt Marian was the one who displayed the larger musical talent and she developed herself as a singer, pianist, piano teacher, and would—be composer. She never married and never held a job outside the house except for a brief stint as a clerk for Blue Cross during World War II, when virtually every able-bodied person was pressed into the work force in some way as part of the war effort.

She spent her time at home singing and playing piano and serving as companion to her father, Perkin, whose wife had died in 1937, the year before I was born. As fate would have it, my Scots grandfather's wife also died in 1937, so I never knew either of my grandmothers except through family tales and pictures, which were skimpy.

Mom and her sister Marian in their Philadelphia years

My mother worked on and off as a bookkeeper, but also lived at home with her sister and father. She too loved music, although without the more marked talent of her older sister. As an avocation, she sang in the *Mendelssohn Club*, a volunteer singing society in Philadelphia.

The Fateful Meeting

As one of their ventures, the Mendelssohn Club was engaged by Leopold Stokowski to sing Beethoven's Ninth Symphony with the Philadelphia Orchestra. It is a notoriously difficult piece for the singers, and my mother confessed more than once that she could not quite make the soprano high notes. But it was the opportunity of a lifetime.

It also became the occasion for her to meet my father. He appeared to her as a dashing "ladies' man." He was a widower caring for two children following the death of his young wife shortly after the birth of my sister in 1922. It must have been a whirlwind romance, with my father sweeping my mother off her feet.

Unfortunately, the "romance" did not seem to last very long. They were two very different people from two different universes of culture, values, and experience. By itself that says nothing. Some persons of dissimilar background get on quite well with one another, but that was not the case with my parents.

My mother confided in me more than once, when I was very young, that her purpose in having me as her only child was "to save the marriage." This is a task that no small child can ever take on. She apparently had counseled with our family physician about ending the marriage early, but she did not believe in (*or want to face*) divorce. He advised her to consider having a child "to save the marriage," so here I am.

I thank God for my life, but I was not cut out to be anyone's savior. None of us is. It took me years of spiritual development to come to the simple truth that only Christ is Savior. It is not for any child to be the salvation of their parents' dysfunctional marriage.

Joy Despite Strife

I was afraid of my father although he never struck me as a child. His temper was enough to strike terror in the heart. On the other hand, he coddled me and protected me. My mother related to me that when I was a very small child, I had pneumonia and ran a fever of 107 degrees F. During World War II with no car and limited ambulance services, Dad sat up with me all night long, rubbing my head and chest with alcohol every 15 minutes until the fever broke. After the War when we did manage to have a car again, he showered great attention on me with long summer vacations when the orchestra was not playing. One year we drove all the way to New Orleans—quite a feat in the days before the Interstate. We dined at Antoine's, and I had sole amandine which Dad had recommended.

Despite open and visible strife between my parents, with ugly episodes of screaming and shouting, I had, on the balance, a cheerful childhood. Between the sometimes terrifying outbursts of rage on my father's part and my mother's consequent weeping, we had a happy household much of the time. My father had a great ability to pour out his effusive charm on my mother, creating an almost party atmosphere for the three of us, as whim would carry him. The good times were very good.

My sister Hope was 16 when I was born. She was soon out of the house with an early marriage (I think to escape her father), so I grew up as an only child. Whenever we met or she did visit, she always took my mother's side in any dispute and the hostility between her and her father grew through the years, with only an occasional rapprochement. She has been a generous friend to me.

My Enigmatic Father

My mother and I both attributed Dad's complex makeup to "an artist's temperament," which I must admit has been helpful training for me to deal with church organists all of my life. Many years later, with the help of a perceptive pastor friend, I figured out that my father had all the characteristics of being a "dry alcoholic"—the infantile rages, the out of control behaviors—although he had never taken a drink. He described himself as "all Scotch, but my breath." He said that when he was young, he had carried too many drunken musician friends home on his back ever to want to touch alcohol himself. I shudder to think what would have become of him if he had been a drinker.

I have never had a doubt, then or now, that both of my parents deeply loved me—sometimes to the point of doting on me, as one might expect with older parents and an only child. They were not overly protective and I was at times on the verge of being spoiled. God save me from that. They permitted, even encouraged, things that would be unthinkable today. For example, when I was 14 they let me travel to New York for several days on my own, so that I could walk about and experience the Big Apple at my own speed. Philadelphia was only 90 miles from New York and we had been there many times. We had driven there often as a family, and from time to time I would accompany Dad on the train when the Philadelphia Orchestra played Carnegie Hall in its regular series there. So for this solo trip of my own, Dad helped pick out a hotel he often had used, which was conveniently located across the street from Penn Station. All went well, even though I was solicited once or twice by prostitutes on Seventh Avenue. I was too interested in the general sights and sounds of the city to pay any attention to them. Dad had schooled me well enough on the dark side of life that I was nothing more than a bit amused by their come-ons. I have since learned to pray for them, that they can find some deliverance from the wretchedness of their lives and discover the abundance of God's saving grace.

We matured more quickly then. Dad functioned as an adult by age 14—out of school, unable to finish the 8th grade, and working as an adult to make his own way in an adult world. So in his mind I too was an adult by age 14 and 15, right? After all, I had been working part time six days a week since I was 13, pumping gas after school every day and all day Saturday. By age 17 I was clearly an adult in my own mind—out of high school, renting my own accommodation, working at my own job to pay my way through college. Today we wonder about the maturity of folks who are 35 or even 40 years old, living at home, emotionally and financially dependent on their parents to take care of them. The world has changed.

Parental Nurture

My mother was a Christian and my father was an agnostic. These are contradictories, but they were not a source of conflict within our family life or for myself in my own spiritual formation. My mother freely shared her faith and taught me what she was able to teach.

Religion for my father, on the other hand, was more of a "zero" than anything to argue about. As I was growing up I would ask him from time to time if he remembered any church connections of any kind for anyone in his family, even generations back, that he might have heard about. He would tell me *No—no one I can remember ever had any church involvement at all.* His was an example of the purely secularized European family. Faith or church was nothing for him to quarrel about because there was nothing there. My mother simply did her thing and that was that.

Despite Dad's lack of any clear spiritual interest, it does continue to surprise me that my first Bible was given to me at birth by my Dad. I know this because I keep it on my bookshelf for reference. It is a leather bound prewar edition of the Authorized Version (*King James translation*), and inside the front cover is pasted Dad's own music bookplate inscribed with my name and Ambler, PA, 1938, in his own recognizable handwriting.

Why this from my agnostic father? It is by the grace of an inscrutable yet providential God that this should be Dad's first gift to me.

The Deadly Shears

The *deadly shears* on the other hand were quite a different story. My mother had romantic visions of what she thought I should become in life, and she pressed them onto me with a gentle but subtle and powerful force that I could not argue with or rebel against at a tender young age. In her mind I was to become the artist that her dead brother had no chance to become when he died of tuberculosis in his early 20's. So she signed me up to take an expensive course in drawing from a correspondence school in Minneapolis. Despite her spending money on this project that she really did not have to spend, it all came to naught. The mailings of instructions and exams piled up, unopened and unused, until we had to thrown them away in the trash. It did not matter to her that, while I had a rudimentary talent to draw, it was clear to me that I did not have the motivation or the aptitude to make my way in the world as a latter day Rembrandt or Van Gogh, much less even as an industrial designer or advertising illustrator.

More devastatingly, she also had romantic expectations that I should fulfill the unfinished business of social reform and political advocacy that her father, Perkin Warbeck, had undertaken but not achieved. When I was 13, she managed to obtain tickets to take me to a political rally in Philadelphia in the summer of 1952 to hear Adlai Stevenson speak during his run for President. She never thought that I might become a pastor. Her father had tried that and had left the ministry for brighter fields. She did not oppose my own pastoral calling, but she never seemed very thrilled about it.

For her, Stevenson seemed to be the anointed agent for the salvation of the world against the dark forces of reactionary primitivism and nationalistic xenophobia. After all, he had been a prime mover behind the creation of the United Nations—the post–WW II reincarnation of Woodrow Wilson's failed League of Nations and its romantic vision of *"world peace through world law."*

The rally at a University of Pennsylvania auditorium was an exciting occasion for me as a young teenager. Stevenson was a great orator. But unfortunately for Mom's hopes for me, I had no taste for the argumentative arena of public politics.

My father, on the other hand, had a hard-headed expectation that I should succeed in some form of commercial venture—anything but becoming a professional musician like himself, which he saw as a calling doomed to poverty. He sought to train me to be shrewd, even cutthroat if necessary, in human relations, so long as anything I did would be to my own advantage. He would lecture me for hours at the Saturday breakfast table, all to my mother's horror. As I look back, his perception of me seemed to be that I was languid and plodding where I ought to have been aggressive and confrontational. He never quite called me slow and stupid, but that was the subterranean and unspoken script.

At the bottom line, these were the two blades of a scissors that threatened to dismember me as I grew up. In their most rudimentary, subconscious and devastating form, they were: (1) a message from my mother that I was to become the savior of the modern world that her father, Perkin Warbeck, had been destined to be, but failed; and (2) a contradictory message from my father that I would never amount to a hill of beans unless I were to shape up and cunningly take advantage of every opportunity that beckoned, no matter what the cost or damage to others.

Neither my mother or father ever said such unsavory things to me openly, of course. But as the years went on, I slowly became aware of these sub–rosa suggestive images at work within me, in part with the help of spending more than 15 years with Jesuit spiritual directors.

I resisted these forces to define me, and I have survived, even thrived. On the balance, I would say that I had a happy childhood and learned early on how to maneuver around these pressures to become things I was not.

In time, I would learn both to love, and to forgive, each of my parents—frail mortals like myself. I did not choose them, but they brought me into being without any selecting on my part. I simply woke up one day to discover that I was alive on this transient earth, and glad to be here. Hallelujah.

A Countervailing Third Force

The two blades of the deadly scissors that menaced my early life were subtle but formidable. They were palpable threats at the time. They are still vivid to me now.

Against these dark forces stood another truth. It is this: the hand of the Lord was upon me. The Lord had laid claim to my life long before I was aware of it. I am certainly not alone in this. Scripture testifies repeatedly to persons the Lord has chosen who had no clue to it at the time.

The Lord told Jeremiah (*Jeremiah 1:5*):

> "Before I formed you in the womb I knew you,
> and before you were born I consecrated you . . .

Not everyone is called to be a prophet to the nations like Jeremiah, but the underlying truth applies. It applies to me and it applies to you. God called you in the womb to be his own. How you respond to him is up to you. You don't need to become a pastor or a religious professional to serve the Lord. Christ calls everyone to follow him. Some respond sooner than later. Some take years to find their calling. Some never do.

When the Lord called Samuel, he was slow to respond because he didn't know what was going on. It took him three failed tries before he got the message (*I Samuel 3:1–10*). Like Samuel, I had no clue early on about the power of the Lord in my life. In these later years the truth has become obvious to me that the Lord was there from my earliest childhood. It was never about just me alone against the threat. His influence was like a countervailing Third Force exerting an inexorable persuasion over me when I was oblivious to his effect. He rescued me from the deadly shears.

Mustard Seeds

In St. Mark's Gospel (5:30–32), Jesus tells us:

> *"With what can we compare the kingdom of God, or what parable will we use for it? It is like a mustard seed, which, when sown upon the ground, is the smallest of all the seeds on earth; yet when it is sown it grows up and becomes the greatest of all shrubs, and puts forth large branches, so that the birds of the air can make nests in its shade."*

The countervailing Third Force against destructive forces in my life has been *the guiding grace* of a providential God. He plants the mustard seeds of grace in particular and specific ways.

I remember a church during my college years whose sanctuary was open during weekday hours for quiet contemplation and prayer. It was an Episcopal parish just off Germantown Avenue in Chestnut Hill where my mother had a small apartment over a beauty salon. I was drawn there as if by a magnet to sit quietly and savor the gothic quiet and magnificent stained glass, all the while eagerly preparing to become an Industrial Engineer. Little did I know . . .

Seeds in Childhood

I was baptized on Easter Sunday, March 24, 1940, at the family church in Philadelphia. When infants are baptized, we do not choose this any more than we choose to be conceived in our mother's womb. We grow into our new Christian identity, or reject it, as the case may be, just as we grow in the flesh—or reject that too, as the case may be.

As the nation proceeded into World War II, we lost the family car and Sunday transportation into Philadelphia for church became nearly impossible. So my mother enrolled me in a local Sunday School close to home. She could have selected the large and imposing Presbyterian

Church directly across the street from where we lived. She did not. I know why. She was wary of a stern Calvinism that was big on Double Predestination and short on redeeming grace.

Instead, she chose St. John's Evangelical Lutheran Church, a half block in the other direction. It was a small stucco building, very different from the imposing Presbyterian edifice across the street. The Lutheran Pastor was a quiet, gentle soul whom she quickly befriended after worshipping there herself on a few occasions.

I was a regular at Sunday School and rarely missed a class. I remember a comment by our teacher Mrs. Ziegler, a small, squat, chunky woman with a steady will and encouraging smile, who told us, *We all love the 23rd Psalm, because the Lord does shepherd us through life, but do not overlook Psalm 24, which comes right afterward. It reveals his glory.* Her word has stuck with me for a lifetime. So has the key passage she unlocked for me as a child, which is this *(Psalm 24:10)*:

> *Who is this king of glory?*
> *The Lord of hosts, he is the King of glory.*

One year when I was 11 or 12 we put on a class pageant during Sunday worship. I do not remember what the theme of the pageant was, but I do remember that I was chosen to play the part of the Pastor in it. So they dressed me in the appropriate black shirt with white neck band. I remember feeling very comfortable in this, although quite surprised that they had selected me. This mustard seed of my Lutheran Sunday School and consequent Confirmation was a significant milestone. As I said, *little did I know.*

The Power of Baptism

Many years later, at the annual Karl Barth seminar I regularly attend, we drifted into a discussion about the efficacy of the sacraments. We spent time on the meaning of Baptism. We had about 15–16 participants that year, as we usually do. Nearly all of us were Reformed Pastors, and all were of the New England Congregational variety except for me with my Pennsylvania background. Everyone quickly agreed that Baptism was the Entrance Rite into the Body of Christ, not primarily a family baby-naming ceremony. Then we hit upon the hard question, *Is there spiritual regeneration in Baptism, or is it only a welcoming event to bring us into the community of the church?*

A lively discussion ensued with a lot of energetic back and forth. So we decided to take a quick straw poll: *Yes or No—Is there spiritual regeneration in Baptism*? (The same question would apply to the Eucharist as well, of course—and to other sacramental events like Confirmation). To my shock and surprise, every single person around the table, but two, said *No*. The only two persons who affirmed that *Yes, there is spiritual regeneration in Baptism* were myself and Fr. Ed O'Flaherty, a Jesuit priest who was the Ecumenical Officer for the Archdiocese of Boston and a regular participant in our annual Barth seminar.

It is worthy of note that John Calvin's *Geneva Catechism* spends an entire page defending and interpreting *Spiritual Regeneration* in Baptism. Calvin also upholds *the Real Presence* of Christ in the Eucharist. The New England recalcitrance on these matters confirms the observation by Howard Hageman, a Dutch Reformed Pastor, that Reformed piety in New England resembles that of Ulrich Zwingli, not John Calvin, despite the New Englanders reputation as "Calvinist" Puritans. More on this later.

The mustard seed of my Lutheran Confirmation has borne fruit, and I thank the Lord for it.

Three

Assertion

Elkanah knew his wife Hannah, and the Lord remembered her. In due time Hannah conceived and bore a son. She named him Samuel, for she said, "I have asked him of the Lord.
—I SAMUEL 1:19b-20

Growing Up, 1938

I WAS BORN IN 1938, three years before Pearl Harbor. Ambler, Pennsylvania, the town where we lived, was in those days a gritty blue collar working class community dominated by a series of Asbestos factories. I remember a school tour where we went from one mill to another to learn the whole process. The first mill separated the raw fibers from the way they were mined to prepare them for processing. Another was a rolling mill that produced large flat sheets for use as wall board. Another produced floor tiles. Yet another molded round pipes and pipe coverings for insulation.

These days we hear a lot about the horrible medical consequences from breathing asbestos dust. I have great sorrow for those mill workers who spent their lives there and now suffer debilitating sickness from the air they breathed. I have sometimes wondered if I would suffer any ill effects merely from living in such a town. But here I am, eight decades later, and my lungs are fine. The Lord is merciful.

The Boy Samuel

When the boy Samuel was growing up, he had no idea what he was to do in life or what he would become. Neither do most of us. Surely those mill workers in my home town had no idea what fate was in store for them.

Samuel's mother Hannah had been married for years without a child. She wept over her estate in life as a barren woman scorned. Her husband loved her despite this, and she pled to the Lord for a child.

When Samuel was born, she dedicated him to the care of the sanctuary at Shiloh as an act of thanksgiving for receiving her precious gift. In due time, she bore three more sons and two daughters. Her prayer of thanksgiving, the *Song of Hannah* in *I Samuel 2*, prefigures the *Song of Mary* in St. Luke's familiar Christmas story (*Luke 1:47–55*). Set these two texts beside each other and you will see the parallels:

Song of Hannah
Hannah prayed and said,
"My heart exults in the Lord;
my strength is exalted
in my God . . .
There is no Holy One
like the Lord,
no one besides you;
there is no Rock
like our God . . .
The bows of the mighty
are broken,
but the feeble gird on strength.
—I Samuel 2:1,2,4

Song of Mary
And Mary said,
"My soul magnifies the Lord,
and my spirit rejoices
in God my savior . . .
He has shown strength
with his arm;
he has scattered the proud
in the thoughts
of their hearts.
He has brought down the

> *powerful from their thrones,*
> *and lifted up the lowly . . ."*
> —*Luke 1:46,47,51,52*

Mary knew her scripture. She most likely was singing *Hannah's Song*, which then led to her own.

None of us knows the details of what life has in store for us in the years that lie ahead, or what shall later become of us. The story of Samuel's Call to Ministry (*Chapter 3 of I Samuel*) tells us in verse 7 that the boy Samuel *did not yet know the Lord*—even though he had been working diligently in the temple for some years. He was *in the dark*, literally. The text goes on to tell us that when the Lord called to him three times in the night, he couldn't figure out who it was. He kept running to the old priest Eli, mistakenly thinking that it was he who had called. We do stumble even—and maybe especially—when important things lie ahead and beckon us. As the story unfolds, Samuel does finally assert himself appropriately just as his mother Hannah had done before him.

Dark Days

The World War II years were stark. We had to give up the family automobile, a large Packard sedan, because tires for it were no longer available and gas was nearly impossible to obtain. Everyone was issued small red and blue ration tokens to buy what limited groceries there were. They looked as if they had been made of something like cheap hard—pressed masonite to conserve metal. Streetcar lines were abandoned and the rails ripped up from the street to be melted down for bullets. In school, everyone brought in pennies every week to purchase savings stamps to help finance the war. These were pasted into a small booklet—something like the Green Stamp books from retailers in later years. When the savings book was full, we would take it to the Post Office to be exchanged for a War Bond.

When we were able to go out for the occasional restaurant meal, butter was limited to a single pat for the whole table. The local dairy two blocks from our house was closed for the duration of the war, so I had no idea where the milk came from for the limited ration we had. I would walk past the dairy on the way to school and look at the shuttered windows and door. When the war was over it started right up again just as before. Then on the way to school I would look into the open door and see the conveyor belt going under a spout, chugging milk into large metal cans for wholesale transport to a bottling plant to be put into individual glass bottles for retail. Like many, we had home delivery from a dairy truck.

Those were the days before television. The main entertainment was a large console radio, plus Saturday children's movies at the local theatre in town. Before the Superman episodes and Mickey Mouse cartoons, there was a black and white newsreel to give news events for the week—mostly battle clips taken live at the front lines to measure the progress of the war. I remember the newsreel for Franklin Roosevelt's funeral procession. The entire nation wept. And the war was not yet over. We did not know what would become of us. There were frequent air raid drills with sirens blaring in the street. We had to pull down the shades or turn off the lights completely so that no lamplight could shine out. All we could see when we peeked through the curtains were Civilian Defense Wardens with their hard hats and flashlights, checking on everyone's compliance with *lights out*.

The War Ends

First came VE Day (*Victory in Europe*) and then VJ Day (*Victory in Japan*), both in 1945. In an unusual convergence of events for our family, VE Day on May 8 also happened to be my mother's birthday, as well as President Truman's birthday. When the war was over, everything changed. There was hope. There were also the ghastly revelations of the true extent of the holocaust, with unbelievable news footage at the Saturday movies of the liberation of Nazi prison camps. We saw cadavers piled high that had not yet been fed into the ovens, and emaciated prisoners hardly able to walk. These were searing images for a small child. This was life. And this was cruel and savage death in monumental proportions.

I had my first crush on "the girl next door" when I was about 8 or 9, but nothing came of it. It was my first taste of unrequited love—if you can call it that at such an innocent age. Actually, she lived across the street, not next door. Her father was a radio repairman with his shop in their house. He had an oscilloscope with a 3 inch green screen, which he had converted into a makeshift television to receive the first TV broadcasts from Philadelphia in the late 1940's. He invited some two dozen neighborhood children to watch the Mummers Parade on New Years' Day, and we crowded around and strained our eyes at the tiny screen in amazement to see the fancy costumes and the endless string bands playing *I'm*

Looking Over a Four Leaf Clover—It was the promise of greater things to come.

Years later I would explain to my own children that I grew up before there was television, and their jaws would drop. *How is that possible, Dad?* they would ask in astonishment. Today we need to explain to some that *there was life* before there were cell phones and computers. My father would tell me about the days when he concocted a device to listen to the first radio broadcasts by using a safety pin with a tuning crystal attached to an open spring mattress for an antenna. Time moves on.

Growing up in the 1950's was like being part of an alien universe compared to what confronts today's youth. In my high school, it was a punishable infraction to be caught chewing gum in the hallway or walking up the down staircase. The few who got caught smoking cigarettes outside were in real trouble. Today we worry about assault weapons, heavy drugs, and military hardware, at the least.

In the 1950's we made jokes about an alleged remark by President Eisenhower that "*Things are getting to be more like they are now than they ever were.*" The war was over and things were returning to "normal."

We had thugs in my high school, but I never ran afoul of them. We did have one fellow who seemed a bit intimidating just by his description. I never really met him, but apparently he was a benign sort of character, maybe a bit slow. He was described as "Big Ed" because in the seventh grade he drove his own car to school, smoking a pipe. He had flunked a few grades in grammar school and at 18 or 19 years old, he was still in Junior High.

We moved when I was in the tenth grade. This was traumatic at first, but in my new school I quickly developed a devoted circle of new friends—all boys—who were united by a love for classical music combined with the emerging technologies of the LP record and stereo preamps. One friend (with more money to spend than I could muster) had purchased a "binaural" record player with two separate parallel needle arms, which played special two-rack "binaural" records with separate stereo grooves. One track was on the inner half of the record, the other on the outer half. It was a fascinating technology, but was plagued by the aggravating difficulty of trying to get two separate needles into the proper matching tracks of a spinning record. If you put each needle down correctly, you had stunning stereo. If you got one needle just one groove sideways from where it belonged, you had a ghastly mishmash. The whole apparatus quickly disappeared from the market when the stereo record was introduced—two separate channels all from one needle in one groove. It was *amazing*.

Things That Move

And then there were cars—prewar models reintroduced in the late 1940's while the necessary time was taken to design new post-war models. No cars were built during the war—only military vehicles like trucks and tanks and jeeps. Our first post-war family car was a 1937 DeSoto that coughed and leaked oil. When it broke down trying to climb the hills around West Point on the Hudson River during a family vacation, we moved on to a 1935 Studebaker.

Although it was illegal then to obtain a Social Security card before age 16 because of child labor laws, I somehow managed to get my card and number when I was only 13 so that I could go to work pumping gas every afternoon after school and all day Saturday. By working in a mechanic's garage at the gas station, I learned to drive when I was 13. I stayed in the parking lot and did not venture out into the street before I was allowed to.

More than cars, there were trains. Most small boys seem to have a fascination with trains—often along with trucks, cars, fire engines, planes, and other conveyances that move. Then some, like myself, discover a special curiosity bordering on fanatic devotion with one particular category of transport. For me, it was trolley lines. This can be a passing stage or it can lead to a lifetime calling.

My younger son was, for a while, so taken by large 18 wheelers that he was sure he wanted to be an overland truck driver when he grew up. But that passed away in time. He became a physician.

For me, I was enthralled by trains when I was small—but especially with trolley cars and interurban railways. By my early teen years, I must have driven my mother crazy with a desire to follow, investigate, and track down every possible variety of railway transportation—but especially interurban trolley lines. She was indulgent enough to drive me around endlessly in search for the grand and the novel.

Philadelphia was an obliging environment for this. There was, of course, the Pennsylvania Railroad—which at its heyday boasted to be the world's largest corporation (*or so I thought*). If you are familiar with the *Monopoly* board, there were also the Reading Railroad and the Baltimore

& Ohio. (The Monopoly board *Short Line* did not seem to exist in real life, so far as I ever new). Then there were streetcars and the subway in the city, the Red Arrow line and the Philadelphia & Western in the suburbs, and that prince of all Interurbans, the *Liberty Bell Limited* from Norristown to Allentown. The opportunities seemed endless.

While living in Ambler, I could walk to school and to work. After we moved, I suffered under having to take a daily school bus ride of 45 minutes each way over bumpy back country roads for a less than five mile trip to school. So at 16 I had earned enough to buy my first used car for $100. That was a lot of money then. It was a 1947 Frazer, which looked something like a giant bathtub turned upside down, but it was truly elegant in its time. It could seat three across the front and four across the back, and a person even 6 feet tall could stretch his legs forward from the back seat and not touch the seat in front of him. It was old, but it was smooth as a dream and it got me to school on time. I was on top of the world.

College

As high school drew near to a close, the question of college began to loom. I was not quite at the top of my class, but I was close enough that a lot of attractive alternatives were possible. I loved mathematics and physics, chemistry less so, and was not much for biology. I had almost failed 10th grade botany because I could not seem to find enough wild flowers to press under plastic for a term project. I also loved history, English literature, poetry, and art.

Music, of course, was a prime mover in my life, but it required skills and aptitude I did not possess, so the point was moot. In any event, that was the one calling my father was dead set against because of his dark experiences as a musician during the Great Depression. He also doubted why college should even be important at all since he had never completed the 8th grade but had made his way in the world.

The possibilities seemed many, but with one major impediment: *money*. The thought of going to any of the better private colleges or universities was entirely out of the question because of the cost involved. Circumstances soon pointed clearly toward a technological university with a work–study program, where it was possible to earn enough through internship placements to self-finance my basic college expenses.

Moving Out

I was graduated from high school when I was 17. My father had ended school to function as an adult by age 14, so at 17 I was ready to function on my own in the adult world.

I applied, and was accepted, into the one school that was financially possible, Drexel Institute of Technology in Philadelphia—now renamed Drexel University. We called it *the poor man's MIT*. I entered a program called *Commerce and Engineering*. It was a course of study jointly administered by the school's *College of Engineering* and *College of Business Administration*. It was a program closely allied to what is called *Industrial Engineering*, a specialty pioneered by Frederick W. Taylor, Frank Bunker Gilbreth, Sr., and others. Gilbreth's life and career were popularized by the book and the movie, *Cheaper By the Dozen*. It seemed to be just the right ticket for me. I was eager to start and, once on my way, had dreams of becoming a city planner, transportation engineer, management consultant, or perhaps even an architect.

Our course work involved math, physics, and chemistry from the Engineering College, along with cost accounting, corporation finance, and personnel management from the Business College. It was challenging and rigorous. I had no idea at the time that the demands on us were not the norm for colleges everywhere. Our typical schedule was five or six courses at a time, with more than 30 hours a week in the classroom or the lab. Laboratory courses made the hours longer because they took extra time. I was shocked to learn some years later that friends who had gone to high end liberal arts colleges typically had only three or four courses at a time, with nine to twelve hours a week in class. It sounded to me like indolence.

My day began with Calculus and Analytic Geometry, five days a week at 8 o'clock in the morning. I loved it. I got high marks in the course. For it we had three hours of homework every night to be turned in the next day, and a pop quiz at the end of every week. We used the same 800+ page textbook for three years, sometimes proceeding only half a page a day, because higher mathematics is very compact.

I still keep that textbook on my bookshelf, and I open it once every year or two and look at a page of *differential equations* for comic relief. I did so well with it then, but now I haven't the faintest idea of what the peculiar signs and symbols mean. I might as well be looking at the indecipherable characters from an ancient language lost in the mists of time before the Rosetta Stone.

I enjoyed my college work, although one disability began to rear its ugly head, which—although it abated after a few years—would return with demonic force later on. We will come to more about this affliction later. But in my sophomore year, I began to find our physics course so demanding that I would break out in a cold sweat before every final exam and would need to run to the toilet to vomit up everything before going in to take the test. Yet I passed the course with high grades.

Money

I am almost embarrassed to admit—in these days of soaring financial burdens for higher education—what my college cost, and how I was able to finance it. As a work-study school, the Bachelor's Degree was a five year program: freshman, sophomore, pre-junior, junior, and senior years. The freshman year was nine months, but the remaining four years were six months each, with the other six months scheduled for work placement in industry.

Ours was a private college with no public money, unlike a tax supported State University. It had only a modest endowment fund, unlike those of historic Ivy League schools. But my freshman year tuition starting in 1956 was $565 for the entire year. My work-study appointments would pay about $2000 for the half-year, so I made this stretch to cover tuition, rent, food, and transportation. When I fell slightly short I was able to obtain modest financial aid from the school, including one $500 student loan. I paid that off in ten years at $50 a year, plus interest.

Money was worth a lot more then. I calculated that my $2000 salary doubled to $4000 if it had been for a full year. Then I raised it a bit for an engineer after graduation instead of being for a student co-op job before graduation. This would mean some $5000–6000 for an engineer's starting salary.

My boss at my work-study job had married during my years there, and he bought a brand new suburban ranch house across the bridge in southern New Jersey for about $13,000. These days, wages and housing costs have inflated at different rates (not to mention college tuition), and today it would be very difficult for a new graduate to find a family-sized house for not much more than double his starting salary.

What's in a Name?

For most of my appointments, I returned each year to the same office in the Industrial Engineering Department at the American Sugar Refining Company, although I did work one quarter for IBM.

When I was growing up, my mother had always insisted on *Sunny Cane sugar* at the grocery store. She said it was much better than any other brand.

During my first week on the job at the "sugar house," as it was called, I was standing on the packaging floor talking with my boss while the conveyor belt was passing by with empty five pound bags going underneath the chute where they would be filled and sewed shut to be sent to the warehouse. They were for Sunny Cane sugar, so I knew that my mother would be pleased. Then all of a sudden I turned my head and saw that the bags coming along, without the conveyor belt ever stopping for a pause, were for *Benjamin Franklin* sugar, one of Sunny Cane's strong competitors. I was astonished at the revelation.

I went back to the conversation with my boss only to see, a few minutes later, that the bags had been switched again, this time for *Domino* sugar, another competitor. So I asked him about it and he said, *Oh, it's all the same sugar, but we do have three separate sales departments that compete with each other for business.*

"*Commercial smoke and mirrors.*" I thought to myself. When I later told my mother about this she was incredulous, then appalled.

In ancient times, a *name* represented the reality itself. If a Roman Centurion came up to you and said, *In the name of Caesar, I command you to . . .*" it might just as well have been Julius Caesar himself giving you the order. A name carried the same authority as the reality behind it. These days we say, *Oh, its only a name*—meaning it doesn't mean much of anything.

An old Chinese proverb says, *The beginning of wisdom is to call things by their proper names.* Christians should take this to heart for the realities we deal with.

God told Adam to *name* the animals. After telling Adam and Eve to *be fruitful and multiply—and have dominion over—every living thing that moves upon the earth (Genesis 1:28)*, the next assignment that God gave us was to name them *(Genesis 2:19)*:

> So out of the ground the Lord God formed every animal of the
> field and every bird of the air, and brought them to the man to

see what he would call them; and whatever the man called every living creature, that was its name.

The giving of names is a foundational human activity. In addition to naming our children, new endeavors we undertake, projects and productions large and small, it is essential that we accurately name the dark and demonic powers that come against us. It is easy to see both visible enemies and friends. It is not so easy to identify the invisible forces that work to do us in, but they are there. If we do not recognize them and call them out for what they are, we are at their mercy. We master them by naming them correctly.

The First Turning Point

I enjoyed my school, and math most of all. But I also had to confess that the exclusively technological focus was wearisome. We had only one survey course in English and American poetry and prose in my freshman year, and nothing more until a senior year course in grammar and sentence diagramming. The college bulletin board had an instructional letter posted on it to guide graduating engineers on how to speak and write for job placement interviews. It suggested they be sure to check their spelling and avoid using terms like *ain't.*

I needed more. Despite the endless time demands of schoolwork, I sought out a local church near the campus during my freshman year and soon found myself deeply involved in parish life.

Sunday worship was a must. The choir and organist were first rate, and provided a 15 minute choral Prelude each week before the Opening Hymn. There were Bach Cantata pieces and Baroque chorales. It was heaven—especially since I no longer had the fellowship of my musical companions from high school or the regular Saturday evenings at the symphony I had known when I was young.

As a child, I often sat on my father's 'cello trunk in the greenroom in my short pants. I met many of the great soloists of the day who came to play with the Philadelphia Orchestra. Gregor Piatigorsky was especially impressive. The orchestra musicians had nicknamed him "Piat," and he had the habit of striding on stage holding his 'cello so high that his 6 foot plus height made it look like a violin.

I remember asking Ralph Kirkpatrick why his massive harpsichord had six or seven pedals, and what they were for, since I had never seen more than three on an ordinary grand piano. Perhaps he was bemused by a small child's curiosity or he knew that he could not explain such things in a short time to a child's question, so he simply said, *Oh, I don't know what they all are for. I just step on them.* And we laughed. All of that was gone by my college years.

The campus church provided a lot more than music and Sunday worship. I quickly became involved with parish programs, especially with a Young Adults' club. I soon became a prime mover in its program planning and honed my relational and organizational skills. It was both fun and challenging. We reinvented the group from a modest clique to a major urban ministry, called the Communitarians. We learned how to squeeze 60–80 people into one or another of many small two room urban apartments for roaring social party events. It was wall to wall people. I remember an especially energetic conversation about the Seven Cardinal Sins with a certified intellectual, whose eyeglass lenses were so thick they put Coke bottle bottoms to shame. He was a young math professor at another university. We debated whether it was possible to be guilty of both *Lust* and *Sloth* at the same time. The general conclusion was *No*. This was, after all, the 1950's, on the cusp of becoming the 1960's when everything changed.

Summoned like Samuel

A transformative moment came near the end of my pre-junior year when I was sitting quietly one evening at the small desk I had purchased during high school. I still keep that desk in our front hall, a place to store pens, pencils, checkbooks and other household items.

In a contemplative mood, I slid open one drawer on the left where I had accumulated years of railway timetables from middle school and beyond. Then I slid open a drawer on the right where I had in recent years collected a pile of adult education pamphlets from the church literature rack. I stared at the one, and then at the other. And it struck me in a flash: *I am not really cut out to be an industrial engineer or corporate accountant or architect or transportation planner or business executive. My only attraction is to be a pastor in the church.*

At the time, it seemed a clear-cut turn in the road, but I did not think of it then in especially spiritual terms. I was naive about such things at that early age. It was a call in the dark like the summons to Samuel who couldn't figure out what was going on. It was only many years later when I embarked on serious spiritual direction that my first Spiritual Director took me back to that moment to explore it more deeply, and help me uncover it as a true epiphany—a comprehension of reality I was unequipped to see at the time.

I remember vividly that first meeting with my first Spiritual Director, many years later in Chicago. I stumbled around, mumbling what probably were incoherent things about my then current struggles and confusions. He was leaning back, listening. Most of the Jesuit Spiritual Directors I have had listen most of the time, more than anything. They do not really "direct" in the ordinary sense of the word. Finally, he leaned forward and said, "*Tell me about your original call to ministry.*»"

Then I really stumbled, because I had never quite thought about it. I had to rack my brain for the appropriate memory. Then I remembered the incident with the timetables in one drawer and the church literature in the other. It had seemed so trivial then. So I described the moment to him, along with my immediate confidence at the time that this was what I was to do. He leaned back and smiled and said, "*That sounds authentic to me.*»" We moved on to other things and began to make progress.

A Blessed Meeting

A church in the Germantown neighborhood of Philadelphia, where my mother's family home formerly had been, featured for years an "ecumenical pulpit" with a steady stream of notable guest preachers throughout each season. Paul Tillich and Reinhold Niebuhr were among the luminaries who were guests there several times each year.

I visited there on a Sunday morning in December 1960, to hear Martin Luther King, Jr., who was the guest minister that day for the regular Sunday worship. He was ten years older than I and this was one day before my 22nd birthday, and about a month before his 32nd in the January following. The *Letter from a Birmingham Jail* was a little more than two years away in April 1963.

We shook hands after the close of worship and passed a few minutes of casual chit-chat, as is customary in many churches. I told him that I was off to seminary the following September. He was very pleased to hear it and was quite encouraging about what might lie ahead. We discovered that my soon-to-be Professor of biblical studies at St. Lawrence

University, Morton Enslin, had been his professor at Crozer Theological Seminary in Chester, Pennsylvania, some years before.

Who of us could possibly have imagined what portentous events in this nation lay before us in the decade just then unfolding? But this was a quiet encounter with a truly kind and gracious person, and a moment to be savored. These days, too many forget that King's primary calling was to be *a pastor in the church*—as was mine—whatever secular society would later make him out to be. He was faithful to that pastoral calling to the end.

A New Direction

My original call event with the timetables and the church literature was the summer of 1959. It was clear to me then that my life had taken on an entirely new direction. The practical evidence of this was incontrovertible. But it immediately brought into play its own challenges and stumbling blocks. I could clearly see these obstacles as they were appearing, but I could not comprehend why. I thought that choosing one new career over another was a simple matter of selecting one fork in the road over another—but that is not true where the Lord is concerned.

It would have taken a lot more spiritual wisdom than I had absorbed at that early stage in life to know that choosing in favor of the Lord will immediately bring down upon you the opposition and even condemnation of the world. Jesus told his own first disciples as much the night before he died (*John 15:18,19a*):

> *If the world hates you, be aware that it hated me before it hated you.*
> *If you belonged to the world, the world would love you as its own."*

Hate is a strong and vicious word. Jesus uses it to expose the fault line between the ways of this world and the kingdom of God.

His disciples didn't really understand what he was saying at the time. How could they? They had Easter to face before they would be able to comprehend the depths of what was going on. How much more so was this true for me, a simple college student struggling to respond to a new and transcendent call on my life.

Even so, the evidence of the yawning gulf between faith and world soon made itself known. One unhappy episode quickly unfolded when I returned to my co–op job at the sugar refinery. My boss and I had enjoyed a convivial relationship up until then. He was young, intelligent, and only a few years older than I. We got on well together.

He had displayed a real fondness for me as a supervising mentor might with an eager but novice student. More than that, he had professed himself a regular church goer and believer, and we had shared positive reflections on his church wedding when he recently had married. But as soon as I told him of my new direction, his demeanor changed. He began to treat me as if I had just arrived as an alien refugee from an unknown galaxy. He no longer knew how to relate to me. Life on the job was never the same again. Our relationship was corrupted with undercurrents of condemnation mixed with disbelief, almost as if I were an undercover spy whose cover had just been blown.

There is a truth to that. All Christians are called to be *covert spies* working on behalf of a foreign entity in this current world. That *foreign entity* is the Kingdom of God. St. Paul calls us *ambassadors* of that kingdom *(II Corinthians 5:20)*:

> "*We are ambassadors for Christ, since God is making his appeal through us.*"

Find Your Own Calling

While cutting his hair, Martin Luther's barber, Peter of Wittenberg, asked him how to pray. So Luther wrote him a 40 page letter on prayer, going over the Lord's Prayer, the Ten Commandments, and the Creed. He begins by calling for our *conversion*, but he never tells his barber that he should go to seminary and seek to be ordained as a pastor. He says that our Christian calling is to perform our life's vocation with as much skill, devotion, and attention as our God–given talents enable us to do. If your calling is to cut hair, then do it with all the craftsmanship and honor you can demonstrate.

Not every Christian is called to be a pastor. Our basic calling is our baptism, which summons us to live a Christian life in whatever vocation we follow and to witness Christ to others whom we meet along the way. Baptism levels the playing field for all vocations, including pastors. Ordination is subsumed under baptism as one vocation among many. Ordination is only one calling among others, no less and no more worthy than anything else you might do in life. If your vocation is to pick up trash for the city Sanitation Department, then do it with devotion and skill, as Luther told his barber to cut hair.

The Lord is the author of our true calling. This text from Isaiah applies to you and to me and to every human person: *(Isaiah 49:1b).*

> *The Lord called me before I was born,*
> *while I was in my mother's womb he named me.*

Every person on earth has a calling, however humble, implanted in us while we are still in the womb. Pray to the Lord to find yours. Nurture it, realize it, build on it, fulfill it. You will be blessed.

There is an old saying in ministry that some pastors do it as a *job*, others do it as a *profession*, while still others do it as a *calling*. Whatever you do in this life, seek to do it *as a calling*. You will be richly rewarded. If your work is not a calling, then maybe you ought to try another line of work. Our talents and skills differ. The Lord will show you what is right.

Another Test

A more serious confrontation than my new struggle at the sugar refinery occurred at my school. I went to the Dean and said, *I am fulfilling all of the course requirements listed in the curriculum, but I have a few electives available in my last two years. We do have English and History departments in the college. I want to take humanities courses for my electives.*

His response was uncompromising: *No way.* He stated that the electives were to be chosen from the Engineering school, with no exceptions. Otherwise, I would not qualify for a degree. And that was the end of that. I had no choice. Any attempt to transfer to a liberal arts college was out of the question as financially impossible, and would have cost me who knows how many extra years to obtain a Bachelor's Degree. So I had to soldier on where I was.

The Dreary Basement

Perhaps my most depressing challenge in those final two years of college was a laboratory course called the *Thermodynamics of Heat Engines*. The lab was in a smelly and dreary basement room of the school, with a cranky old Diesel engine as its centerpiece. The main point of the course was to demonstrate the principle of *entropy*.

Technically, *entropy* means *lost heat* or *lost energy*, which can never be recovered. For example, if you had a perfectly level bowling alley, with a perfectly polished ball on a perfectly polished surface extending for as long as you wanted it to stretch, the energy you put into rolling the ball would always be—in an ideal universe—the same amount of energy that the ball would take to be propelled down the alley. The result, of course—in such an ideal universe—would be that the ball would roll on forever, the energy going in being equal to the energy needed to roll the ball.

As we know, such a thing is not possible. Eventually, the ball will roll down to a dead stop. This is because the energy you put into it is always greater than the energy you get out as the result. The difference is due to friction. Friction is a simple fact of this mortal life. Friction is *lost heat*, called *entropy*, which cannot be captured or reclaimed.

Entropy works like a leaky bucket. You patch the bucket as best you can and put in the water you need for your journey. But along the way some water leaks out, and what you have available to use is always less than what you put in to start.

The obvious example of this is the romantic notion of creating a *perpetual motion machine*. This has been the fanciful, and futile, speculation for centuries of philosophers who have no proper grasp of reality. A *perpetual motion machine* always fails in the real world because the energy you put into it is always more than the result you get out. You lose some along the way. The machine stops when the energy you put in runs short. Most of the energy you put in to run the machine does run it, but some is diverted into friction. Friction takes its toll. It is *lost heat*, forever gone.

The lab course in the basement of the school with its archaic Diesel engine made its point. I soon was glad to be rid of it at the end of the quarter. I was graduated on schedule and in good order, all the while grieving the humanities education I had sought but could not obtain.

Upstate New York

After a short and eventful summer following graduation, I was off to seminary in September—ironically at St. Lawrence University in Canton, New York, the same school that grandfather Perkin had attended in his preparation for ministry.

I was impressed by our first event when we arrived at school. It was an orientation session for incoming students, led by the Dean. He told us the story of St. Lawrence, for whom the school was named.

Lawrence was a third century deacon who served as Treasurer of the church in Rome. He suffered a martyr's death under the persecutions of the Emperor Valerian, who ruled in the years 253–60. The Roman Empire sought to confiscate the wealth of the church, which Rome had heard was great. Lawrence was given three days to empty the treasury of the church and present it to the Imperial Court. By the third day Lawrence had assembled a large a crowd of lepers, orphans, cripples, the blind, the lame, and the destitute.

He declared, "*Here is the wealth of the church: the poor of the world, on whom the light of God has shined.*" For mocking the Emperor, Lawrence was condemned to be roasted alive on a gridiron.

It is said that he demonstrated heroic humor during his torture by exclaiming after a time, "*I am done on this side. You can turn me over to broil the other side . . .*" Little did I know that this would be a prophetic word for persecutions I would later suffer in years to come.

Philosophy?

The very first semester at seminary we were given a course in *Philosophy of Religion* as groundwork preparation for later courses to come in theology, biblical studies, and church history. We were given a textbook that explored various classic arguments for the existence of God. A number of these had originally been developed by the great medieval Doctors of the Church, and before them the ancient Greeks, beginning with Plato and Aristotle, and proceeding on to St. Thomas Aquinas, the greatest of the medieval schoolmen. The classical proofs were several, later classified by Emmanuel Kant as *ontological* proofs, *cosmological* proofs, and *teleological* proofs. It was all very exciting—a whole new world of thought I had never before encountered.

The *Ontological Proof*, developed by St. Anselm in the eleventh century and later refined by Descartes, seemed intriguing and convincing. It rests on notions that nothing greater than God can be conceived, and that an infinite and perfect God who exists in fact is greater than one who exists only in thought. This has been surpassed in modern times as somewhat heady and speculative.

Cosmological proofs go back to Plato in the *Timaeus*, and revolve around notions that every created thing must be created by some previous cause. So for all created things, the chain of causality runs backwards, step by step, each to the previous. But an infinite chain of causes going backwards forever is logically impossible. Therefore, by default, there must be a *First Cause*, itself uncaused and self-existent and giving rise to all the secondary causes in the series. That First Cause is God.

The third great proofs are *teleological*. Teleology means *destination*—an end point. As the old saying goes, *If you don't know where you're going, you'll never know when you get there."* In practical terms, this means that life has a *purpose*. It is not all random chaos. From this purpose derives *the Argument from Design*: For example, you cannot create an omelette *by throwing a dozen eggs out the window*. It takes deliberate and careful preparation, according to a plan. And if there is a *design* to this world, there must be a *designer*, an *architect*, and that is God.

Entropy, Again!

As we moved along through these various ancient debates, considering how they have been impacted by modern science and the evidence of evolution, we came finally to a chapter on *The Second Law of Thermodynamics*—which led to the *Argument from Entropy* for the existence of God.

I couldn't believe it! I thought I had left all that behind. What on earth could theological seminary have to do with that cranky old Diesel engine back in the basement lab of engineering school?

Yet I had to admit that the application was simple and made sense: The universe is like an alarm clock. You wind it up to get it started, but eventually it runs down to nothing and you have to wind it up again to get it running. *Entropy* is the nature of all mortal reality. Entropy is *decline*. We are born. We grow up and grow older, and eventually we die. Even mountains crumble and rocks disintegrate.

Pastors know this better than doctors. We do funerals. When the doctors are done, the pastor takes over. When the pastor is done, the lawyers take over to probate the estate. All Creation is in a state of decay. Every created thing is in the process of dying. All life is *entropy*. The only countervailing force against entropy is the power of God—the *inexhaustible source* of all that is. So I swallowed my astonishment and moved on.

All of this discussion, however, *was in the head*, not in the heart. It was, after all, *Philosophy of Religion* and not theology or scripture. Philosophy will not save you. God alone saves. When entropy threatens to drag you down, the Lord will lift you up—as Hannah knew and Mary sang.

Covenant

Christian faith is not philosophy. Christian faith is not primarily a matter of correct belief. Christian faith is first of all a matter of *adoration, devotion, belonging,* and *worship*. *Belonging* runs deeper than believing. Belief is important of course, because if you follow strange gods and worthless idols you are in deep trouble. Correct belief guides us toward authentic belonging. Wrong belief is delusional and destructive—as the sorry history of twentieth century ideological warfare so sadly shows.

Faith is a *personal relationship* with God. God is a Person. We belong to him and he belongs to us. Covenant is a binding relationship of *espousal*, like marriage. The prophet Isaiah tells us this (*Isaiah 54:5*):

> *For your Maker is your husband,*
> *the Lord of hosts is his name;*
> *the Holy One of Israel is your Redeemer,*
> *the God of the whole earth he is called.*

God loves us, cares for us, protects and provides for us like a husband. In the most Paleolithic and aboriginal model, the wife carries the household goods on her head, while the husband carries the spear and the sword and the shield to protect them from enemies and wild beasts. If God is our husband, then every believer—whether male or female—is the *wife of God*, spiritually speaking.

Admittedly, it is more constitutionally difficult for men to come to this truth than for women. That is why so many men more easily leave it "all in the head" as a philosophical proposition. This also is why so many men more easily fall away, or never come to the truth of God in the first place. We shall return to this matter again, later.

Faith means *trust*. We trust our mother. We trust our spouse. But these relationships can fail us, as in divorce. Or they end when the other person dies. God is the *Covenant Partner* who does not fail. Faith means to *rely* on him.

Theological school soon moved on from Philosophy of Religion to biblical studies and church history, which was a welcome blessing. David

Parke, our Professor of Church History, gave us two memorable guidelines: *(1) If you want a proper study of church history, begin with the Book of Acts. It all starts there. And, (2) read original documents and sources whenever possible instead of relying only on second—hand commentaries about what someone else said or did.* David was a University of Chicago product, as I was later to become.

A New Opportunity

Half way during my first year, the Dean arranged an appointment for me as a student pastor for a small parish in Dexter, New York, a village about an hour from the school. This was a great benefit not afforded to every student. It provided a fertile environment for learning at the intersection of classroom and parish. I marveled at the vitality of such a small church in what was largely a very depressed area of New York State's north country. This was a village of less than 800 people, with five churches in town. This was one of the strong ones.

In time, I began to perceive why they had thrived over the years. On my very first Sunday, a deacon showed me the hymnal they had in the pews, and on the inside of the front cover was pasted their order of worship. "*This is how we do it*," he said. He was not giving a command. He was just giving helpful orientation. So I followed it. It was classic *Morning Prayer* as it has been done down through the ages, about which too many good Christians are oblivious. The robed choir processed down the centre aisle to an Opening Hymn. The pastor led the opening versicles, with the choir and people all chanting the response from memory, set to classical Anglican chant by Thomas Tallis:

> *O Lord, open Thou our lips,*
> **And our mouth / shall show / forth Thy / praise.**

Then the choir and the entire congregation moved directly into chanting *Psalm 95*, in the 1740 Anglican plainsong setting by William Boyce:

> **O come, let us sing / unto the / Lord!**
> **Let us heartily rejoice in the strength of /**
> **our sal / va / tion.**

At the end of Psalm 95, everybody turned toward the large central cross over the altar and continued chanting the *Gloria Patri* to the same William Boyce plainsong, bowing down at the waist:

**Glory be to the Father, and / to the / Son,
and / to the / Holy / Ghost; /
As it was in the beginning, is now, and /
ever / shall be, /
world / without / end. / A / men.**

I loved it. It was heaven. I was *home*. It was shades of the family church in Philadelphia where I grew up, even before Lutheran Sunday School. I came to understand that this rich and rock solid liturgy gave this small church the stability to survive, even thrive over the years, despite the callow preaching of a long parade of novice seminary students like myself.

There is the old story, long told, of the proverbial young pastor in his first parish and the legendary little old lady in tennis shoes sitting in the back pew. On his very first Sunday, he preached at length about sin. When worship was over, she greeted him at the back door and said, *"Well, young man, that was an impressive sermon, carefully prepared and elegantly delivered. Unfortunately, you haven't lived long enough to have sinned enough to have even the faintest idea of what you're talking about.»*

Chicago, Illinois

In time, the limitations of grandfather Perkin's small seminary began to show. I knew I needed more preparation than was available there, especially given the educational poverty of my engineering school background in matters of history, literature, psychology and related humanities studies. At the end of my second year, I managed to transfer to a seminary in the University of Chicago complex of interconnected theological schools. It was a grand opportunity to study with the best of the best. At the time, it was said of the Hyde Park neighborhood on Chicago's south side that it was home to more seminaries and theological students than anyplace in the world except for the Vatican. It was also said of the University of Chicago that it was *a Baptist school where atheist professors teach Jewish students about medieval Catholic philosophy.*

On the other hand, there was a signal graffito etched into the wall in the men's toilet at a popular pizza hangout two blocks from the campus that reads:

Neitzsche is dead.
—God

In between St. Lawrence and Chicago, I was able to enroll in a full time summer quarter of ten weeks, 40 hours a week, of Clinical Pastoral Education at the old Mattapan State Hospital (now closed) in Boston, sponsored by Boston University School of Theology. I learned an important lesson there about myself. Out of of 30 theological students in our group, 29 were intimidated by the psychiatric wards more than by the general medical ward. I was the only one who was less comfortable in the medical ward than the psychiatric wards. I had a hard time with the blood drips and urine bottles and smells of the medical ward, but I had an easy time sitting around and chatting with an endless number of folks who clearly were completely out of their minds. I guess that says something about me, but I'm not sure how deeply I want to explore what that is.

The University of Chicago was a heady environment. But there were many faithful Christians in the faculties of the University Divinity School and the other connected seminaries where I studied, and I was enriched in faith as well as learning. I found professors who were at the top of the list in academia, who were kind and personable out of the classroom as well as in, but who also were persons of faith: Bernard Meland, Mircea Eliade, Martin Marty, Joe Sittler, and others. Marty was an especially pastoral person. So was John Godbey, of blessed memory.

In addition to classwork, which was magnificent, my school placed me into a new internship program in urban ministry—hands on, in the street. The city itself was the place and time for great events like the Martin Luther King rally in Chicago, including more than half a million people in a quiet, peaceful, and determined march through Grant Park and the adjacent downtown. It took my breath away to look back and see the waves of people coming without end from behind, and to look forward and see the same thing moving on ahead.

Along with local neighborhood work, there were the long conversations in the student lounge at odd hours of the day and night that enriched both street experience and classroom.

I thrived.

After another two years in Chicago, there came graduation and the placement at my first church. I was called to be the Associate Pastor at an urban parish in Brooklyn, New York, with a special portfolio for social justice work. This was, after all, 1965, and the nation was in an upheaval. This seemed like the perfect placement for me.

Brooklyn, New York

When I arrived in Brooklyn, everything in life was brimming over with promise. I was young, enthusiastic, and we went right to it. A task force of dedicated parishioners and I initiated an ambitious outreach program that included establishing a storefront community action center in Fort Greene, one of Brooklyn's more troubled neighborhoods about 20 blocks away from our church. I ran around with Richard Neuhaus who then was a Lutheran Pastor at St. John the Evangelist parish near the Williamsburg Bridge and of later fame as editor of *First Things*.

This was the decade of the 1960's, where it seemed that everything was permitted and nothing was impossible. Programmatically, our storefront center was a bold new venture for our parish. It was there that I began to comprehend the limitations of benighted liberal social action efforts among the poor. For example: the typical liberal assumption was that people in such neighborhoods were suffering from police brutality. Quite the contrary—we quickly learned that the chief complaint was lack of police protection.

We did our part organizing protests and carrying placards in the street reading "*No Rent for Rats.*" We took photographs of police officers sound asleep at noontime in their patrol cars in Fort Greene Park. We had community meetings at our center, where neighborhood residents could converse with police officials about drug gangs and the desire for a more active police presence.

Spiritually, I began to learn that the most powerful force for the improvement of life was not protest in the streets, but the preaching of the Gospel in indigenous, and mostly Pentecostal, local churches. That is where lives were being changed and where new generations were advancing beyond anything their parents had imagined. At one small street demonstration we led, I remember Mrs. Wallace, a large and formidable woman who was a deaconess at a neighborhood black church, stepping onto her front stoop and calling out, "*Where are the police when we need them? They need to get these thugs and hoodlums out of here who are selling drugs to our children on the street corner.*" She was a voice of sanity and authority.

The Brooklyn Heights neighborhood where my church was located was close to the eastern end of the Brooklyn Bridge, and the Esplanade provided a stunning view of New York harbor, the Statue of Liberty, and the Manhattan skyline. When I came to Brooklyn in 1965, the Twin Towers of the World Trade Center did not yet exist. Construction began in

1968. Tower #1 was completed December 1970, about the time I left New York. Tower #2 was completed the following year, July 1971. By 2001 they were gone. In addition to all the other horrors of that event, it was a shattering lesson in the transience of all things on this mortal earth.

In 1969, my church partnered with *M.U.S.T*, a large ecumenical organization in Manhattan that did urban ministry training for community action groups. It was another new venture for the times. The acronym *M.U.S.T.* originally had stood for *Methodist Urban Service Training*, but as its mission developed, it was changed to mean *Metropolitan Urban Service Training*. Its Executive Director, Bill Weber of the East Harlem Protestant Parish, had been its driving force. He had moved on to become President of New York Theological Seminary, so we were housed in the New York Theological Seminary building. M.U.S.T. received most of its funding from the national missions boards of several major denominations. My own parish provided half the salary for my own position there so that I could work full-time for M.U.S.T. as a member of their training teams. By 1970, financial funding from both my parish and the national mission budgets that had supported M.U.S.T. began to wane.

All of a sudden, it was time to move on.

Upstate New York, Again

On short notice, I was able to receive a call to a parish in a small city near Buffalo. I soon learned that I was not far from where grandfather Perkin had begun his ministry in 1888. My mother came to visit from Philadelphia. I picked her up at the bus terminal in Erie, Pennsylvania. As we were driving back through the countryside, I was commenting on the names of the small villages we were passing through. All of a sudden at Sherman, New York, she exclaimed in surprise to herself as well as to me, *Oh, this is where my brother was born in 1890!* (He was the uncle for whom I was named). There was hardly a traffic light in the town for us to pause, and the church that had been there was long gone. We moved on with hardly the time for the blink of an eye.

My new church had special challenges and my years there were to be short. But I was the Pastor of my own parish for the first time and that was exciting.

At the Annual Meeting of the parish my very first year I sat with some astonishment while the budget was being voted on. The proposal being passed out was a bare bones budget of about $18,000 (*that was worth a lot more then than it represents now*), while the projected income listed was less than $12,000. Anyone with a minimal sense for numbers knew that this could never work—but it passed unanimously with barely a word of discussion. I soon figured out that they had just sold the church's Parish Hall across the street the year before I came, and were making up the deficit by spending down the proceeds from a savings account where the money from the sale had been placed. There is no future in that.

Quite some years later in Massachusetts, I met the Pastor who had been my immediate predecessor there. He told me that he had to leave because they could not pay him on time. It became clear then that their remedy for their deficit was to sell the old Parish Hall just after he left and live off the proceeds. Not good.

Conflict

This small corner of Americana had culture-conflicts of its own. There were three basic constituencies in the church. One was a group of old-timers who had been there for generations, mostly Swedes who had emigrated in the nineteenth century. They were plain people, rock solid and generous of heart but of limited means. They were not moving on to anyplace else. We got on together very well.

The second group were young political assertives, a number of them attorneys, including the Executive Assistant to the Mayor. They were restless and eager to move up in the world. The Mayor was positioning himself to run for the New York State Assembly, with his band of supporters strongly behind him. This was the smallest constituency in the church of the three, but the one with the money and the energy.

The third group were essentially hippies, graduates of and fallouts from Woodstock and other period places. They had settled mostly on farms near town in a kind of back-to-the-land movement. They were loyal to the church, but sought to refashion it into an advance guard of an envisioned new world order, although without much energy and with very little means to bring this about. They were *"like, laid back, man."* I remember one fellow rhapsodizing about *being glad to get out of the city*. I presumed that he was talking about Greenwich Village in New York, until he corrected me. The "city" he was referring to was the small town where our church was located.

I tried to balance my relationships with all three groups. Group One was not going anywhere. Groups Two and Three, as it turned out, deeply resented one another for their entirely different and incompatible world views. Group Two was hanging in because they saw me as the sophisticated emissary from New York who had trafficked successfully with Wall Street brokers who were members of my church in Brooklyn. I think they were expecting me to drive out Group Three—which I did not do, and probably could not have done. Fairly shortly, Group Two evaporated from the church to seek other things. The two remaining groups had a very hard time trying to sustain the place. It became clear to me that I was not going to have a lasting or fruitful ministry there. It was, however, a valuable training time for me.

In 1974 I received a call to serve a substantial metropolitan congregation in Toronto, Ontario, just a few hours drive away. It seemed like a whole new universe of opportunity. A new horizon beckoned.

Four

Confusion

*Remember the long way that the Lord your God has
led you these forty years in the wilderness . . .*

—DEUTERONOMY 8:2

Wandering

IT HAD BEEN A rocky road from Brooklyn. I yearned for something new, but I was wandering lost, and searching. I was not confident that my three year ministry outside Buffalo had added anything significant to advance the beachhead of the Kingdom of God on earth.

As I began to look back in later years, I was not entirely sure about the previous five years in Brooklyn either. What I did know was that all this had been, as they say, *a learning experience*.

What I certainly did not know at the time was that all this had been a type of kindergarten, perhaps grammar school. It was preparation for a greater school of hard knocks to come.

Later on, in my middle years, I complained to my Spiritual Director that I had always yearned to see the blueprint of my life that lay ahead. With a wry smile he said, "*Well, if you saw the blueprint, then you would have to live through it twice.*» So we wander, sometimes not knowing where or why—sometimes not even aware that we are wandering.

Lost and Enslaved

Israel wandered in the desert wilderness for 40 years, lost. They were lost spiritually, not geographically. Egyptian astronomers were very skilled in reading the stars to guide them on any journey, and some of the Israelites would have learned these skills during their many long years in Egypt. Geographically, they would have been able to find their way.

Their wilderness journey was little more than 200 miles from the Nile to the Promised Land. At five miles a day, you could have pushed a donkey cart through the mud and gotten there in 40 days, not 40 years.

Why did it take them so long? There is an old saying: *You can take the slaves out of Egypt, but you cannot get Egypt out of the slaves.* It took them 40 years because the Lord was leading them, and he was leading them in circles in order to test them—and to teach them. They needed this in order to be delivered from enslavement to the Egypt they still were carrying around within themselves (Deuteronomy 8:2):

> *... your God has led you these forty years in the wilderness ...*
> *testing you to know what was in your heart ...*

I too was wandering, lost. I was a slave to things I did not understand. My Egypt included dark influences from my parents, romantic assumptions from faulty doctrines in my inherited religious tradition, unsavory shadows from the revolutionary fervor of the 1960's, and other inculcated values and corruptions ingrained from our culture.

It was harder for the Lord to get my Egypt out of me than to take me out of my Egypt. I was 35 years old when I moved to Toronto. I was confused and in bondage to varieties of darkness, and did not know it. It has taken me years to come to a new life in Christ.

Toronto, Ontario, 1974

When I received the call to go to Toronto I felt like I was on top of the world. This church I was called to serve had been established in 1845, partly through missionary efforts from a sister church in Montreal that had been gathered by Presbyterians from Northern Ireland, and partly from missionary visits from the pastor of a church in Chicago gathered in 1836—the same church I would later be called to serve.

To us mortals, such connections sometimes make it seem like a very small world. In the grand economy of God, such connections are part of a large tapestry for our lives that we can scarce comprehend—except as later hindsight gives us a more panoramic view.

I was puffed up. I felt invincible. I was feeling on top of the world because this appointment was to a parish that had been the "mother church" to a whole series of congregations in Ontario. A rapid expansion of population, along with tectonic shifts in the culture of Southern Ontario following World War II, had brought about the establishment of new churches in unthought of places during the 20 years before I arrived.

In addition to my Toronto responsibilities, I was asked to travel once a month to preach at these various spin-off congregations throughout Ontario. It was exhilarating. I felt like a missionary bishop traveling to the hinterland to nurture a far-flung progeny.

An invitation to preach in Thunder Bay introduced me to the vastness of the Canadian landscape. I could not possibly think of driving and the airline options did not seem inviting, so I took the train. It was the Canadian Pacific Railways' superliner from Montreal to Vancouver.

We left Union Station in Toronto at about 5 PM on a Friday afternoon. Dinner in the dining car was first class. Conviviality in the lounge car afterwards was charming and lively. The sleeping car was well—appointed, and with the gentle rocking of the carriage I slept like a baby. The next day, much of our travel was along the shoreline of Lake Ontario with the sunlight glistening on the water and the waves lapping the rocks only a few feet from the tracks.

We stopped at many rural villages that had no visible outside highway access. Their only contact with the rest of the world was by rail. We did not arrive at Thunder Bay until Saturday afternoon, nearly 24 hours later. It was then that it dawned on me that we had not yet left the Province of Ontario.

The Storm Gathers

It was not all glory. At the same time that I was exuberant over my new pastoral position, I began to come under fire for my theology. The church I was serving was having a strong counter-reaction against the conservative Calvinism that many had known from their Scottish parents and grandparents. They wanted to move in a liberal direction that seemed to me to abandon completely their Christian roots.

I remember an especially sad episode during Coffee Hour following worship on one Easter Sunday morning. Margaret, a long-time and devoted parishioner, started screaming at me for everyone to hear: "*What do you mean I crucified Christ? That was 2000 years ago. I was not there! I am not a sinner.*" I guess she was confident about her own holiness—but of course, since she was an agnostic rationalist, she would never have used the word *holiness* to describe herself. I could always handle such blatant and above board attacks because they were self-revealing of the attacker. What were more difficult were the sly, devious, and insidious intrigues that wanted to hide themselves from scrutiny.

This was a congregation that over a span of 50 years had drifted away from having a gentle but nominal Christian perspective toward being primarily Bertrand Russell devotees—a rationalist and skeptical outlook on life that, as they say, liked to have things *crisp*. But "rationalism" escapes you when you are filled with rage.

Après moi, le déluge?

Rationalism has severe limits as a framework to understand life. When I came to Toronto, some in the congregation had already begun to tire of the atmosphere of "crisp" and dry logic as the prevailing tenor of things. No doubt this dissatisfaction was behind the enthusiasm of many who at first were eager to see me as their new pastor. I did not base my faith on agnostic rationalism.

It happened that a few in the congregation who were poetically inclined presided at the occasional lay-led Sunday. One of these, Jack Robertson, was a theatrical sort of fellow in everything he said and did. He had a ruddy red face and snow white hair, and delighted in wearing a white suit with white shirt, white tie and white shoes at almost any season of the year. One Sunday he presented a "program" that offered poetry readings instead of book reviews in order to nudge things away from the dry. After hearing his presentation, it led one wag in the congregation to comment: "*When the dam of rationalism bursts, it releases a flood tide of sentimentalism that knows no limits.*»"

The Drift

Although I did sometimes feel confused about what I was doing there, I was not confused about why or how these folks came to represent what they represented. They described to me what "the old Toronto" was like in the 1950's, and it certainly was entirely different from the Toronto I saw when I arrived in 1974. As an old line institution from the nineteenth century, this church was more than eager to identify with "the new Toronto" of the time.

The Toronto I saw was a thoroughly cosmopolitan and international city. There were immigrants from all over the world, especially from Third World countries that formerly had been British colonies. They brought with them new languages, foods, cultures and customs which were evident everywhere. The city was an energetic place, brimming over with activity all hours of the day and night.

The Toronto of the 1950's, as they described it to me, sounded more like a stodgy, backwater place that resembled my father's descriptions of the old Scotland he had left behind, where all you were allowed to do on Sunday was pull down the shades and peek out underneath if you wanted to see any daylight. One fellow in Coffee Hour commented, *"Today they talk about sex without guilt. I grew up in a Scotland where it was guilt without sex."*

The older folks in my church described 1950's Toronto as a place where not even restaurants were open on Sundays. Their incumbent pastor at the time had made headlines by announcing that he would no longer wear a preaching gown in the pulpit and by managing to have his sermons published in the major daily papers, where he paraded what many in the public thought were scandalous heresies, but which delighted his congregation for the attention it brought them. He then engineered the sale of the old and majestic gothic church and developed the design of the new one by his own force of will. He was an "in your face" sort of character.

They bought into his program. They thought it was "progress" because it so shook the established order. Yet barely two decades later, the "novelties" they had pioneered no longer seemed novel. They were restless again for something "different." When they interviewed me, they claimed that I was the "different" they needed. Little did they know. Little did I know.

Confusion

Outward Signs of Inner Truth

They did possess a congruent harmony between outward form and inward spirit. The architecture of the new 1950's building reflected exactly the inner spiritual state of the majority of the people at the time. By design, it had been stripped down from having anything "churchy." I give them credit for being honest.

Unfortunately for me, I did not care for it at all. I saw it as arid, flat, and sterile. It was the least attractive part of my new calling, but it did have the virtue of correctly reflecting the truth of who these folks thought they were. During the interview process they had asked, with some pride, "What do you think of our building?" I stammered and blurted out: "*Well, it looks something like my junior high school auditorium.*" I thought I had lost the job right then before it even had been offered. But we quickly moved on to other things. Maybe they were impressed by my bluntness. I was not proud of my performance.

The previous nineteenth century building was an impressive gothic church, from the few old photographs of it I was able to find. The congregation had sold it in the years following WW II in order to relocate a short distance farther north from the downtown to a flourishing new neighborhood. The old church was demolished to make way for a department store office building.

The new structure was designed to be as "modern" as possible to reflect the new spiritual focus, which it did. It was an almost square brick box, with several floors of offices and classrooms attached. The inside walls were plain concrete. New names were given to the interior space to indicate their function. Instead of a *sanctuary* it was now an "auditorium." It was designed to be a multi-use space with movable chairs instead of pews to make a separate parish hall unnecessary. They were Art Deco armchairs from the old Eaton Auditorium on College Street when that building was remodeled—perfect for armchair philosophers to sit and listen to a studied discourse. (Incidentally, Glenn Gould said the Eaton Auditorium had the best acoustics in Toronto. It was his favorite place to play and he used it frequently for many of his recording sessions).

In front, instead of a *chancel* our building now had a "platform" that contained a *pulpit* (they did retain that customary name though many preferred "podium"). There was a grand piano instead of an organ. Pipe chambers for a new organ were included in the building's original design but never used. They remained empty because the majority thought an organ would be too "churchy." Besides, they wanted to save the money.

Instead of a *sacristy* (a place to store and maintain worship implements and materials) there was the "hydro room" (the place for electric meters for *Toronto Hydro*, the power company). They used this room to store microphones and audio equipment.

I spent some time digging through an old storage trunk in the church basement and came upon their magnificent set of nineteenth century Communion silver. The Eucharist had been a steady and constant source of grace in my own spiritual life, so I brought it out for display one Sunday morning. It was all there: hand wrought silver chalice, paten, and tankard to pour the wine. People had been inquiring into the roots of their own congregational history, so I thought it a valuable lesson about how much they had abandoned. I was shocked to discover that many thought that the large and splendid wine decanter was a coffee carafe, and they pondered using it for after-church Coffee Hour. I managed to derail that program by explaining what it really was.

And the Music

The organist/choirmaster from the old church was still with us and he did quietly lament to me that he missed the organ that had originally been planned. His job was to play the piano and recruit musicians from the Toronto Symphony to play chamber music with him for a long performance "Interlude" between the "Opening Words"(not *prayer*) that were to start things off and the "Address" (not *sermon*) that I was supposed to "deliver" (not *preach*). Some spoke of this in reverentially hushed tones as "The Platform Address."

The music was excellent in quality but it was as completely out of place as a third eyebrow. Purely secular music does not belong at the center of worship.

One small musical blessing did come my way when one family arranged for a bagpiper in full Highland dress to play a traditional Scottish funeral lament to process the casket down the centre aisle for a funeral at which I presided. The wailing of the pipes was bone-chillingly appropriate, and it helped me move beyond my father's distaste for bagpipes.

There were no hymnals and very little singing on Sunday mornings. Occasionally they sang "songs." They wanted to "listen" not *worship*. And they preferred that I preside over things in a business suit, not a robe or vestments, which again were seen as too "churchy." I disappointed them on that one. I said that if I were to wear only a business suit to lead the "program," I would need to stride down the centre aisle with my sermon notes and other worship items in a briefcase to complete the secularization process they had set in place. I wore vestments. And I preached sermons. And I prayed. They did not quite know what to make of it.

The Old Affliction Returns

I began to experience a disconnect between pastor and people that was akin to marriage incompatibility. The old physical nemesis from my college days began to rear its ugly head again. It returned for the first time since I had been a college sophomore, struggling with the challenge of final exams for my especially rigorous Physics course. In fact, this disability had dogged me since I was a small child. I would describe it as a hair–trigger stomach.

The most familiar manifestation of this was motion sickness in a moving car. I would be OK as a passenger until I might want to look at a map or read a magazine on a long trip. I could read on the train or in an airplane but not in a moving car or bus. Everything was fine so long as I looked out the window. But as soon as I would try to read in a moving car, everything and anything in my stomach would come up and out—and quickly.

I had long been intrigued about how such afflictions would pass along from generation to generation. My two children are only one year apart in age, yet totally different in personality and other aspects of their makeup. Often we would be riding in a car with the two of them in the back seat. My older son was heavily into books and later became a librarian. He would enjoy reading in a moving car without difficulty. But his younger brother could not restrain himself from looking over his shoulder at his brother's book.

Then I would hear the plaintive cry: "*Dad, stop the car. I'm going to be sick.*" I knew I had to jam on the brakes immediately, no matter what the traffic situation. There was never time to admonish him: "*I told you not to look at your brother's book.*" We always had to instruct him beforehand. Sometimes he would heed the warning. If not, the result was very messy. Ironically, he is the one who became a doctor when he grew up.

When I was small, I would regularly vomit my breakfast before leaving for school in the first or second grade. I was given a series of hospital tests, with barium ex-rays of my esophagus and stomach, which reported no physical abnormalities. The affliction was diagnosed as anxiety over schoolwork. By middle school, this affliction disappeared as I adjusted to classroom routines. It reappeared in my college Sophomore year at engineering school when I was taking my Physics course. By the mercy of God, I passed the course because I actually did enjoy Physics.

In Toronto, the affliction returned. Again, by the grace of God, the architecture of the building had provided a Pastor's Study just off the chancel, and the study included a private toilet. On far too many Sunday mornings than I care to remember, I would be sitting in a large pastor's chair near the pulpit while someone else led the opening parts of the service. When the time came for the long musical interlude prior to the sermon, the attack would come on with a bout of heavy sweating. I would slip out of my chair, make it into the study and vomit my guts out in the toilet. I would clean my mouth and wipe the sweat from my brow, which was then as cold as an Arctic storm, and crawl back to my chair just in time to rise up and preach.

The Lord is merciful. If they ever caught wind of what I had to go through to make it to the pulpit, they never said so—either out of politeness or because my stratagem of quick departure and return did not interrupt anything and was not intrusive enough to elicit unusual attention. The Lord always granted me the strength to preach, and I was grateful.

And the Nightmare . . .

From time to time I also had a recurring nightmare in which I would open the door of my study to go into the chancel and find my way blocked by two enormous grand pianos. As I would try to crawl over them, my vestments would get snagged in the piano strings. There is not much convoluted *interpretation of dreams* required for that one.

Under the Gun

Early on, along about my second year, the leadership of the parish appointed a *Ministerial Review Committee* that took on the task of engaging in private interviews with whoever had a gripe to express. After quite some months, a special congregational meeting was held to receive and discuss their report. It was pages and pages long, detailing every perceived violation I had committed against the core values they felt were important. It was a reasonably civilized meeting without a lot of shouting. After all, they did prize some sense of parliamentary decorum.

Some several hours into the meeting, an older man stood up to speak. Edgar was a reserved and dignified character. He had only recently joined the congregation and did not possess the institutional memory of the church's long drift away from its roots. He was generally respected by all as a steady and reasonable person and he quietly said, "*Well, it appears to me from reading this report that Mr. Gray is guilty of everything but last January's crippling snowstorm in Buffalo.*" Then he sat down. Not much more was said except for nervous chatter around the room. I was exonerated. No vote to discipline or dismiss me was proposed or taken. The report of the Ministerial Review Committee gathered dust on the shelf.

How It Went

Even most of my enemies thought my sermons were challenging and valuable, even when they disagreed vehemently with what I had to say. Every Sunday we had a "sermon talk-back" session in a lounge just off the sanctuary, a few minutes after Coffee Hour had convened. Most often some angry voice would challenge me to a debate with a leading question, "*What right do you have to say xxx about yyy*? " I would never answer the question but would cheerfully toss it back with, "*Well, tell me how you see it.*" As a pastoral tactic this began to elicit various peoples' hidden fears and hopes. And I listened . . .

Ida Kent was one of the saints of the church, easily old enough to have been my grandmother. She and her husband Bernie had grown up in Dublin, Ireland, as members of an historic Presbyterian Church there that had helped sponsor the original Montreal mission that later sponsored our church in 1845. She once described to me the public reputation that our church had earned. She said that friends who were not our members would say to her, "*O you belong to that church where they grill the pastor after every sermon.*" Word gets around.

Her remedy was to invite me to Sunday lunch from time to time and serve, among other things, Irish Coffee. It was strong—and delightful— just the ticket after being "grilled." I once asked her, "*Ida, explain Irish*

Whiskey to me." (*I was familiar with Scotch, but not with Irish. As an aside, Canadians, Americans, and Irish spell it "Whiskey" while the Scots spell it "Whisky."*) She replied simply in her flowing brogue, *"Well, there are two kinds: There is Protestant Whiskey and there is Catholic Whiskey."* She was droll. We left it at that. Those of us who are Celts are deeply connected.

The very first funeral I did upon my arrival in Toronto was for her husband Bernie. The last funeral I did just as I was leaving was hers. She had remained a steadfast and rock-steady supporter of everything I said or did for my entire time there. I bless the Lord for her to this day.

After seven years, I had had enough. It was a congregation that loved to debate and argue with me, but they never attacked my Person directly—only what I said and stood for. That was a blessing from the Lord. I could probably have stayed there for some years longer, so long as I was willing to tolerate the extremes of the debate. But I was done.

I loved Toronto. I enjoyed my Canadian environment. They might have tolerated me for a long career, but it was time for me to look elsewhere and move on—primarily for the sake of my sanity and self-respect, not to mention the chronic assault on my stomach.

I Was Not Alone

At the same time, I had my own issues of spiritual confusion, which were not fully revealed to me until a later time. I had a number of Pastor friends who struggled with similar issues. One dear friend, Michael Boardman, about my same age—and now deceased—described it to me this way: *After many years of trying to square the circle, I gave up—knowing that such a task was futile.*

I have had a long struggle coming to face the fact that for much of my career, I have been a *reformer*—and too often I have been unwilling or unable to admit this, either to myself or to others. Reformation in society usually means moving ahead from a bad practice to something better—like abolishing slavery, for example.

Reformation in the church classically has meant quite the opposite. *Reformation in the church* has historically meant a *restoration of the faith*, once held but then compromised, lost, or corrupted.

Reform in the church means a return to *authentic roots*, not the introduction of novelties. Cut flowers don't last—no matter how pretty the arrangement. I was a reformer—too often a thankless task. Perhaps that is why I resisted owning up to what I was doing.

Facing the Truth

Years after Toronto was over I had to face the truth in an unexpected way. I was having a business conference in my office in Chicago with the head custodian of the parish over property matters. We had a custodial staff of three and he was the supervisor. He was also a church member.

All of a sudden the conversation shifted from custodial routines to liturgy and theology. He confronted me straightforwardly and said, "*The trouble with you, Gray, is that you're a reformer, and we're not ready for your reformation.*" I stammered and stuttered and objected saying, "*No, no, I'm not introducing anything new. I'm trying to rebuild what this place has lost.*"

He spoke the truth on two counts: (1) I *was* a reformer, and (2) *they* weren't ready. What I said about not introducing something new was also technically correct, but that didn't matter. What did matter was that I didn't want to face up to what he said. I was confused.

Even Jesus was not the 100% perfectly successful evangelist. He was not confused, of course. He knew exactly what he was doing and the price he would have to pay for it. But on matters of "success," consider the *Rich Young Man* in *Matthew 19:22*. When Jesus told him what to do, he was crestfallen. He went away sad, and we never hear of him again.

Nicodemus too was a tough case, but he fared better. In *John 3*, he questions Jesus extensively, but goes away confused and perplexed. Yet in the end, he shows up in *John 19:39* with a hundred pounds of burial spices to anoint the dead body of Jesus. He had become a believer.

Martin Luther remarked: *The pagan trembles at the rustling of a leaf. The uniform teaching of Scripture is that fallen men are fleeing from God.*

The Dynamics of Confusion

I was not fleeing from the Lord. I was searching—like Nicodemus. I knew that I had a calling from the Lord, but like static on the radio when you are too far from the broadcast tower to get a proper signal, I was roving in the dark as much as walking in the light.

I also was grasping at straws in a whirlwind. I remember clearly some grace-filled moments that helped me retain my sanity. As had been true for much of my life, many of my most comforting and converting moments were in church. I admit that this is a grace not too many people can confess.

Occasions of Grace

Good Friday was a blessed day in Toronto. Despite the growing secularization of Canadian society, Good Friday—following the traditional European pattern—was a total public holiday. I remember walking down Yonge Street—the main drag—on a Good Friday morning. Normally it was a bustling cosmopolitan thoroughfare, but on Good Friday it was dead as a doorpost—except for the churches.

I stepped into Trinity Church by the Eaton Centre for the 11 AM worship. It was appropriately stark for Good Friday. All of the statuary was covered in purple. The sanctuary had movable cathedral chairs and these were arranged in a circle around a huge wooden cross placed at the center of the nave. The *St. John Passion Narrative* was read *(John 18:1—19:42)*.

We were invited to place nails into the cross in silence as a sign of our own participation in the Passion. The priest wore only a simple black cassock—Good Friday being the only day on the ancient calendar of the church when the Eucharist is not celebrated. We prayed a penitential litany for the sins of the world, and for our own. Then we departed quietly without a Benediction. A reserved sacrament was placed on a rude wooden table by the exit door so that we could partake of the Body and the Blood in silence, each at our own pace, as we left the church. It was a rich and redeeming event. I wept—for the sins of the world, for my own wayward church, and for myself. And I received a deep and quiet peace.

Two other occasions sustained me during those troubled years. One, I attended my first Easter Vigil at St. Thomas Church on the University of Toronto campus. Traditionally, this is called *the First Mass of Easter*. It starts by lighting a bonfire outside the church and ends with the glory of the Resurrection at midnight, when all the lights go up and the *Gloria* is sung for the first time since the beginning of Lent. The bonfire is lit to signify the New Creation, which is Christ, just as light came into the darkness at the First Creation *(Genesis 1:3)*:

> *Then God said, "Let there be light;" and there was light.*

From the bonfire a new Paschal Candle is lit, to be used throughout the coming year as a sign of the Risen Christ who shines in the darkness of the world. When we stepped into the church, everything was in total darkness except for the small vigil candles we were given to signal the coming of Christ.

Then the singing began. I was stunned to hear an entire congregation singing all the Psalms and responses from the *Book of Common Prayer* from memory in the dark, because even with a small vigil candle it was impossible to read the prayerbook in the darkness.

I began to realize then how much we had lost in our churches when we stripped down the liturgy to nothing more than idiosyncratic novelty, reinvented from week to week by whatever imagination the pastor possesses—which too often is not much. There is no point to trying to memorize novelties because, by their nature, they change from week to week.

The other sustaining occasion was attending Holy Week services at the Church of St. Mary Magdalene. This was a small parish in a blue collar working class neighborhood of Toronto where Healey Willan had been the organist and Music Director for much of his career. He had died in 1968 only a few years before I arrived in Toronto. They sang *Tenebrae* services three nights in a row, with both a sanctuary choir (seated in facing pews in monastic fashion at the front) and a gallery choir (on a shelf at the rear). It was *heaven on earth*—which is what the liturgy is designed to be.

Tenebrae is Latin for *darkness*. *Tenebrae* is a form of monastic Morning Prayer, typically done in the early hours of darkness before sunrise, but transferred for parishes to an evening service the night before to make it accessible for ordinary working people to attend. So Wednesday evening *Tenebrae* is based on Thursday Morning Prayer for Holy Week, and so on. The basic format is the singing of penitential Psalms with readings from the Book of Lamentations, along with the progressive extinguishing of candles to represent the falling away of the disciples in their hour of testing. All of this reflects the solemnity and agony of the Passion in preparation for Easter. The agony, of course, is not only that of Christ facing the Cross. The true agony is our own infidelity and running away, as the disciples did at Calvary.

Some of our churches do celebrate a Tenebrae during Holy Week on Maundy Thursday evening. And that is good. But to do this three nights in a row as preparation for Easter is a seriously transforming encounter with the Lord and not easily forgotten. I was deeply blessed by this encounter. It centered me in the midst of my own confusions like tuning out the static on an old radio when you finally get the dial adjusted properly to the exact frequency of the signal.

The Bare Bones Church

Celebrations like this are a reminder of what our churches have lost when we strip down our worship practice to the convenient cultural expectations of our day.

I remember once sitting behind two young women at an ecumenical conference and curiously eavesdropping on their conversation. The one said to the other: *Oh, our church is just great!* "*First we listen to 15–20 minutes of praise music, then we have an intermission break for coffee and chit-chat. Then we go back, and the pastor steps out and just talks to us for an hour.*"

I thought to myself, "*How dreary. Nothing but musical entertainment and talk, talk, talk.*" Although their church was more faithful in doctrine than mine, it was no different *in form and function* from the secularized congregation I served in Toronto where everything is stripped away but the talk and the music, where you only listen and no one sings.

This is *consumer religion*, where church is a product to be ingested like any other commodity from the supermarket shelf. Where is the prayer, the devotion, the *covenantal belonging* to a sovereign and saving God? It is *the sin of nonchalance before the holy*—a domestication of the awesome mystery and majesty of Almighty God to trivial categories we can manipulate to our own taste and preference.

An Unexpected Truth

At another large ecumenical conference I once attended I went to a workshop led by a Youth Pastor from Willow Creek Community Church in South Barrington, Illinois. The workshop gathering was small enough to provide for easy discussion with a question and answer time after the main presentation, as such workshops are designed to be.

The Youth Pastor was competent and well-informed about his work, and he gave us a detailed picture of how his youth ministry operated. It was impressive and unusual. Afterward I asked him, "*Would you describe the shape and pattern of your youth ministry program as a general design for the whole church in the future, or do you see it as a highly particular design for a specialized target population i.e., teens?"*

He was quick to pick up on what I was asking and said, *"No, it is not at all a pattern for the shape of the whole church—it is a particular design for teens."* So I asked a follow-up question: *"Do you see any discernible trend about where these teens go and what they do with their spiritual lives after your program?"* He paused for a moment and said, *"No, not really—they go off in a number of directions and to a variety of church involvements as they become young adults."* Then he hesitated a bit more and added, *"But if there is any one trend, we see a number of them move on to the Greek Orthodox Church because as adults, they find something rich and satisfying in the liturgy that we never provided."* He had a touch of wistful surprise in his voice when he said this, but it came as no surprise to me.

Chicago, Again

Relief came for me in 1980 when I was called to another metropolitan church in Chicago after nearly seven years in Toronto. At the time, this seemed like pure deliverance from torture to tranquility.

How sadly mistaken I was.

We started out well. This was a unique parish first gathered in 1836 by missionaries from Boston. The church had survived the Great Chicago fire of 1871, but by the turn of the century it found itself in a depleted condition at its location just south of downtown (*known by everyone as "the Loop"*).

Revival came in the 1920's when the Hull family—who had helped establish the pioneering work of Jane Addams at *Hull House* in Chicago—provided the means for the church to move and rebuild farther south next to the new campus of the University of Chicago.

Through the Depression years of the 1930's, the church then flourished. This renewal had three different but deeply interconnected aspects: (1) the <u>architecture</u> of a new building, (2) the development of a sophisticated <u>liturgy</u> for worship, and (3) the gathering of new people into a spiritually revived <u>congregation</u>. Who could ask for anything more—especially during the dark years of the Great Depression?

The foundation of this renewed and revived congregation was the vision of *Isaiah 6:1–8*, which has five distinctive steps in its spiritual progression:

- **Confrontation** (Isaiah is caught by surprise at the intrusion of God into his ordinary routines): "*I saw the Lord sitting on a throne, high and lofty; and the hem of his robe filled the temple . . .*" Angels flew and called to one another: "*Holy, holy, holy is the Lord of hosts. The whole earth is full of his glory . . .*"
- **Confession** (This awesome spectacle overwhelms Isaiah, and he acknowledges his mortal frailty in the face of this divine majesty): "*Woe is me! I am lost, for I am a man of unclean lips, and I live among a people of unclean lips . . .*"
- **Cleansing** (One of the angels takes a live coal from the altar with a pair of tongs and flies to Isaiah): "*The seraph touched my mouth with it and said: 'Now that this has touched your lips, your guilt has departed and your sin is blotted out . . .*' "
- **Summons** (God then addresses Isaiah directly): "*I heard the voice of the Lord saying, "Whom shall I send, and who shall go for us?"*
- **Response** (Isaiah answers): "*And I said, 'Here am I. Send me!'*"

Can we imagine what kind of chair is big enough to hold God? "*I saw the Lord sitting on a throne.*" Can we imagine a garment where merely the fringe fills the entire space? "*and the hem of his robe filled the temple . . .*"

One of the most overused words in our culture is *awesome*. Even when you order an item from the menu for lunch, the waitress is likely to say that your choice is *awesome*. A chicken sandwich at the deli is not awesome. Only God is awesome in his majesty.

For quite some years I had been a student of this Isaiah text and its application to the life of this Chicago church. I knew the history of the rebirth that had taken place there inside and out. So now, to be asked to go there as Senior Pastor seemed like coming home to heaven. Little did I know the hell I was being invited into.

Five

Conversion

*The Father has rescued us from the power of darkness
and transferred us into the kingdom of his beloved Son,
in whom we have redemption, the forgiveness of sins.*

—COLOSSIANS 1:13-14

The Landscape of a New Calling

IN OCTOBER OF 1980 I landed in Chicago on the rebound of a severe flagellation in Toronto. I was like a battered woman escaping from an abusive marriage and then falling into the arms of someone who seemed like the perfect lover—only to discover, in time, that this new relationship was worse than the one before.

Of course I couldn't see that then. Few of us do. After all, this new parish promised to be the liturgical showpiece with the magnificent architecture and the spiritually sophisticated congregation. I presumed that they worshipped with deep reverence and gratitude for the work of an awesome God. Or so it seemed. More than that, I was just the right person at just the right time who had been rightly schooled in this church's remarkable legacy. I was therefore equipped to enhance its vision forward. Or so it seemed.

I had spent years pondering and praying over the text from *Isaiah 6:1—8* that had shaped this church. So too it came to have a large influence on my own ministry. Yet I had failed to factor sufficiently the next part of the text that begins with *verse 9*. Romantic interpretations of the faith stop at *verse 8* and end there. I was guilty of that romantic blind spot.

After his glorious vision, Isaiah was given a distasteful task that was decidedly inglorious. He was told to prophesy *the Babylonian Captivity* that would take Israel back into slavery again, despite already having spent centuries of slavery in Egypt. He would also prophesy the Assyrian invasion of the north that would wipe out the Ten Northern Tribes forever. Who wants to tell people things like that?

A lot of people read this *Isaiah 6:1–8* text and then drift off into a romantic reverie as their eyes glaze over in halcyon bliss. They never read on through *verses 9–13* to reckon with the task that Isaiah is given to do. Failure to read *beyond verse 8* is a deadly trap that leads directly to the abject failure of sentimental religion. I know. I have been guilty of this too—until later trauma knocked me back to reality.

Pain

At my new post in Chicago I began to learn about pain—*real pain*. Most of us have experienced something like a toothache, here or there. Many of us see extreme physical pain when police or firefighters or military personnel are wounded in the line of duty. Much of it seems unbearable. But physical pain has a way of getting resolved by time and medical intervention.

Psychic, emotional, and spiritual pain are quite another matter. More public attention is being given to these now than generations ago and that is good. Post traumatic stress and other psychic disabilities are real. Returning soldiers suffer from having seen unspeakable atrocities in the line of duty. The emotional trauma they suffer can often dwarf the pain from their physical wounds.

War is not the only source of these things. Too many ordinary folks bear crippling personal and private scars, sometimes without any acknowledgement. I am sometimes astounded at the range of suffering I perceive on an average Sunday morning when I look out at a typical gathering of God's people assembled for worship.

When I started out in 1965 I was oblivious to such ubiquitous pain. It took only a few years before I was introduced to this reality in a personal way. After being whiplashed by events in Toronto with more to come in Chicago, I was hurting badly. We sometimes have to hit bottom before we can be turned around.

I hit bottom.

I fell into a pit from events and circumstances I did not foresee. In my life, confusion led to pain, and pain led to conversion. I thank the Lord for that.

The Clues Were There

There were some early clues about what lay ahead in Chicago, but I didn't see them or didn't want to see them. I had just begun to settle into place and I certainly was not looking for rocky shoals just beneath the surface of the tranquil sea.

I had known Etta Gibson for years through a civil rights project that had involved her church in Chicago and my former church in Brooklyn. She served as Chair of the Chicago Search Committee that had nominated me for this new position, and had been an eager advocate to bring me there. She made an offhand remark while giving me a "get acquainted" tour of the church and community. We were walking along the street and she said, "*Well, you have to watch out here—this is a warping place . . .*" (She was referring to the church, not the neighborhood). We both laughed it off.

In time, she would turn out to be a deadly enemy, as Search Committee people can sometimes become when we fail to fulfill their expectations or to do their bidding. Some years later she declared to others in the parish: *We brought him here. We can take him out.* She thought she owned me. She did not. Only the Lord owns me. And he rescued me from being warped.

The District Executive for our area (the staff person responsible for coordinating things among 60–75 parishes) gave me what seemed like an offhand warning the first time we met. He was an affable Icelander from Manitoba and was looking out for my welfare as he did for all the pastors in his District. He said, in a reflective moment in the corridor outside our parish office, "*You need to watch out for Pastor Cliff. He's like a little kid at the zoo. Just when all the monkeys are sitting quietly on their roosts, he likes to run along the cages banging on the bars with a stick, just for the fun of it, until all the monkeys are jumping and chattering and screaming for no good reason."*

I heard him but did not compute the seriousness of what he said. I was too enthralled with a vision that later turned out to be an illusion.

Corporate Challenges

The church was a sprawling enterprise that included four major community programs initiated by the parish, with several still under its direct supervision. This meant that 45–50 adult staff people (*full and part time*) passed through the building every day. The first battleground was the weekly Thursday morning staff meeting for which I was the nominal chair, with some 16–18 of the more significant players attending. Much of the time I felt like a playground supervisor trying to restore order to a bunch of unruly children in the sandbox who were throwing sand into each others' eyes. Many of the squabbles were over space usage and custodial routines, and who was accusing whom of leaving this or that room in disorder for the next occupant instead of properly putting away the toys. The pattern of this staff meeting was a strong undertow that masked the tidal wave to come.

I had been called to the position of Senior Pastor. At the time, it was a five pastor church. This meant that I was the point person for preaching, public worship, and basic pastoral care. The other four pastors were not young or novice "assistants" just starting out. They were not in a hierarchy like the military to be given orders by me or be delegated whatever tasks I had when I didn't want to do them. They each were seasoned directors of parish sponsored Associated Programs with unique skills of their own in the specialties under their watch. According to the parish Bylaws, however, I was the designated institutional CEO of what was, in fact, a chaotic corporate institution.

I welcomed the challenge and I felt qualified to handle it. Preaching and public worship were always my first gift. These were skills I had honed over the years and I had often received confirming feedback about the worthwhileness of what I had to offer. Add to this my college background in business management and corporation finance and it all seemed to fit like a custom made shoe. Moreover, I had always been a teamwork person and I welcomed the opportunity to work together with other pastors who were my peers more than underlings.

Then there was my experience in Brooklyn, where I had been an Associate with a specialized portfolio in a cooperative relationship with a Senior Pastor who had treated me as a peer. Everything made sense—until undercurrents deep below the surface began to exercise their deadly pull.

I encouraged each of my four Associates to assist with worship, including sharing the pulpit by having them preach on a regular schedule. On these occasions, I would take on the assisting roles at the lectern and altar. This was important to me because I had always believed that the whole Body of Christ was more important than any one person. I believed that pastoral teamwork was far more rich than personality cult ministries where parishioners too often end up worshipping the charismatic cult leader instead of the one true God.

I soon learned that this was not to be. Each of the four other pastors demurred, claiming to be not especially skilled at preaching or public worship. Each had specialty skills that I did not posses: one for music, one for social work, one for psychotherapy and clinical pastoral care, one for the sometimes tedious administration of a crypt chapel in the undercroft of the church with columbarium vaults for the interment of ashes. This frequently included the difficult task of chasing down families of the deceased who would deposit cremains with the church and then fail to make any followup arrangement for their final placement.

How Senior Was "Senior?"

Pastor Cliff, the "senior" of my four Associates whom our District Executive had warned me about, had been there for more than 25 years. He had served "under" (*pardon the expression*) three previous Senior Pastors and I was the fourth to have that dubious honor. He was always cordial, but he was the most reluctant of the four to be seen in any public worship position. It was all I could do to get him to preach once a year—which he did under duress, often repeating himself from the previous year.

I also soon learned, however, that he saw himself as the *defining pastor* of the parish (*my language to describe him, not his*). He wanted to call the shots about the life of the parish and its direction, while never admitting so. He never wanted to preach, but he carefully monitored everything I said and sought to "instruct" me on my mistakes—and, more especially, about my "deviations" from what he perceived to be the spiritual norms of the congregation.

Pastor Cliff's most destructive behavior was the easy access he afforded to receive the murmuring complaints from parishioners who did not want to speak directly to me. He invariably took sides with them to validate their dissatisfactions with what I was doing.

He did this openly and he explained to me what he was doing and why. His justification was that he believed his validating of contrary positions held by disaffected parishioners against initiatives I was taking was a helpful way of creating a "balance of power" in the congregation between them and me. He saw himself as "the defender" of the oppressed and me as "the oppressor." He said it with a smile.

Twisted.

The *Rule of St. Benedict* is the granddaddy of all documents that lay out *a rule of life*, the necessary ground rules for maintaining harmony, order, and virtue in a close-knit community. It has sustained the common life of Benedictine monasteries for nearly 1500 years. The *covenanted community* of a Benedictine monastery is in its interior dynamics very much like that of the *covenanted community* of a congregational church. The *sin of murmuring* is identified at several places in Benedict's Rule as one of the grievous practices that disrupts community life. This, in turn, is based upon the *murmuring* of Israel in the desert against the leadership of Moses *(Exodus 17:4)*:

> Moses cried out to the Lord, "What shall I do with this people? They are almost ready to stone me."

When we paper over the *sin of murmuring* and make it seem innocuous by calling it "gossip," or see it as a virtue in the name of a "constructive" balance of power, we court serious harm to our common life.

Who Calls the Shots?

My conflicts with the power structure proceeded on two different levels. These were essentially unrelated, but they converged in the real world to bring almost irreparable harm to my position as Pastor. They were: (1) Administrative, financial, and managerial issues, and (2) (*much more importantly*) theological issues. Theology is, after all, the discourse that defines the church. If we don't know what we stand for or cannot agree on what we uphold, what is the point of all the rest?

My "number one" Associate, Pastor Cliff, had started out by trying to call the shots on the spiritual focus of my public leadership. In time, my relationship with him proceeded on to include severe financial and administrative conflict. He was in charge of the largest of our four Associated Programs, a music ministry for children that provided a striking alternative to street gangs and the drug culture of Chicago. 25 years earlier he had begun with a small Sunday School choir, and then expanded the church's outreach when the public school system scaled back its music programs. Over the years he had developed a venture that included more than 600 children enrolled in after school singing groups, along with intermediate and senior performing choirs. He had a staff of 18 people to assist him—conductors, piano accompanists, and administrators.

The program budget for this most unusual ministry was larger than the basic parish budget, and it included a complicated bookkeeping system of commingled funds in the same checking account. His idea was that cash shortfalls in the parish budget would temporarily be covered by choir income, and the opposite when his revenues fell behind. Hopefully his shortfalls would occur in different seasons of the year from parish needs. This needed to be untangled.

It Gets Worse . . .

To complicate matters, the church Treasurer—responsible for monitoring all of this—was an engineer with absolutely no financial or accounting background. He prided himself on providing an early version of electronic bookkeeping—on a gerrymandered home computer he had built himself. Remember, this was the early 1980's when desktops had hardly appeared. The memory system for his computer was small cassette tapes which invariably missed the mark at every start and stop of the cassette, resulting in lost digits and compromised data.

I remember many sorrowful conversations in my office with Mr. Epstein, the outside Auditor whom the church engaged to provide an Annual Audit. He was a kind and patient man. Each year he would make an appointment with me and come in with essentially the same sad message—year after year. He would lament the high fee that he was obliged to charge us, explaining that the bookkeeping provided by the Treasurer was so botched up that he could not audit it. He first had to hire an independent professional bookkeeper to go back to the original bank statements in order to reconstruct the books for the entire year, so that his auditing firm had something reliable to audit. I knew exactly what he meant. He would plead with me to go back to the parish Board of Trustees, explain the problem to them, and ask them to appoint a competent Treasurer so that he could do his audit in routine fashion and save us a staggering fee. I did this, of course, but to no avail. The Treasurer was a fixture in the congregation and no one had the courage to nominate anyone else for the office of Treasurer at the parish Annual Meeting.

In addition to Pastor Cliff wanting to call the shots on my preaching and worship leadership, I realized that the Trustees were the ones who wanted to call the shots on management issues—despite my being the designated CEO—but they were incompetent to manage.

Congregational Polity Unmasked

Congregational polity originally developed in the seventeenth century to liberate the people of God from oppressive bishops, synods, and presbyteries. In its original form, the Annual Meeting for church business was conducted as a prayer meeting. But when Christ is banished and the Holy Spirit departs, congregational polity descends into a hellish parody where the inmates are in charge of running the asylum.

A More Egregious Corporate Crisis

I had arrived in Chicago in October of 1980. Before the month was out, my "number two" Associate Pastor approached me to talk about "a problem." He was a reserved and gentle soul whose expertise was family therapy, not financial management.

He was the Executive Director of the parish's second most formidable Associated Program. This was a comprehensive therapy and crisis intervention agency that received most of its funding from public sources through referrals from the family court system, which sent us persons and families in need. It employed a substantial professional staff of MSW counselors and therapists, along with the necessary administrative support people.

In his conversation, Pastor Ethan confided in me that his agency was in financial trouble. *Deep trouble.* He gave me his report in a calm but serious manner. I never knew whether this was because he did not understand the gravity of the matter, or whether he was so grounded in the reality of life that he could accept the worst with a higher trust that

God was sovereign and would care for him no matter what. I prefer to believe the latter.

In any event, his report was simple and matter-of-fact. He said, *I knew last spring that we were in trouble, so I had to terminate our bookkeeper to save on her salary. I took the books home to work on them myself. We missed the June 15 IRS deadline for remitting the Withholding taxes from our staff for the second quarter because we just didn't have the money. Then we missed the September 15 third quarter deadline for the same reason. We are less than three months away from the January 15 fourth quarter deadline and we cannot make that one either.*

I knew what this meant, because his agency was still a corporate entity of the parish. I told him: *You know I cannot receive this as a form of private and confidential confession. This is a serious administrative breach of financial trust. I have to report this to the next meeting of the church's Board of Trustees.* He simply said, *I know . . . .*

Jail Time?

The parish Board included a number of attorneys, business people, and bankers. They were more than alarmed when I reported the situation. It is one thing to fail to pay your own taxes to the IRS. That involves only you and the Tax Man, your own money (*or lack of it*) and what the law requires. It is quite another matter to fail to remit other peoples' money when you have collected their Withholding taxes on their behalf, and you are supposed to remit them as a third party fiduciary. To fail to do this borders on fraud, or worse.

The Trustees immediately knew that they were personally liable and in serious danger. They did not want to envision themselves in Federal Tax Court or serving time in the Big House. So they voted on the spot to raid the church's endowment funds to pay the IRS nearly $40,000 before the next deadline on January 15. Pastor Ethan's head rolled quickly. He was summarily dismissed and I never heard from him again. I pray to the Lord in his mercy for him.

I quickly turned to my "number three" Associate Pastor and asked him to become a candidate to be the new Director of our family therapy agency. Pastor Timothy was a fully credentialed pastoral psychotherapist who also possessed a sound and practical business head. He knew the situation and was reluctant to touch it. He was fully employed at another church agency in the city and served pastoral care needs in our parish on a volunteer basis. He was understandably hesitant to trade away his own family financial security by giving up his position at a large and reliable agency for the improbable future of ours. But I prevailed on him, and he applied for our position. He was quickly confirmed and took up his new post. It was a highly successful move. He restored stability and financial health to a struggling enterprise and the entire church was grateful. Among all of the contending personalities and fiefdoms in our highly complex institution, I was able to count on his wisdom and confidentiality to the end. Pastor Timothy was a Prince in the company of the saints. I thank the Lord for him.

Following in the Footsteps of a Tyrant

Other things were deeply wrong in our day to day administrative life. They had roots in the practices of decades before, as most things do. My predecessor, Pastor Richard, had been Senior Pastor for ten years during the troubled 1970's. He spearheaded many public initiatives to speak to the times. He dominated the pulpit, demanded the spending of money the church didn't have, and defined the church's public persona. He was an egocentric and overbearing character, but he also radiated a magnetic charm that inveigled almost everyone to cower to his whims rather than risk his rage.

This was true even for the most seasoned officers of the church who might have had the mettle to stand up to him, but did not, or could not. At his very first Board of Trustees meeting shortly after he had arrived on the scene, things began in a routine manner. An eyewitness related to me what had happened next. It came time for the Treasurer's Report and the Treasurer at the time, a distinguished elder of the parish and a competent financial person, quietly related that the church was facing a substantial budget deficit—a proper report to help orient a new pastor. Pastor Richard abruptly interrupted his report, stood up from his chair (he was a tall and commanding figure), and banged his fist on the table saying, *We'll have no more negative talk here about money*! and sat down. They then moved on to other things. After the meeting was over, the Treasurer submitted his Letter of Resignation without finishing his term of office and quietly disappeared from the church, never to be seen again.

This had paved the way for several of our financial catastrophes. These continued to play their way out after Pastor Richard's departure, leaving me to clean up the debris as the next occupant of the office of Senior Pastor. In a different environment, he could have become a very dangerous cult leader.

I learned later on from a very wise counselor who ran her own corporate head hunting firm that this problem of leadership style was not unique to the church. She explained that throughout the industrial world, when an overly authoritarian executive departs, his successor is typically doomed to failure unless he can successfully mimic his predecessor's every gesture, footstep, and commanding tone. Otherwise, a thoroughgoing reform of the entire enterprise is needed to replace a dysfunctional system.

This counselor was a blessing to me that the Lord provided unexpectedly, just when I needed it. God is Providence (*provision*).

When you are groping your way through a dark tunnel, it is always a healing balm to learn that you are not alone The Lord is with you. Others have been there too and you can know that you will pass through your challenges victoriously, by the grace of a merciful God.

The Newsletter Deception

What I learned about the weekly parish newsletter was another revealing indicator of dysfunction. Pastor Richard's unbending expectations were obvious to the office staff and program administrators under him. The church office had a variety of responsibilities to look after and the weekly newsletter was only one task among many. Articles had to be solicited, coordinated, edited, and jockeyed around for space. Then the 10–12 pages had to be typed, folded, stapled, addressed, and bundled by zip code. I told the office staff that it was important to do it right and do it well, and that if the newsletter was a day late in the heavy seasons of the year it was better to be late than to be sloppy. It was, after all, our basic face to the public.

My encouraging words to the office staff were taken with deep suspicion. I learned that they had been bullied into a deception that they were still too frightened about to want to abandon. But one secretary finally had the courage to spill the beans. She explained that Pastor Richard demanded that the newsletter be completed and given to the Post Office by noontime each Tuesday, no matter what.

He had a practice of working at home several mornings a week to achieve solitude and not be disturbed. On Tuesday afternoons he would show up at the office around 2 pm for a long day that often stretched into the night with appointments, committee meetings, and other claims on his time. I knew that schedule too, often having three committee meetings in one afternoon: at 5, 6:30, and 8 pm.

He would stride through the office around two, monitoring things to be sure that the newsletter had been completed. More often than not, it had not been completed. So the office staff had a regular practice of bundling it up, unfinished, and stuffing it into a canvass post office bag and hiding it in a mop and broom closet down the hall. Pastor Richard would survey the situation and, satisfied, move on. Then early the next morning the secretarial staff would drag it out again, finish the project, bundle it into the postal bags and cart it to the Post Office by Wednesday noon. Apparently he never discovered the ruse, to their great relief.

The Deeper Issues of Faith

In my scale of priorities, these vexing institutional conflicts all were secondary to the focus on faith that is our basic calling in the world. The primary business of the church is, after all, to witness Jesus Christ.

In Toronto, I had upset the complacent vanity of an apostate congregation by rummaging through the basement and uncovering the abandoned silver Communion ware. In Chicago, I again went rummaging through the church basement, there to discover a large Tenebrae candelabra gathering dust. It obviously had been custom made for our sanctuary because the dimensions fit perfectly the massive marble altar at the center of the chancel.

I began to ask questions. Some elder parishioners with long memories were quick to validate what I had suspected. *Oh, yes*, they said, *we used to celebrate a choral Tenebrae every year for Maundy Thursday, but this was abandoned in the middle 1960's.*

I then checked in with a Christian fellowship group that consisted of members of the parish but which did not meet in the church. They met regularly for Eucharist and Bible study in the student lounge of the seminary across the street. Several members of this group were faculty of the school who had been my professors and mentors when I was a seminarian there 15 years earlier. Now they were my parishioners.

Outcast Allies

I had already made a "mistake" in the eyes of many in the parish because I started to be a regular member of this group as soon as I had arrived in my new post. Why not? A regular prayer group for Eucharist and Bible study was what every church serious about its faith ought to have. They were able to minister to me as much as I to them. In this case, however, the forces of skeptical rationalism had taken sufficient hold of a majority of people in this University campus congregation that this group was frowned upon by the majority as being "divisive."

I had asked them early on why they met across the street in a seminary lounge instead of in the church parlor, since they all were members of the parish. They had answered that *"another member of the church staff"* had advised them some years earlier that their presence in the church building would be *"disruptive"* to parish harmony—so they quietly demurred and chose to meet across the street to keep the peace. I should have taken the hint then that I was wading into treacherous waters.

I discussed with this Christian fellowship group what they thought of reviving the Maundy Thursday Tenebrae for the coming Lenten season and Passion week. We had several months to plan ahead. They were reserved about it—privately enthused but publicly fearful that it would negatively impact their already precarious position in parish politics.

An Unexpected Defender

News quickly spread about our conversation over reviving Tenebrae, with a lot of negative responses. It came as a surprise when one of the voices that spoke up clearly and convincingly was that of Walter Russell, a retired professor of history from one of the colleges in the area. He was known by all to be a champion of the rationalist/humanist sympathies in he congregation. He was a devotee of Robert Ingersoll who during the nineteenth century had fashioned himself as *the Great Agnostic*. Ingersoll was a gifted orator whose public speaking career had blossomed when the "Free Thought" movement was the rage.

Walter had confided to me early on about how influenced he had been by the story of Ingersoll's dramatic challenge to the existence of God. As the story goes, Ingersoll would stand in the middle of the stage and say, *"If there is a God, I challenge him to strike me dead as a blasphemer."* He would then pause for silence as the hushed audience waited in rapt attention. After a few moments he then would say, *"There, you see! I am still alive! There is no God,* "and the crowded theater would break into thunderous applause. (*This is actually an atheist declaration, not an agnostic position, but Ingersoll knew exactly how to appeal to his audience.*)

God is not in the business of striking us dead for our sins. He is in the business of saving us from our sins. Jesus had to rebuke his own disciples about this. After he had passed through a Samaritan village that refused to receive him, James and John said *(Luke 9:54–56),*

> *"Lord, do you want us to command fire to come down from heaven and consume them?" But he turned and rebuked them. Then they went on to another village.*

Walter described this Ingersoll story as having a transforming impact on his own personal life. But Walter was a very principled person as some devoted rationalists can be. When the subject of Holy Week came up, he said that the Christian fellowship group should be given the opportunity to hold whatever form of worship they wanted to sponsor in church space for Maundy Thursday, since the church is not a private club and public worship is always open to everyone.

Christian faith was, after all, the genesis of the parish. So we brought out the hidden Tenebrae candelabra, dusted it off, and celebrated Holy Week as it had been done before in that place.

When the murmuring against me tuned up, Walter was even more outspoken in his response. He said to all who would listen to him, *You know that I disagree completely with just about everything that Mr. Gray says from the pulpit, but I totally support his right to say it because freedom of the pulpit is one of our foundational principles.* He was a faithful supporter of my position as Pastor, to the end.

And There Was More . . .

Walter also took the lead in untangling the related situation of meeting space. When he heard that the Christian fellowship group regularly met across the street in a seminary lounge because they had been surreptitiously told that their presence in the church building would be disruptive, he was furious. *Where is our freedom of speech?* he demanded to know. *They all are members of this congregation,* he reminded everyone. He advocated that they be officially invited to hold their meetings in the church, which the parish Board then did.

This was a gracious position because he was a gracious person. He politely shamed the parish leadership into supporting both me and the Christian fellowship group because not to do so, as he pointed out, would betray our core principles.

Our parish was not unique in these conflicts. This was, after all, a University community and varieties of rationalism, deism, skepticism, and humanism were commonplace in many of the neighborhood congregations, which had a variety of denominational connections. At least three other parishes within four blocks held multiple affiliations with Congregational, Baptist, Presbyterian, Disciples, and Methodist denominations. Several belonged to three different denominations at the same time. And all had suffered varying degrees of strife, sometimes dismissing the Pastor on short notice with rancor and bitterness.

Because of the many seminaries in the neighborhood, most of these congregations had a special relationship with one or more schools as we did. Seminary students and faculty were at the active core of our parish life, and I took this as a special blessing because it was an opportunity both to learn from seasoned colleagues and to mentor upcoming students. I was glad to have seminarians assist me on Sunday mornings and to preach for us whenever I could invite them. And I was able to do this officially, because the seminary had granted me a University of Chicago staff card as an adjunct faculty field education supervisor. This provided the teamwork I had sought for but could not obtain from the Associate Pastors on our staff.

Help with the Truth

Among these seminarians, Carly Murray was a young woman from Texas, a clear-headed Calvinist and a gifted preacher. She was a regular participant with me and a favorite among the students I invited to share in leading worship. She had sought us out because the denomination in which she had grown up frowned on women pastors.

We were in the sacristy early one Sunday morning, putting on our vestments and having a spirited theological conversation. All of a sudden, with energetic pluck, she confronted me with a truth I had been trying to avoid. She waved her finger in my face and declared, "*The trouble with you, Duke Gray,*" she said, "*is that you don't want to admit that in this outfit, freedom of the pulpit means the freedom to preach anything but the Gospel.*"

She was right of course. By relentlessly preaching the Gospel, I was constantly offending this unspoken rule while not owning up to what I was doing. That same morning she confessed to me that she did, in fact, compromise her own principles. She said, *To earn my keep as a student and help pay my tuition, I do trot out my little humanist homily to accommodate the audience at some of the small outlier congregations who hire me as a Sunday Supply preacher. But as a Calvinist, I know that I will have to pay the consequences for this in the end when I meet the Lord.*

I cherish her memory as a truth teller. I never saw her again after she was graduated and ordained, but she had a stellar career as a beloved pastor.

The Lord Provides

Things were calm for a while following the debate over the existence of the Christian fellowship group and their return to the church premises for Maundy Thursday Tenebrae. But things soon got ugly again. My tenure was to come to an end early in 1987 after nearly seven years in the caldron.

Several years before the worst was to hit, the Lord stepped into my life in a dramatic and unexpected way. He had been there all along, of course. And I had many times cried out for help. Small occasions of grace came my way, but this was different.

How different, I did not recognize at the time. When it happened I saw it as a moment of blessing for a difficult day. Years later when I looked back with the help of a Spiritual Director, I saw it for what it was—the *turning point of a lifetime*, a converting event at the Lord's initiative.

We sometimes appreciate the gravity of an event only long after the passage of time. I have learned to look for what I call the *Providential Thread*: Life often seems like a container full of marbles, randomly rolling around with every shift and shake of the box. Then one day you realize that the hand of the Lord has drilled a hole through each marble and inserted a strong cord through the center of each. He lifts it up, and all of a sudden your random marbles are a string of pearls.

Lady Luck and the Lord of Life

When we assume that the events of our lives are like disconnected marbles randomly rolling around in a box, we speak about a positive break as "a stroke of luck" or "a lucky draw." or "my lucky day." I used to speak like that. But I have learned better.

Our lives are more than a roll of the dice or a game of roulette. The sovereign hand of the Holy Spirit should never be confused with "chance." And do not confuse *the Lord of life* with *Lady Luck*.

Lady Luck is a fairy tale and the goddess *Fortune* is an ancient idol. Idolatry is the worship of false gods, and the worship of phony gods is the foundational human offense against the Holy (Exodus 20:3,4):

> *You shall have no other gods before me. You shall not make for yourself any idol.*

Today, Lady Luck is a laughable superstition unless you get enticed into believing its lie. Then you are on the pathway into darkness. When you become ensnared in idolatry you will never see the *Providential Thread*.

The Lord continually provides us with blessings, great and small. When you fail to see the *Providential Thread* you will miss your blessing when it passes by. When it passes you by, it is gone.

The prophet Isaiah tells us *(Isaiah 55:6)*:

> *Seek the Lord while he may be found, call upon him while he is near.*

An Epiphany at Midnight

It was February of 1984. Life seemed very dark. I was in the sanctuary of the church at midnight—after the 10 pm security checks had been done through our complex of buildings. After all, as Senior Pastor, I had a key. I needed to be alone.

The sanctuary was the most visible sign of the revitalization of the parish in the 1920's. It provided the foundation for the development of the liturgy and the revival of the people. It was classic fourteenth century English Gothic, built of massive grey stone blocks with a black marble floor. It was deliberately small in scale, not huge, successfully designed to capture both majesty and intimacy. These are the unmistakable marks of a God who awesomely created all things, yet condescended to take on our mortal flesh and walk with the lame, the broken, and the stricken down.

At Christmas we celebrate the *enfleshment* of God, *the Incarnation of God in Christ Jesus.* Here is how St. Paul speaks about this: *(Philippians 2:6–7)*.

> *Who, though he was in the form of God,*
> *did not regard equality with God as something to be exploited,*
> *but emptied himself, taking the form of a slave,*
> *being born in human likeness.*

Our sanctuary was <u>an incarnation of God in stone</u>.

The church did not have pews, but cathedral chairs that could be rearranged or stacked and moved away as the occasion might suggest, just as in ancient cathedral design.

I knelt down at the altar, facing forward toward the empty chairs in the empty church, and began rambling on to the Lord all manner of complaints about my agendas and achievements, pain and struggle, disappointments and defeats. I mumbled along until all of a sudden, without warning, I broke down and began to weep inconsolably. All I could manage to say between the tears was, *Oh God, it's so hard . . . . . .it's so hard*. My pious posturing had been swept away in a flash.

I struggled to wipe the burning salt from my eyes. I looked up and just as quickly, without warning, I began to laugh with a holy joy—because I saw a vision of the Lord emblazoned in the giant tinted glass tracery window at the rear of the sanctuary. It was pitch dark and the only natural light was moonlight coming through the window. But this was not natural. I will leave the further details of this to the intimate conversation I had with my Spiritual Director in Boston many years later. Enough to be said here: This was a *type* of Isaiah's vision in the temple that had given shape to this whole church in the first place *(Isaiah 6:1)*:

> *I saw the Lord sitting on a throne, high and lofty; and the hem of his robe filled the temple.*

The Lord was my evangelist, without any human agency. He continues to abide and guide me, indwelling until now.

The Power of Christ

We do not convert ourselves. We are converted when Christ intervenes in our lives. The conversion of Saul, whom we know as St. Paul, begins with this *(Acts 9:1–2)*:

> *Saul, still breathing threats and murder against the disciples of the Lord, went to the high priest and asked him for letters to the synagogues at Damascus, so that if he found any who belonged to the Way, men or women, he might bring them bound to Jerusalem.*

Jesus interrupted his journey on the road to Damascus and turned around his entire life, including his change of name from Saul to Paul. Notice in this passage that these first Christians were called the people of "the Way." This means "the Way of Christ," not our way.

The power of Christ converts. The power of Christ heals. The power of Christ forgives sins. The power of Christ brings new life. The power of Christ baptizes with fire. The power of Christ plants the seed of the Lord Holy Spirit within us.

Turning Points

Much is made of conversion as a once-in-a-lifetime thunderbolt from the sky that dramatically turns around a life forever. That is only one part of it. There is more. We have a part to play if our conversion is to be effective.

There are several steps we must take to accompany our conversion. These may come before Christ intervenes, or they may come after. First comes shame. Shame is the motivator of remorse. After remorse comes renunciation, followed by repentance. When we renounce our familiar habits and perceptions, we open the space for Christ to enter.

Modern culture is a severe stumbling block against a remorseful and penitent spirit. We live in a shameless society. When you feel no shame, it is nearly impossible to come to remorse.

Full conversion consists of a *whole series of turning points* in our lives. To repent is to turn. This means turning away from the familiar path of the world, and turning toward the new path that Christ opens for us. Our turning points take time and turmoil to bear fruit. Sometimes we can identify one large turning point, but it is the cumulative impact of many smaller converting events over the years that shows the result. That has been true for me.

This was true for St. Paul. His pivotal encounter with Christ on the Road to Damascus in *Acts 9* is not the whole story. It took time for his fruit to ripen, but when it did, he made a complete harvest.

By his own account in *Galatians 1 and 2*, he spent three years in Arabia following this event before he went to Jerusalem to confer with

Peter. Then he went back to Syria and Cilicia for another 14 years before returning to Jerusalem again with Barnabas and Titus to meet the other apostles. Along the way, his name was changed from *Saul* to *Paul*. We can reckon from this that he spent years in spiritual formation for his new life in Christ to mature.

Christ took the decisive initiative to turn around Saul's life. After that, many other steps followed to give shape to his Apostolic ministry. The Lord did this for me too.

Standing at the Crossroads

Imagine that you are standing on the street corner at a busy intersection. In one direction there is Main Street. You know where it goes. Or at least you think you know. You have been traveling on it for quite some time. All your life, actually, until now. You know it well. Main Street is a bustling boulevard, lined with shops and attractions, taverns and cafes. Everyone in the world seems to be on it, or so it appears.

But at this corner, you stop. You notice a narrow side street that veers off to the right. You can't remember seeing it before. If you have, you gave it no heed. It is a winding way, called Providence Lane. It has leafy green trees and curves in the road that block any long term view of where it goes. It looks attractive, even beckoning, but since you don't know where it leads you are not sure you want to try it. Yet you are enticed and intrigued.

So you decide to check it out. You turn into this unknown street. Very soon a thought enters your mind—almost like a voice in your head. The message sounds familiar, like something you once read. It goes like this *(Joel 2:32a)*:

> *Everyone who calls on the Lord shall be saved.*

Or perhaps something like this *(Romans 10:9)*:

> *If you confess with your lips that Jesus is Lord, and believe in your heart that God raised him from the dead, you will be saved.*

Whoa! *What's going on here?* you ask. You stop in your tracks as another lost memory or stray thought crowds into your mind, something like *this (Romans 10:11)*:

> *No one who believes in him will be put to shame.*

That seems like a word of comfort, but now you ponder, *Maybe I should go back to Main Street, which is familiar and I know where I'm going* . . . *After all, it's only half a block back, just a few steps* . . . So you start to reverse course, just as another half—remembered thought comes (Matthew 7:13–14):

> *The gate is wide and the road is easy that leads to destruction . . .*
> *the gate is narrow and the road is hard that leads to life, and there*
> *are few who find it.*

With this, the Lord whispers to you: *remorse—renounce—repent.* So what do you do now?

Providence

We call this alternate path "Providence Lane" because the term *Providence* carries two different truths: (1) *provision*—the Lord *provides* what we need, especially in distress, and (2) *destiny*—the Lord has a *destiny* for our lives. Your destiny, and mine, is to live with him in everlasting joy.

The point of this parable about crossroads is that we have free will. The decisions about what to believe and what or whom to follow are always ours. And there is a second point: it takes only a few steps down one side or the other of this fork in the road to have the easy choice to turn back. But once you have gone 30 miles or 30 years down one or the other, the decision to turn takes a lot more undoing and back–tracking from where we have been.

Darkness to Light

St. Paul in his *Letter to the Colossians* speaks about our *being transferred* from darkness to light (*Colossians 1:13,14*):

> *The Father has rescued us from the power of darkness*
> *and transferred us into the kingdom of his beloved Son,*
> *in whom we have redemption, the forgiveness of sins.*

This transfer is a work of God. Our part is to receive this or reject it when it comes our way. Our transfer begins when we confess Jesus as Lord. This reveals the truth that a confession of sin is also a confession of faith: We are mortal and he is holy.

When our transfer is complete and we no longer belong to the darkness, we see with new eyes and speak with a new voice. This does not happen overnight. There are turning points and stumbling blocks along the way. I have faced more than I can count.

Some ask how we can reconcile the notion of free will with the will of God, if God has a destiny for our lives. The answer is to look at Adam. Adam had free will, but he did not exercise it well. He stumbled big time. Adam was intimate with God. He walked side by side with his Creator in the primeval garden, yet he stumbled. The Lord told Adam what to do and what not to do, but Adam did otherwise. We have been paying the price ever since.

Is there anyone reading this who has never stumbled? If so, you are uniquely blessed.

Stumbling Blocks

Some of us stumble in serious ways that do great damage to ourselves and to others.. Some of us have done vile and reprehensible things—whether from malice or from good intentions gone sour. Some of us are not guilty of grievous sin, yet we slowly come to realize that our lives are blemished by a thousand petty peccadilloes we have intentionally or blindly committed over the years.

Some of us stumble without even knowing it. We think we are on the high road, anointed in our calling, yet we blunder into places we should never have been. Then, looking back, we discover that it took years of regret before we were ready even to admit that we made a wrong turn or that our lives were not right. Sometimes we do have to hit bottom before we can come to terms with our stumbling. Conversion, for many of us, is a slow and painful process.

Another World

In 1998, my wife Gloria began serving as a volunteer for *Renewal Ministries* of Ann Arbor, Michigan—a lay-led Roman Catholic evangelization ministry that sends volunteer mission teams all over the world to do preaching, teaching, praying, and evangelizing on invitation from local bishops, priests, and prayer-group leaders.

Gloria has continued in this ministry for more than 20 years now. In recent years, the Lord has called her to do a solo mission in Slovakia for three months each summer, evangelizing both Gypsy and Slovak youth and adults. This itself is its own remarkable story.

In 2003, I was invited to join one of their teams for a two week mission tour to Eastern Europe. Tom Edwards, the team leader, is a full time lay evangelist in Florida. I spent four or five Octobers with them in Slovakia, with a number of trips to the Czech Republic. The first time I was invited to go, I reminded Tom that I was not a Roman Catholic. He said, *So?* Charismatics are ecumenical and open-ended at the grass-roots of Christian faith.

One year we spent nearly a week at a local Gypsy, or *Roma*, Bible school and community center. I learned an important lesson there about the depths of true conversion.

Roma culture is tight-knit and thickly bonded. In many Roma communities there are only two sources of income: the women do fortune-telling and the men are pick-pockets. Often they are living in a bleak public housing quarter of grey cinder-block apartment houses like the one we visited.

In sharp contrast, the Bible school/community center was a jewel in the midst of a depressing housing compound. It was clean and sparkling and we learned that the Roma men had built it themselves after being taught carpentry, brick-laying, plumbing, and other building trades. It was theirs and it would not be trashed as many of the surrounding apartment blocks had been.

Conversion is *Personal*—and a Whole Lot More . . .

One evening we took part in a roaring prayer meeting with vigorous Gospel preaching, loud music from a Roma praise band, and dancing in the aisles. The place was packed and was swarming with children. Then I caught sight of *what full conversion means*: I saw a group of angry-looking and grim-faced older women staring out the windows of the apartment block just across the alley, leaning on their elbows, looking down on this boisterous prayer and praise party. Then it struck me: I was seeing *two entirely different worlds in conflict*. The one was *darkness* and the other was *light*.

These sad and angry women were watching as their familiar world of darkness was slipping away. At the same time, they were witnessing a new world being born. The old world being challenged was a forbidding realm of occult magic, superstition, fortunetelling, tarot cards, sorcery, spells, and curses.

The new reality now breaking in was the kingdom of God, the Light of Christ, a bright and joyful world of promise for the next generation but also for whoever of this older generation wanted to receive a new and blessed life. Some did.

Here, conversion meant not only that individual lives were being transformed. It also meant that persons were being *transferred* from one world to another, from one jurisdiction to another, from one culture to another, from one universe of meaning to another. By this transfer, an entire culture is converted.

Just as St. Paul Said

It is just as St. Paul described it in *Colossians 1:13*: *The power of God transfers us from darkness to light*. I saw that while conversion is, of course, *personal*—it also is *a transfer of citizenship*, the issuing of a *new and different Passport*, the severance of our belonging to one kingdom and our admission into another. This *transfer* is from slavery to freedom, from a carnal dominion of bondage to the blessed kingdom of God.

Elsewhere, Paul tells us that although we live *in this world*, we are *ambassadors* for another *(II Corinthians 5:20)*:

> We are ambassadors for Christ.

The Christian does not live in some detached realm of heavenly bliss. The Christian lives *in this world*—with all of its challenges and promise, grief and hope, sickness and health, violence and glory. However, we do not *belong* to this world. We *belong* to another. Our task is to represent the kingdom of God on earth as it breaks into our present reality at the initiative of Christ.

Conversion Gives Gifts

Conversion confers many gifts. Chief among these are two: (1) the humility to *repent*, and (2) the ability to *forgive*.

Following his adultery with Bathsheba and his plot to have her husband Uriah killed in battle, King David is confronted by his court prophet Nathan, who reveals the tawdry truth.

This is the major turning point in David's life. He could have denied it all and perhaps even have had Nathan killed to cover up the whole mess. Instead, David repents, as we hear in his extended prayer of confession *(Psalm 51:1-2,10-11)*:

> *Have mercy on me, O God.*
> *according to your steadfast love;*
> *according to your abundant mercy*
> *blot out my transgressions.*
> *Wash me thoroughly from my iniquity,*
> *and cleanse me from my sin . . .*
> *Create in me a clean heart, O God,*
> *and put a new and right spirit within me.*
> *Do not cast me away from your presence,*
> *and do not take your holy spirit from me.*

There is an important double message in this.: (1) Yes, God forgives David and puts aside his sin. (2) Yet even though his sin is forgiven and removed, the *consequences* of sin remain: Uriah still is dead, and the remainder of David's life is plagued by turmoil.

Our Forgiving and Repenting

Most importantly, the forgiveness of God is a template for the forgiveness we must show to others. The forgiveness of God is absolute. God's forgiveness overcomes David's terrible transgression. Prior to David's violation of three of the Ten Commandments (adultery, murder, covetousness), God had made a Covenant with David that his throne would be everlasting, and from his throne would come the Messiah, the Christ. Despite David's sinful behavior, God does not remove this Covenant. He is the Promise Keeper, not a promise breaker. When David misbehaves, the Lord maintains the Covenant he made. God keeps his Promise for us too, even when we stumble.

Our own repenting and forgiving lays the groundwork for other gifts that bless a converted life *(Galatians 5:22-23)*:

> *The fruit of the Spirit is love, joy, peace. patience, kindness, generosity, faithfulness, gentleness, and self-control.*

Fruit requires seed–planting, growing, ripening, and harvesting. God is the seed planter. The fruit grows within us, and this takes time. So does the ripening. Further, the harvesting must be done at the right time, or the fruit will rot on the vine. We are the harvester. We harvest this fruit by our behavior as we live out a converted life.

Notice also that this fruit is the "fruit of the Spirit." John the Baptist speaks of Jesus like this *(Luke 3:16)*:

> *I baptize you with water; but one who is more powerful than I is coming... He will baptize you with the Holy Spirit and fire.*

Jesus, who is God the Son, plants the seed of God the Holy Spirit when he baptizes you with fire. Don't let this fruit rot on the vine.

Harvest Your Fruit

From the time I was a small child, my father gave me a negative message that I would never amount to anything if I did not shape up. He never said the worst of it openly in words, but the subconscious impact of his attitude was that I was slow and stupid. That is not true. Part of the fruit of my conversion is to know assuredly that I am not slow, stupid, or impaired. Quite the contrary. I am gifted by God in many ways, not of my own making, and these are still unfolding before me.

After my midnight epiphany in the darkened church, it took me another 15 years, with the help of hindsight and monthly spiritual direction, to comprehend that this was a life–turning *conversion*. When it happened I saw it as an event that had *saved the day*. In time, I was able to comprehend it as an event that had *saved my life*.

Hindsight is a magnificent blessing: witness the *Providential Thread*. We often cannot comprehend the meaning of things until years after they happen. What is important then is not to luxuriate in our wisdom, but to apply to the future the revelation we are granted.

Some of us do this less quickly than others. Nicodemus was slow to catch on *(John 3)*, but he did come around in the end *(John 19:39)*. The woman at the well was quick to get it *(John 4:19 and 4:29)*.

The Unlikely Evangelist

When Jesus met the woman at the well, she had no idea what would unfold from their extended conversation (*John 4:5–42*). She had three counts against her: (1) *she was a woman* in a culture that placed women at the bottom of the social ladder and forbid them to talk with a man not their husband, (2) *she was a Samaritan,* one of the despised enemies of Israel, here talking openly with a rabbi, and (3) *she was an outcast* from her own community because of her wanton lifestyle with a series of men. She came to the well in the heat of the day instead of the cool of the evening when the other women from the village would gather.

In baseball, it is *three strikes and you're out.* Here, it is *three strikes and you're an evangelist.* John 4:28–29 tells us:

> *The woman left her water jar and went back to the city. She said to the people, "Come and see a man who told me everything I have ever done! He cannot be the messiah, can he?"*
> And then *John 4:39: Many Samaritans from that city believed in him because of the woman's testimony.*

When the Lord gives us a gift, it is not for ourselves alone. We are called, each one of us, to respond as did this unlikely evangelist whom Jesus met at Jacob's well. She ran with joy to broadcast to her neighbors that she had met the Messiah. So should we.

Conversion is a gift of God. It is not a static object to be placed on a shelf and admired. It is a dynamic seed that cries out to be planted, cultivated, harvested and shared. Do it.

Terminal Individualism

The emblem of our times is the "selfie." This is a sign of *terminal individualism.* This goes even beyond narcissism. In this advance guard of the twenty-first century, a concern for ultimate truth has evaporated into a private realm of "individual preference" and personal choice.

In spiritual matters today, the stark contrast St. Paul lays out between the kingdom of darkness and the light of Christ devolves into "*I like Jesus—who do you like?*" This is the equivalent of saying, "*I like marmalade on my toast—what do you like?*" Here, the question of human destiny disappears into triviality and the issue of *conversion* is lost in a jungle of "options."

Our conversion, or the lack of it, sets in motion the direction of our lives. In today's culture, the ultimate question of *destiny* is not often asked any longer.

We are uncomfortable with ultimates. Yet the question remains: either we are lost in the carnal or we delight in the divine. Today, speaking of our destiny in Christ or our destiny in Hell dies the death of a yawn—unless we wake up.

Part Two

Harvest

"'Master, did you not sow good seed in your field? Where, then, did these weeds come from?' He answered: 'An enemy has done this . . . Let both of them grow together until the harvest; and at harvest time I will tell the reapers, Collect the weeds first and bind them in bundles to be burned, but gather the wheat into my barn.'"

MATTHEW 13:27B–28A, 30

Six

Darkness

And the Spirit immediately drove him out into the wilderness. He was in the wilderness forty days, tempted by Satan; and he was with the wild beasts.

—MARK 1:12–13A

Testing

I WAS TESTED SEVERELY in Toronto. I was tested even more severely in Chicago. Too many people these days expect spiritual curiosity to lead directly to comfort and solace. It does not. It invites you into the pathway of a pilgrim, and almost every serious pilgrimage involves challenge and testing. You don't need to be a pastor or even a Christian to face a time of trial. Every human person faces life challenges. And every devoted Christian will be tested by this world if you are serious about your faith.

The tests you face—like the tests I have had to face—are not necessarily over spiritual issues. They may be over things like paying your mortgage when you loose a job that you thought was secure. It may be the terrifying prospect of finding a new place to live and the rent money to pay for it if you have just gone through a traumatic separation and are now facing the inevitable divorce. It may be needing to cope with angry or destructive or dysfunctional people at work.

Every issue we face in life has a spiritual component because both God and Satan are active agents in the events of this world, however "secular" some folks think these events are. If you are alive, you *will be tested* on this mortal earth whatever your age or station in life.

The Tunnel at the End of the Light

When we stumble in this life—and we will stumble—we face a choice: (1) does this disaster mean "the end?" Or (2) can something good come from this?

The darkness can come in many forms. Circumstances beyond our own stumbling can cast us into the pit of darkness. We can face unforeseen sickness and disease; the death of a loved one or the loss of our livelihood; divorce and the loss of family, dignity, and home. Or, we can be the cause of our own stumbling. The list is endless.

How we respond to darkness is largely a matter of what we believe. If we believe that darkness essentially means defeat, then we will be defeated. If we have the faith to see beyond our present darkness, then there is hope.

Biblical testimony about darkness is clear: While the darkness itself may be the work of Satan, the grace of God has the power to turn darkness into a womb for the seed of the Holy Spirit. The Holy Spirit brings new life.

I Thought I Was Lost

I had gone to Chicago thinking I was entering into the Light. Very shortly, the light began to dim. Then came my converting epiphany after some years. This did not lead directly to a burst of new light. It led to a very dark tunnel at the end of the light.

For the next several years I felt truly lost and abandoned. Yet all the while my Lord Holy Spirit stood at my side, preventing my stumbling from casting me into the pit, though I hardly knew it.

I had yet fully to receive *John 14:18*:

> *I will not leave you orphaned . . .*

And, *John 15:26;16:13a*:

> *When the Advocate comes, whom I will send to you from the Father, the Spirit of truth who comes from the Father, he will testify on my behalf. When the Spirit of truth comes, he will guide you into all the truth.*

In these passages, Jesus is speaking about the Holy Spirit, whom the Nicene Creed calls the Lord, the Giver of life. Truth is life. The Lord Holy Spirit is the one who will keep you from the Pit when you stumble, no matter how deep the darkness.

Winter Wheat

I first heard about winter wheat in a high school geography class. It sounded crazy to me. *How can you grow wheat in the snow?* I thought. Then the truth dawned. The seeds are planted in the autumn. The seed germinates slowly, protected by the cold and the dark. When the snow melts, it is watered. The seed sprouts and produces a hardy durum. It flourishes well in places like Montana and Manitoba, even Siberia. The Lord works like that. He plants his seed in the cold and in the darkest places of our lives. When the season is right, the harvest is ready. If we wait on him, the Lord will bring about his harvest in our lives like a crop of winter wheat.

Pilgrimage

One of the most arresting steps on the footpath of the pilgrim is to consider what happened to Jesus at the beginning of his adult ministry. All three Synoptic Gospels (*Matthew, Mark, Luke*) record essentially the same event, which has two distinct components:

- The *baptism*: Jesus is *commissioned* to his ministry by his cousin, John the Baptist. God the Father confirms this calling through the anointing of the Holy Spirit who appears in the form of a dove, and identifies him as the Beloved Son of God. Then:

- The *wilderness*: *Immediately* afterward Jesus is led into the wilderness to be tempted by Satan.

As often is the case, Mark's Gospel gives us the most terse and blunt chronicle of this event. Matthew and Luke give us a more extended report of the three temptations—crucial data in themselves, but elaborations nonetheless on Mark's essential narrative.

The point here is that too much conventional piety misses the direct connection between these two steps: (1) the *commissioning*, and (2) the encounter with *darkness*. Jesus did not receive his commissioning in a burst of divine majesty and then say, *"Well, I think I'll take some time alone in monastic quiet and savor the implications of this exalted calling."* as if he were signing up for an extended retreat at a spa resort in California, there to spend his time in a hot tub overlooking the Pacific.

Two Clues

Two key words disabuse us of this romantic perversion of the Biblical witness.

The first key word in Mark's report is *immediately*. Immediately after what? All three of these Gospel accounts answer that one: It is *immediately* after his baptism by John. His baptism is confirmed by the anointing of the Holy Spirit, who descends in the form of a dove.

The second key word is *drove*. Most of us know what it means to be *driven*. It means to be *pushed* or to be *pulled*—perhaps both at the same time. It means to be drawn into a situation that we would not necessarily seek by our own devices. As St. Mark tells us (*Mark 1:12*),

> *The Spirit immediately drove him out into the wilderness.*

Wilderness indicates one thing if it refers to an inspiring hike in the forest, a camping vacation in Yosemite, or a majestic vista from Mount Washington. It means quite something else when it is an encounter with darkness. As Mark says (*Mark 1:13*),

> *He was in the wilderness forty days, tempted by Satan; and he was with the wild beasts.*

I don't know about you, but I am not too eager to spend forty days in the desert with Satan, in the company of wild beasts.

The Nature of Darkness

We cannot understand what any of this means unless we come to grips with *the meaning of darkness*. Darkness is *distance from God*. The corollary to this is just as simple: The Light of holiness is *intimacy with God*.

My first clues about darkness began to take shape during my years in Brooklyn. That is when I began to realize that social justice initiatives from the middle class toward the poor could harbor shadows not easily seen. Chief among these shadows is the reliance on human justice agendas instead of making the Gospel of Jesus Christ the basis for change.

Human justice is not the same as the justice of God. Human justice means giving everyone a fair shake, an equal cut of the pie, an appropriate reward or punishment for deeds that are done, good or bad.

This is not the justice of God. The justice of God is holiness. Amid the vast variety of scripture translations available today, many words that are rendered as *righteousness* in one version are rendered as *justice* in another. This can be very confusing. It can do great mischief to our understanding if we are not careful. This can put us far away from the Lord, into a very dark and empty place.

We stumble on this because the word *righteousness* in scripture comes from the word "right." When our efforts *to do things* "right" become simply *a human justice program* instead of a *quest for righteousness*, this can be wildly different from the Lord's expectation that we have a "right relationship" with him.

As a result, a lot of churches today are <u>preaching human justice</u> while thinking they are <u>preaching righteousness</u>, which they are not. In the extreme, this becomes the pursuit of purely human social programs as a substitute for preaching the Gospel of Jesus Christ, which it is not.

Deluded

This self-delusion can be very powerful for those who believe it. I know. I too bear the shame for having been held in the thrall of such notions. For years, I preached my own human agendas about social justice, thinking it was the righteousness of God, while Christ stood on the sidelines, shaking his head in sorrow. I thought I had it all whipped, even as my own emptiness was whipping me on. It took the sorrows of Christ to become my own sorrow before I was able to repent.

The Dark Truth beneath the Sunshine

The holiness of God pours an enriching grace into us when we turn to him. This enriching grace is the binding glue for a *relationship of espousal* between God and ourselves. God *espouses us* when we espouse him, and he endows us with his majesty when we draw close to him. This majestic endowment is the Gospel of Jesus Christ.

This rich process of relationship-building is an entirely different matter from pursuing human justice programs. The more romantic and perfectionistic our justice agendas become, the more ideological they become. The more ideological they become, the more detached from Christ they become. And the more detached from Christ they become, the more fierce and unbending they become in their application.

Then, what starts out sounding like compassion ends up being an iron fist in a velvet glove. What starts out sounding like welcoming hospitality ends up being a wall of hostility against anyone who demurs from the ideological foundation of our own action program. The sunshine of a human justice agenda is not the Light of Christ.

Failing the Gospel

For example, a high-placed church executive recently admonished all pastors in his jurisdiction to preach on "climate change" one Sunday every month. Add to this another Sunday for police brutality offenses, another for gender identity issues, another for abolishing national borders to bring immigration reform, and what remains for the week after that? No wonder Christians seeking to deepen their relationship with Christ leave the church. They are not being fed.

The *loss of the Gospel* is the curse of the modern church. This loss comes in many disguises, some subtle, some blatant and virulent. All these lead us astray when we fall for a masquerade that poses as Gospel.

In 1960's Brooklyn, I was enticed into a timely but romantic piety not really centered on Christ. In 1970's Toronto, I ran afoul of a more vicious ideological substitute for the Gospel. In 1980's Chicago, the iron fist came out of the velvet glove in the full force of a violent attack. All were in the name of human agendas that had replaced the Word of God, which is the proper witness of the church.

God is Unfair

Jesus tells us a parable about laborers in the vineyard. The landowner goes out early in the morning and finds day workers standing idle in the marketplace, so he hires them for the customary daily wage and they go off to the vineyard. He does the same thing at 9 o'clock, at noon, at 3:00 PM, and even at 5:00 PM in the evening. When the work day is over, he instructs his paymaster to give them all the same daily wage. Most of the workers are indignant—this is <u>not fair</u>, they said (*Matthew 20:10–15*):

> *Now when the first came, they thought they would receive more; but each of them also received the usual daily wage. And when they received it, they grumbled against the landowner, saying, "These last worked only one hour, and you have made them equal to us who have borne the burden of the day and the scorching heat." But he replied to one of them, "Friend, I am doing you no wrong; did you not agree with me for the usual daily wage (a denarius)? Take what belongs to you and go; I choose to give to this last the same as I give to you. Am I not allowed to do what I choose with what belongs to me? Or are you envious because I am generous?"*

Of course this is not fair. It is *outrageous*—in the eyes of the world.

The "landowner" in the parable is God—and the Lord does not operate according to the ways of this world. He is abundant in his outpouring of grace (*favor*), even to the unworthy or the Johnny–come–lately.

The issue here is the difference between *our human judgments* and the commanding reality of our *relatedness to God*, which the Lord invites. If we *belong to God* as our first priority, the deeds we do will follow after this. If we do not belong to God, the deeds we do will seek some other basis or have no basis at all except for whim or fortune or human judgments about what is right.

The Gospel of Jesus Christ is first of all about establishing our *belonging to God*. Faith calls that the *Good News*, which is what the term "Gospel" actually means.

Too many churches today are preaching ethical imperatives, urging what we should do about this or that aspect of world affairs, while spending little or no energy cultivating our relationship with the Lord. Our relationship with God is fed through scripture, sacrament, liturgy, worship, and prayer.

Those churches who are failing to feed the spiritual hunger that is the famine of today's secular culture are in trouble. They wonder why people are not flocking to their doors to listen to their moral proposals about how society should be reorganized. We can hear all about that in the television talk show panels that accompany the evening news. The evening news on TV is not the Good News.

A Stranger Shows Up

At a church I once served a new fellow showed up one Sunday whom I had never before seen. The following week he showed up again, then again, and again. After a while one of our deacons said to me, *It is good to see Jack Nelson back in church. He used to be a regular.* So one Sunday I sought out Jack in Coffee Hour following worship (*where a lot of serious pastoral work often gets done*). We sat at a table in the corner and began to talk. He had issues. After a while he said, *I used to be a regular here before you came. But one Sunday, after hearing yet one more sermon on climate change, I left to find another church. Then after you came I thought I would come and check things out. I need to hear the Gospel of Jesus Christ.*

He needed help with life issues and he was not being fed. He was seeking a place that would follow what Jesus told Peter to do: *Feed my sheep (John 21:17)*. Certainly we should preach justice when appropriate. But relentless preaching about recycling your trash or government regulation of light bulb wattage does not rise to the level of confronting Adolph Hitler, American segregation a hundred years after the Civil War, Apartheid in South Africa, or the threats of twenty–first century terrorism.

Revisiting Brooklyn

In 1985, I was invited to return to Brooklyn for a weekend to celebrate my 20th Ordination Anniversary. That is when some of my suspicions from 1965 began to be confirmed.

They invited me back with the best of intentions. By 1985, I was seen as the successful Senior Pastor of a significant church in Chicago—no longer as the fresh faced Assistant Pastor of 1965. It promised to be a glad occasion of reminiscing with friends, both of ruminating on the passage of the years and of reflecting on the promise of things to come.

We began with several days of social hospitality, all on an effusive and convivial note. When Sunday morning came, the mood soured. I preached on *Chapter 17* of the *Book of Acts*, which details St. Paul's encounter at Athens with the Epicurean and Stoic philosophers.

This text is a template for our times. Many in our day are *Epicureans* who "savor the moment" in a variety of ways: the "taste" of good manners, of a social occasion, of a personal relationship, of gourmet food and vintage wine, of a night at the theatre or the symphony, even of a "fine sermon" or an "inspiring worship" event. Many others are *Stoics* whose first concern is the morality of things, because the Stoics are strong on connecting the dots between the "moments" we savor.

One Epicurean "moment" can have severe consequences in the next. So the Stoics stress the correctness of behavior, the appropriateness of public policy, a stern application of virtue to every aspect of life. The Greek philosophers to whom Paul preached in *Acts 17* were experts in all of these matters, and more.

After 20 Years, I Was a New Person

I quickly discovered that my former congregation and I were no longer on the same page. In 1965 we were congruent. Now, we were on opposite sides of the aisle. They represented the Epicurean and Stoic philosophers and I represented St. Paul.

I discovered that I was a changed person. I no longer believed what I had believed in 1965. I had seen the cracks in the formidable facade of romantic religion and they loomed large. I had been drawn toward a different foundation on which to stand. That foundation is *the Gospel of Jesus Christ*.

My message that weekend received more negative than positive feedback for relying so steadfastly on Biblical categories instead of secular moralistic imperatives. Although cordial and not hostile, the folks in Brooklyn began to sound a lot like the folks in Toronto and Chicago. I had changed and they had not.

The social justice veterans and I toured the old neighborhood where we had worked so hard to make a difference. Our storefront community center was gone. I came to see that church mission endeavors usually take generations, and often centuries, to take hold and have a lasting impact. Five years in a neighborhood that was not our own had made an effect like a finger hole in the sand when the tide rolls in. By contrast, the small Pentecostal churches that had been preaching the Gospel and changing lives still were there, and flourishing. Against the darkness, they were preaching the Light of Christ.

The World Around Us

We are *culture-trained from birth* by the family and the social environment that surrounds us. Christian conversion means trading in the old world that gave us our original birth for a new one given us by Christ.

Jesus was working overtime with the demands of the crowd and we learn *(Mark 3:21)*:

> *When his family heard it, they went out to restrain him, for the people were saying, "He is gone out of his mind."*

Soon *(Mark 3:31–35)*:

> *Then his mother and his brothers came; and standing outside, they sent to him and called him. A crowd was sitting around him; and they said to him, "Your mother and your brothers and sisters are outside, asking for you." And he replied, "Who are my brothers and sisters? And looking at those who sat around him, he said, "Here are my mother and my brothers! Whoever does the will of God is my brother and sister and mother."*

This does not say much for "family values," which we hear a lot about today.

The point for us is that if we receive family pressures that are out of harmony with the will of God, then we are receiving culture-training that only reinforces in us the carnal thinking of this world.

From Carnal to Christian

In our *cultural formation*, we are cast in the image of Adam. In our *new formation*, we are cast in the image of Christ. Our cultural formation is *carnal*. Our new formation is *spiritual*. There is no such thing as *being born a Christian*, no matter how many generations your family has belonged to the church. Failing to see this is why *Christendom*, or *culture religion*, inevitably runs off the rails. Too many traditional churches of every stripe have substituted moralistic imperatives for spiritual regeneration. They have thereby lost the power to change lives. Any high-minded pagan can be a morally good citizen. You don't need the church for that. Being nice to your neighbor is not the same as being a Christian, no matter how much you paper over your ethical aspirations with Jesus talk.

Cultural formation from childhood goes largely unnoticed, unless we give it attention in some particular way. For example, most Americans eat with the fork in the right hand and the knife in the left, stopping to switch hands in order to cut, then switching back again to eat. Canadians by contrast typically follow the common European custom of eating with the fork in the left hand and the knife in the right so that you don't have to switch twice to cut and eat. When you sit in a restaurant in Canada it usually is easy to tell who is who by watching the table manners of others.

This became newsworthy some years ago when a group of Americans held hostage overseas were taught by some Canadians to switch their forks to the left hand. They pretended to be Canadians and this ruse helped them be transferred to the safety of a Canadian Embassy, where they were successfully sent back to the United States.

In matters of faith, childhood formation can be a significant power to bring you back to the Lord, no matter how far you stray. I know. It was for me. The lesson is this: If you are a Christian, *teach your children.*

New Life

In one short but significant verse, St. Paul declares both our human dilemma and the promise of God *(I Corinthians 15:22):*

> *As all die in Adam, so all will be made alive in Christ.*
> Paul also shows what is required in order for us to move from
> the one to the other. It is not moral striving or even religious
> works of holiness and prayer. What is required is quite different:
> *The Old Self within us (Adam) must die, so that a New Self within
> us (Christ) can be born.*

This means *conversion.* This is not easy. In *Romans 6:6,8* Paul tells us:

> *We know that our old self was crucified with him . . .*
> *if we have died with Christ, we believe*
> *that we will also live with him.*

Our Old Self does not go to the Cross with Christ without a fight. Our culture-training is too ingrained for that. Even with a significant turning point in our lives, it takes more than a single converting event to completely turn us around. It takes many conversions large and small to refashion our carnal selves. As our conversion deepens, each new converting occasion reveals more things that we need to repent for.

The allures of this world are too powerful. Jesus lays this out in the Parable of the Sower *(Luke 8:12,14):*

> *The seed is the Word of God. The ones on the path are those who have heard; then the devil comes and takes away the word from their hearts ... As for what fell among the thorns, these are the ones who hear; but as they go their way, they are choked by the cares and riches and pleasures of life, and their fruit does not mature.*

Martin Luther tells us: "*The devil does not drown easily in the waters of baptism.*" And Karl Barth sums it up even more cogently: *He swims . . .*

Adam

In the Hebrew, the word "*adam*" means Man, or humankind. When the Lord molded us from clay and dust he blew his own breath into our nostrils. The Hebrew word used here is the same for *wind*, *breath*, and *spirit*. The Lord's original design was that we should be like him, as we see in *Genesis 1:27*:

> *God created humankind in his image, in the image of God he created them; male and female he created them.*

By this act, Adam received the Spirit (*breath*) of God in Creation. But it did not remain this way. Adam forfeited this Spirit by his disobedience. Consequently, we are born as carnal creatures. We need *conversion* to restore us to our original design (*imago Dei*).

When we are born of the flesh, we do not burst out of the womb as full-blown adults. We crawl before we can stand. We stand before we can walk. We walk before we learn that some things are good for us and some things will do us harm. Moreover, things that are wrong for us when we are small may be good when we are adult enough to handle them.

Why should it be any different with spiritual birth? We are not converted today and immediately emerge tomorrow as full blown new creatures in Christ. Spiritual formation takes many steps and requires many turns in the road. Spiritually speaking, new-born Christians need someone to nurse us, feed us, and change our spiritual diapers even before we can walk on our own. That *someone* is <u>the church</u>, our *spiritual mother*.

Spiritual Infants

Adam and Eve were spiritual infants when they first walked in that primeval Garden as intimate companions of God. They were told what to do and what not to do. But Adam was like a small child running in the street without knowing anything about the dangers of traffic. I remember a woman in my parish whose child persisted in running around the supermarket parking lot. She had to reprimand him constantly. As small children sometimes do, he wanted an answer about why he couldn't play when and where he wanted. *Why?* he demanded to know. *Because I'm the Mommy and I say so!* was her answer.

Authority comes first before we can understand what is good for us. Adam was like a child running in the parking lot when he was told not to. The *authority of God* is the first rule of Christian faith. If we disobey it, one of two things will happen: Either (1) *the Lord will discipline us*, or (2) *the circumstances, unchecked, will do us in*. Pray for the first.

God does not will to do us harm. Our own free will is dangerous enough. If we listen to him, the Lord will train us how to exercise our free will properly. When the Lord disciplines us, it is a *warning*, not a *threat*. When a Mafia Don says, *"If you do that, this is what will happen to you . . .,"* that is a threat. Never confuse a warning from the Lord with the threat of dangerous circumstances or the bad results that come from our own destructive behavior. God is not a Mafia Don.

The Modern Dilemma

In Western society, the culture-training we receive from the time we are born is at least 300 years in the making. It took three significant steps to set the stage for the modern conflict between faith and world, Christ and culture. These began with what is called *the seventeenth century Enlightenment*.

Some time around 1650 or so in England, the forces of modern <u>rationalism</u> began to dislodge the category of *Revelation* as the touchstone for truth in matters of faith.

Then by about 1750, primarily among German philosophers, the notion of <u>moral striving</u> began to replace the norm of personal *Redemption* as the measure of Christian fidelity.

By the 1850's, mainly in the United States, <u>individual experience</u> began to replace *the test of holy scripture* as the authority for Christian truth.

The cumulative effect of three centuries of <u>rationalism</u>, <u>moralism</u>, and <u>individualism</u> has issued in a variety of romantic visions about human nature. It has created the beast of sentimental religion that we can no longer recognize as Christian faith, despite masquerading as such.

There is nothing wrong with the use of reason, or with moral standards, or with being your own person. But these are worldly categories. They ought to keep good company with Christian faith, but they are neither its source nor its confirmation. Christian faith derives from a different source: the category of *Revelation*. Revelation *is vertical truth*. It comes from God, a source that is *external* to this world. Revelation does not bubble up from our own human consciousness. God is *wholly other*.

The Twentieth Century

Two more major developments began to take shape in the twentieth century—again: slowly and not all at once. First, sentimental religion began to choke on the mustard gas and trench warfare of World War I. Then came the debilitating effects of the Great Depression and the Nazi horrors of World War II. These events sounded the death knell for our romantic notions about human nature.

The second important development is that Revelation, Redemption, and the Witness of scripture made a surging comeback among Christian theologians in the 1920's. These were seen once again to be the authority for truth in matters of life and faith. Many important voices made a contribution to this restoration, but the work of Karl Barth is the outstanding pivot in the return of Christian faith to its authentic sources.

Barth (1866–1968) was a Swiss Reformed pastor and theologian. He was trained in the liberal theology of late nineteenth century Germany. He came to repudiate this with his commentary, *The Epistle to the Romans* (1919, and thoroughly revised in 1933). When it first was published, one Roman Catholic commentator said that it *"fell like a bomb on the playground of the theologians."* Barth is the most significant Reformed theologian since John Calvin, and the only one of modern times that Roman Catholics give any serious attention. Even Joseph Ratzinger, later named Pope Benedict XVI, spent time in Barth's classroom when he was young.

Barth considered the basis of Naziism to be a new form of *pagan religion* that traditional liberal Protestantism had no resources to resist. In May of 1934, a group of German pastors gathered in the small town of Barmen to draft a protest, and Barth was the chief author of the *Barmen Declaration* that resulted. Its key opening text is *(John 14:6)*:

I am the Way, and the Truth, and the Life, and no one comes to the Father except through me.

In the brief commentary that follows, the defining paragraph in Article One is:

We reject the false doctrine that the church could and should recognize as a source of proclamation, beyond and besides this one Word of God, yet other events, powers, historic figures, and truths as God's revelation.

Discern the Code

Four key references in this paragraph are *code words* for what was going on: (1) *events* means Hitler's seizure of power in 1933, (2) *powers* means the pagan exalting of "blood and soil," (3) *historic figures* means the person of Hitler himself, and (4) *truths* means the ideology of the *Volk* (a pagan interpretation of "the people"). Barth himself unpacks this extensively in his *Church Dogmatics*, Volume II, Part I, Chapter 5, page 172ff.

Naziism was first of all *an ideological movement* before it was a political force. Adolph Hitler demonstrated *the power of the spoken word* to shape reality, and the Nazis knew exactly what was at stake in the Barmen Declaration: the issue of *truth*.

Never underestimate the power of the spoken word. The *spoken word* was God's instrument for the creation of the world *(Genesis 1:3)*:

God said, "Let there be light; and there was light."

Adolph Hitler spoke a word of darkness, and then there was darkness.

Barth refused to take the required oath of loyalty to the Führer and was suspended from teaching in November 1934. In March 1935 he was forbidden by the Gestapo to speak in public. Being a Swiss national, he returned to Switzerland in May and received a teaching appointment at the University of Basel. From there he continued to be a vociferous opponent of Nazism for the next decade until its collapse at the end of World War II.

The Church Dogmatics

Barth's major life work is his *Church Dogmatics* in four volumes, with the planned fifth volume never written by the time of his death. At 9185 pages, his Church Dogmatics is nine times longer than John Calvin's *Institutes of the Christian Religion,* and nearly twice the length of the *Summa Theologica* by St. Thomas Aquinas.

Most people today completely misunderstand what the word "dogmatic" means in theology. It does not mean "stubborn" or "unbending." *Dogma* simply means doctrine—a very neutral term. It comes from a Greek root meaning "decent." *Dogmatic* means *a searching quest* for the authoritative truths of the faith. It contrasts with "apologetic" theology, which is the effort to interpret the faith to the world—including those outside the church and arguments to defend the faith against objections.

The story is told that when Barth made his only trip to the United States in 1962, a bright young reporter from the New York Times met him at the airport and asked for an interview. She asked, "*Professor Barth, can you summarize your Church Dogmatics for us in a few words?*" He quickly replied:

> *Jesus loves me, this I know,*
> *For the Bible tells me so.*

While his language may often be thick, I always enjoy reading from the Church Dogmatics because what he says reliably goes right to the heart of the matter. It cleans out your illusions like a strong dose of salts. Reading it involves you so intensely that sometimes it is very difficult to put it down, even when other tasks and obligations beckon you away.

Yes, Politics

Sentimental religion and romantic notions of human nature have had a major impact on politics as well as in the church. I was nurtured in an environment of both. As my conversion has deepened over the years, I have had to confess that much of my mother's faith was sentimental religion. I now acknowledge that she had inherited three centuries of romantic notions about human nature from my grandfather Perkin and his politics. I then inherited the same through her.

We are not alone in this legacy. I remember standing on a street corner in midtown Manhattan one evening around 10 pm, talking with the esteemed Senior Pastor of a legendary and progressive church on Park Avenue. Pastor Gillespie also happened to be the chairperson of the New York State Liberal Party. (*New York has had four active parties in state politics for quite some years, not just two: Democrats, Republicans, the Conservative*

Party, and the Liberal Party). It was the 1960's. I was the novice Associate Pastor from Brooklyn, just starting out, and he was the seasoned warrior in contested issues of both church and state, so he did most of the talking and I did the listening. He was a kind and compassionate man with a deep moral sense of right and wrong, which he applied with a stern imperative to the affairs of state and the destiny of nations.

He carried on for quite some time. After a while, I began to wonder what I was hearing because it seemed to me as borderline unbelievable. His face had a wistful and almost beatific countenance and his eyes began to mist with tears as he waxed on eloquently about the city we both enjoyed. John Lindsay had recently been elected as Mayor, running on both the Republican and Liberal Party tickets. Pastor Gillespie had been a significant player in his victory because of Liberal Party support. He was now relating to me his glimpse of unparalleled hope and a triumphalist vision for the city, the nation, and by inference, for the future of a new world order. His vision had the qualities of the final victory of Christ over the powers of darkness at the end of time.

Not the Eschaton

Eschaton is not a familiar word for many people. It is a Greek word that merely means "the end," like the closing statement on the last scroll of the film at the movie house. In Christian faith, it refers to the Second Coming of Christ at the end of history. You can read all about it in the Book of Revelation.

The election of John Lindsay as Mayor of New York was not an eschatological event. Lindsay did indeed later run for President, despite a mixed and hardly triumphant tenure as Mayor. He was far from fulfilling the vision I had just encountered. Pastor Gillespie's romantic politics were both astonishing and revelatory. He stood in the same shoes as those of my grandfather Perkin, feasting on the legacy of Woodrow Wilson and the *League of Nations* (despite its failure), the language of *World Peace through World Law* and the *United World Federalists*. In this vision, all nations (including the United States) would renounce their sovereignty in favor of a unified world government that would end all wars and usher in a final reign of universal harmony and peace.

The thought of it is breathtaking.

It is one thing to build your politics on this. It is quite another matter to build your church on this. Put the two together and you are far away from the realities of life and from what scripture says about human nature.

A lot of this thinking seems new in world history, from the seventeenth century Enlightenment to our Twentieth Century wars and from twenty-first century political movements. But this is not really new. The forms are new, but the undercurrent is not. It is *Darkness* masquerading as *Light*. We now see this in both the terrorism of our time and our contrasting romantic politics. Darkness masquerading as light is not new at all.

Lucifer

The prophet Isaiah tells us *(Isaiah 14:12,13)*:

> *How you are fallen from heaven, O Day Star, son of Dawn!*
> *How you are cut to the ground, you who laid the nations low!*
> *You said in your heart, "I will ascend to heaven;*
> *I will raise my throne above the stars of God."*

The name used in this Isaiah passage, *Day Star*, or *Morning Star*, is translated in the Latin Vulgate and King James Bibles as *Lucifer*. The name *Lucifer* derives from the Latin *lux*, from which we get the English word *light* and related terms like *luminous* and *illuminate*. Lucifer is Darkness masquerading as Light. Those who fashion themselves as *luminaries* or *illuminati* are usually walking in darkness more than they could possibly know.

This passage in Isaiah derives, in turn, from the Tower of Babylon narrative in *Genesis 11:4*:

> *Then they said, Come, let us build ourselves a city, and a tower with its top in the heavens, and let us make a name for ourselves.*

The Sin of Pride is always pretentious. It wants to reach up and grasp the wisdom of God through human achievement.

When the church was born at Pentecost by the power of the Holy Spirit *(Acts 2:1–13)*, this was, among other things, a reversal of the confusion of tongues at the Tower of Babylon. Then as now, when we hear the truth in tongues not our own it is a sovereign move of God on our lives. The power of Pentecost is not to be confused with World Federalist programs or expectations.

Romantic religion that becomes conflated with the politics of a "new world order" is the end of the line where the trolleys don't run and the tracks turn to rust in the weeds.

Recalling Chicago

It took me time to comprehend how deeply my own church was enthralled with romantic religion, a debilitating Darkness masquerading as Light. As my own conversion deepened, so did the darkness around me. Its malignant character became more evident the more I sharpened my preaching of the Gospel. I needed help. As I poked around the several seminaries and theological institutes in my Chicago neighborhood looking for help, someone asked about *my spiritual director*. I did not have one.

As I look back now, I am ashamed to admit that despite 20 years in the parish ministry, the very term *"spiritual director"* had escaped me. Two decades earlier I had devoured books by Thomas Merton, including his book on Spiritual Direction, yet the meaning of this had never really sunk into my consciousness. Truth sometimes takes a long time to take hold. Like the *Parable of the Sower (Luke 8:4–8,11–15)*, it took repeated plantings of the seed on my rocky ground before fertile soil was discovered.

So I went shopping for a spiritual director and the resources were ample. I settled on a Jesuit director, who became the first of several when I later moved to New England. As an aside, I also have been taken aback more than once over the years by the hostile and derisive reaction from many of my Roman Catholic priest friends whenever I even mentioned the name "Jesuit." The church in its variety is a complex soup.

They Listen

I soon learned that good directors are not all that "directive." They mostly *listen* while you ramble on about your relationship with the Lord. Then every so often a good director will interrupt and say, *Tell me more about that . . ."* and then ask probing questions to uncover more detail about what really happened. The ground rule they give is this: *"If it is important, don't ever forget it. Keep returning to that event to drink deeply from its well, even years later, and you will find out how important a turning point it was for you then, even as it continues to enrich you now."*

So I began to uncover, or recover, small events (*they seemed small at the time*) from years past that were significant milestones for me. At the end of Chapter 2 in the section called Mustard seeds, I related this following example of a recovered spiritual memory:

While I was a college student and still committed to an Industrial Engineering career, I had made it a practice from time to time to step into a church that kept its sanctuary open during weekdays for anyone to pause for a time of quiet contemplation and prayer. I was never there on a Sunday, but I was grateful for this accessible space. I would always head to the same pew, about half way down the middle of the church, and sit in the same spot by the wall directly under a stained glass window. It was not a busy place during the week and I was always alone. But it was a majestic space and I can clearly remember the sunlight penetrating the multicolored panes of glass.

At the time, I saw it only as a place of comfort amid the rigorous demands of schoolwork. Now I know it was *the Lord calling me*. This was a year before my evening epiphany when I was looking at one drawer in my desk, full of timetables, and then the other, full of literature from the campus church I was attending. That event too was one of the first things my spiritual director led me back to recover. *What about your original call?* He had asked. I had to stop and think.

Harold Urey's Apparatus

Spiritual Directors tell us not to forget revelatory events. The same applies to institutions and to the culture at large.

Back in Chicago when I was a seminary student, a classmate and I took part time jobs as furniture movers for the University of Chicago Physics Department. We worked at the Enrico Fermi Institute for Nuclear Physics. Across the street from our building was Stagg Field, an intramural sports field for the Athletic Department. The cement block Stagg Field bleachers housed the Manhattan Project, which split the atom during World War II.

We quickly learned that every graduate student in physics had his or her own private office. (*This contrasted sharply with the cramped study carrels we had at the seminary library—a message not lost on us*).

For 2–3 hours each weekday afternoon, Brandy and I moved desks and file cabinets from one office to another, to set up or set down office space for incoming and outgoing physics students. We learned never to lift when we could tilt, and how to tilt a heavy file cabinet onto a four-wheeled furniture dolly. Invaluable skills—as we debated serious theological issues while rolling desks and file cabinets down the corridors.

One afternoon while we were in the attic, and I noticed a strange-looking apparatus about the size of a 6 foot high by 5 foot long bookcase. Its shelves were filled with an assortment of glass bottles and beakers, connected by spiral glass tubes. It looked almost like something out of a Rube Goldberg cartoon. It was gathering dust and obviously had not been touched in years.

When we returned downstairs, I asked our foreman about it. He replied, *Oh, that's what Harold Urey used during the Manhattan Project to develop heavy water.* Shocked, I asked him, *Shouldn't that be in a museum someplace?* He answered, *Well, the University has been discussing that for years with the Smithsonian in Washington, but they can't decide on who will pay the shipping cost.*

These 50+ years later I have no idea whatever was the fate of Harold Urey's apparatus. But it remains a Parable of a lost fragment of history. Nations too forget. Spiritual Directors tell us not to.

The Word You Don't Forget

I remember vividly a sermon during my college years at the church near my campus. How many thousands of sermons do we hear over the years and never remember a word, even though they were valuable at the time? Faithful participation in worship is like eating breakfast. It is necessary nourishment for the day. But do you remember what you had for breakfast on April 26, 1973? Most likely not. But what you ate then was important for the time.

The Pastor Emeritus was Frederick Griffin. Although he was retired and well into his eighties, he did continue to preach once a year. I heard him several times, but I do not forget this particular occasion. He made one very simple point: "*We all love Christmas and we revel in Easter*, he said, *but these are only two of the anchor points of faith that mark the Church Year. The third is equally important. It is the Feast of Pentecost, and we overlook it to our peril.*"

How right he was. A church without Pentecost is an eagle without wings. The Word of God without the Holy Spirit is dry. You die of thirst.

On the other hand, to be enthralled with the Holy Spirit but ignorant of the Word is fire alone. You die in the consuming blaze.

At my seminary in Chicago, we had chapel four evenings a week at 5 PM, Tuesday through Friday. Most services were led by fellow students and occasionally by a faculty member. I remember one scripture vividly when it was read by a classmate at chapel. It struck me then like a ton of bricks and I constantly return to it over the years for nourishment (*Romans 8:22–23,26*):

> *We know that the whole creation has been groaning in labor pains until now; and not only the creation, but we ourselves . . . Likewise the Spirit helps us in our weakness; for we do not know how to pray as we ought, but that very Spirit intercedes for us with sighs too deep for words.*

This is a statement about the working of the Holy Spirit in our lives, praying in and for and through us when we don't know what to say. Put this text together with that retired Pastor's sermon about Pentecost, and you have the charismatic anointing that both drives the church and keeps it humble.

The Board of Directors

Each one of us has a cacophony of voices constantly cranking in our heads. These voices operate like a *Board of Directors*, with various members telling us which way to turn, what paths to pursue, what is good for us and what is not.

For most of us, this "Board of Directors" is a *dysfunctional governing committee*, a chorus of contradictions, one voice telling us "*go this way . . .*" and another saying, "*no, do that . . .*" They usually conflict with one another, and most of them are dark.

A humorous television ad from some years ago gives us a quick example of how this works. There often is basic truth in what first appears as trivial humor.

The ad features a donut maker sitting up in bed with a clock over his head that reads 4 AM. On one shoulder sits a small angel, complete with halo and robed in white, who whispers into his ear, "*Time to get up and make the donuts . . . Time to get up and make the donuts.*"

Then on his other shoulder sits a small devil in a red jump suit, holding a pitchfork, and with two small horns on his head. He whispers into his opposite ear, *"No, you don't have to get up . . . you can just turn over and sleep in, and forget the donuts.* The donut maker's eyes flit furtively back and forth, caught in a dilemma about who really to heed.

The beginning of spiritual discernment is to learn to *give names to your voices*. Often there is the Siren (or the Gigolo, depending on your gender) who whispers: *I am the one for you*. Everyone, it seems, has the Skeptic: *You know that can't possibly work*. There frequently is the Con Man: *Have I got a deal for you*. Often, there is the Demoralizer: *You know you're not good enough for that*. Sometimes there is the Weeper: *You'll never amount to a hill of beans*. Or the Scorekeeper: *Your marks in school were never up to snuff; you don't have enough education (or talent, or skill) to qualify for that*.

Name your own. They probably are different for most of us, yet some of them seem to show up everywhere. They will tempt us to Vanity, Gluttony, Avarice, and Pride. Some are truly demonic and want to lure us into very destructive things.

Know also that hidden among these many players is the voice of God, the lure of the Holy Spirit. We have free will. Spiritual discernment is learning to listen to the voice of the Lord and to make the right choices.

A Will of Its Own

Know that darkness is not benign or neutral. It is malignant and malicious. Darkness is not merely *the absence of light*. It is a willful and deceptive force, seeking to ensnare us at every turn. This scripture for *Compline* (meaning "completion"), the Night Prayer just before bed, is from the *Book of Common Prayer* (I Peter 5:8–9a—BCP page 132):

> *Be sober, be watchful. Your adversary the devil prowls around like a roaring lion, seeking someone to devour. Resist him, firm in your faith.*

We inherit a very bad idea from Plato, the classical philosopher from ancient Greece, who said that *evil is the absence of good*. This exerts a strong and unfortunate influence on a lot of modern thinking. If you follow this it tells you that evil—being the absence of good—is a *nonentity* like coldness, where there is no more heat.

This is true in the physical world, but it is not true for evil. In the physical world, cold is the absence of heat. Heat is energy—molecules in motion. As molecules slow down, energy drops. Water freezes. When molecular motion stops completely you reach *absolute zero*—the bottom floor of coldness below which the temperature cannot go, because movement has come to a stop.

When we apply this thinking to good and evil, we are dead wrong—with the emphasis on *dead*. That is where the deception about darkness and evil will lead us. Plato is the one who was dead wrong, and he's dead.

The simple truth of history is validated by biblical testimony: Evil is not the absence of Good, like a seesaw that goes down when the other end goes up. History shows us that whenever the Good increases, Evil increases as well, side by side, in parallel like a malignant partner in tandem held by an unwelcome but inevitable yoke. Scripture calls this force Lucifer, or Satan, or the Evil One, the Father of Lies and the Prince of this world.

Sentimental religion and romantic notions of human nature are totally blind to this reality. That is just the way Satan likes it. He wants to hide.

If you believe that God is real but that Satan is merely a superstition, you are deeply deluded. You understand neither the truth of scripture nor the depths of Hitler's Third Reich.

Tradition, and Tradition

Henry was a reliable fixture in one church I once served. He was always gracious and polite, but at the same time he was suspicious of anything new. If I were to pursue an initiative different from what people were familiar with, he would quickly remind me how it customarily was done. He would comment, always calmly, *Well, we've always done it that way.* He had a limited understanding of what the word "tradition" means—a common affliction for many good church people.

His wife was a bit more adventurous. She once asked me: "*How many Congregationalists does it take to change a light bulb*?" I paused, waiting for the punch line. She quickly said, "*Change the light bulb? Why my Aunt Sarah donated that bulb in 1957.*"

We too often fail to distinguish between "*tradition*" (*with a small "t"*) and *Tradition* (*with a capital "T"*). With a small "t," *tradition* in most churches means: *Well, we've always done it that way.* The blind spot here is that *always* usually means *since about 1953*, or as far back as someone's own personal memory goes. On the other hand, *Tradition* with a capital "T" means *the teaching authority* of the church down through the ages.

In the classic understanding of the church, *scripture* and *Tradition* are twin authorities that both emanate from Christ. Scripture alone is never enough, though many like to think it is. Every community of Christians has a *Magisterium*, although many would deny this under the banner of "scripture alone."

The Magisterium

Of course the *essential authority* is scripture. However, along with this is *Tradition*, or the legacy of teaching that guides the *interpretation* of scripture. The Latin word for this Teaching Tradition is *Magisterium*, from which we get terms like master, majesty, magistrate, and teacher. Every church has its *Magisterium*, an accumulation of interpretation about scripture. The problem is that some acknowledge this openly and rely upon it to guide them. Others are oblivious to its existence and act is if it is not there.

I was preaching as a guest on one occasion at a church of another Tradition from my own. Afterwards in the Coffee Hour I was talking with John, a conservative evangelical from one of the plain church Traditions. He told me about many years of Bible study in the congregation where he had grown up. He said that they all were obligated to use only one particular translation that had been deemed as "correct." After some years, he began to realize that his Bible study group spent 90% of its time *discussing the footnotes* that came with this edition rather than examining the text itself. This church community certainly had its own Magisterium—in the form of Bible footnotes—whether or not they were willing to acknowledge it. John was reporting the existence of a hidden Magisterium that nobody else wanted to admit.

How do we know what things are *of the Lord* and what things come from the murk? One of the oldest rules in the church is to seek confirmation from *overlapping authorities* when you get stuck. Among these authorities are the *consensus* of the ages, the *counsel* of peers and pastors, the *trust* of a worthy confidant, the *direction* of a spiritually healthy Christian community, and your own *prayer*. Anchoring these is *scripture itself* and the accumulated *wisdom of interpreting it*—your Magisterium.

Catholic?

And Magisteria differ from one Tradition to another. The Greek and Roman—or Byzantine and Latin—churches split over magisterial disputes in the Great Schism of 1054. One of my teaching friends is Fr. Barnabas, a Benedictine monk at a monastery near home. He likes to pique his mostly Roman Catholic audiences by opening his seminar with the statement, *There hasn't been a Catholic Church for a thousand years* (He is referring to the *Great Schism*).

"Catholic," of course, means *Universal*. In the fifth century, St. Vincent of Lérins laid down *the threefold test of catholicity*, named after him as the *Vincentian Canon*. His definition is: *What has been believed (1) everywhere, (2) always, and (3) by all.* This is what broke down in the Great Schism of 1054, although that universal ideal has been upheld by countless Christians ever since who believe that Christ is *one Body*. Why not? This was the plea of Christ to the Father for all his followers in the *High Priestly Prayer* of Jesus *(John 17:11)*

> ....that they may be one, as we are one.

Jesus Christ did not go to the Cross to establish denominations. Martin Luther, John Calvin, and the other great *Magisterial Reformers* of the sixteenth century were precise about this. They adhered uncompromisingly to the <u>test of Catholicity</u> as it was *before the eleventh century* to make it very clear that their agenda was to clean up the corruptions of the medieval church, not to establish some new kind of religion.

To this end, they based their faith and their teachings on the bedrock Magisterium of the Apostles' Creed, the Nicene Creed, the Athanasian Creed, and the Seven Great Ecumenical Councils that governed the church before the Great Schism. I am always amused by the reaction of Roman Catholic friends who have the occasion to attend a Lutheran or Reformed Church and are surprised to hear the congregation profess either the Apostles' Creed or the Nicene Creed, which both include the line: "*We believe in one holy, catholic and apostolic Church*". (The Apostles' Creed is typically in the singular, "I believe...," as the *Baptismal confession* of the individual believer, while the Nicene Creed is in the plural, "We believe...," as the *Faith of the whole Church*).

Does It Deliver the Goods?

When you receive the Eucharist, does it deliver the goods?

At a monthly meeting of a neighborhood pastor's group I was part of for many years, a Baptist colleague told of an incident in which he was commiserating with some neighbors over a death in their family. They were not Baptists, but he knew them to be faithful Christians in another Tradition different from his. He confessed to being shocked when they said, "*We are so glad that she received Christ just before she died.*"

In his Baptist language, "receiving Christ" meant going down the aisle for the first time in response to an altar call to give your life to Jesus. He confessed to being so perplexed at their comment because he knew that the deceased had been a faithful Christian for most of her life. Then he realized that in this family's Tradition, "receiving Christ" meant receiving the Eucharist. He had said nothing to them but he was confessing to us that he had to forgive himself for missing the message that had brought them comfort.

In matters of understanding the Eucharist, the Lutheran and Reformed traditions went their separate ways at the *Colloquy of Marburg* in 1529, only 12 years after the Reformation got under way in 1517. Delegates gathered at this small German town under the patronage of Philip of Hesse to settle differences that had already emerged.

15 Articles were presented for discussion and debate. The opposing Lutheran and Reformed delegations fairly soon agreed on the first 14. But when it came to #15 the sparks began to fly. The point of #15 was the *Real Presence of Christ* in the Eucharist. Luther and the Saxon delegation insisted on this, while Ulrich Zwingli of Zurich and the Swiss delegation demurred. Luther and Zwingli each stormed out abruptly. As a result, the Lutheran and Reformed traditions remained at odds over this for nearly 500 years until rapprochement was made in the 1990's.

Howard Hageman of blessed memory (*1921–1992*) was a Dutch Reformed Pastor in Newark, New Jersey, for 18 years, then President of his denomination. He was later a Professor at New Brunswick Theological Seminary in New Jersey and finally President of the school. He once famously said, "*We do not gather at the Lord's Table to celebrate the Real Absence of Christ.*"

In an essay on *Reformed Spirituality*, he also observed that the Puritans who settled Massachusetts Bay Colony in the 1630's were essentially Zwinglian in their piety, not Calvinist, as so many people typically presume. If this be true, it explains why Eucharistic piety in New England churches around the Body and Blood of Christ often seems so flimsy.

Two Reformation Streams

John Calvin features so strongly in Reformed theology that we can easily forget that Luther and Calvin were not contemporaries. It was Luther and Zwingli who were contemporaries. Their separate movements began about the same time in Germany and in Switzerland.

I remember visiting a German Evangelical Church in Bremerhaven during a church pilgrimage tour in 1990. This was a seaport town where many emigrants to the United States had departed Germany in the nineteenth century. Because of its strategic harbor, it was severely bombed by the allies during World War II and the parish church was destroyed. After the war, the church building was ingeniously rebuilt from the original stones that had been reduced to a pile of rubble by the allies. It was impressive and inspiring.

Over the main door, which was within a classic gothic archway, there were three stone niches, each with its own statue. At the center, where the gothic arch reached its high point, was a niche with a statue of Christ. Then lower down on each side of the door were the other two niches, one with a statue of Martin Luther on the one side, and one with John Calvin on the other. It was touching and almost cute, but potentially misleading because Calvin was a 2nd Generation Reformer after Luther and Zwingli. Zwingli had already died and Luther was aging when Calvin came to prominence. And when Calvin first came to Geneva he called himself a Lutheran, which got him into trouble with many of his Reformed colleagues.

Here what Calvin himself had to say about the Eucharist in his 1540 *Short Treatise on the Supper of our Lord Jesus Christ*:

> *We begin now to enter on the question so much debated, both anciently and at the present time—how we are to understand the words in which the bread is called the body of Christ, and the wine his blood. This may be disposed of without much difficulty, if we carefully observe the principle which I lately laid down, viz., that all the benefit which we should seek in the Supper is annihilated if Jesus Christ be not there given to us as the substance and foundation of all. That being fixed, we will confess, without doubt, that to deny that a true communication of Jesus Christ is presented to*

> us in the Supper, is to render this holy sacrament frivolous and useless—an execrable blasphemy unfit to be listened to.

In other words, *it delivers the goods*. When you receive the bread and the cup, you receive Christ.

Memorial Day?

Zwingli and his followers had developed the notion of the Lord's Supper as a *memorial* to the Passion of Christ, a purely commemorative observance of "remembering." I must confess that I have never been sympathetic to this "remembering" interpretation, but it explains why a Zwinglian Communion service feels more like a funeral than a victory celebration. It resembles *Memorial Day*, where we remember our dead and fallen hero Jesus, now departed from us, rather than *a victory coronation in glory* for the triumph of Christ over Satan, sin, and death.

I was always bewildered by how Zwingli came to this conclusion until I came to realize how much a prisoner he was of his own century. His argument was based on *medieval science*, which spent a lot of time debating whether two different substances could occupy the same space at the same time, or how one substance could be in two different places at the same time. Zwingli argued that, following the Ascension in *Luke 24:51* and *Acts 1:6–9*, Christ was seated at the right hand of the Father in heaven and therefore could not be present on earth at the altar in the bread and wine.

Then along came Copernicus who, a decade after Zwingli had died, dismantled the medieval and materialistic notion of a three story universe with heaven above, hell below, and the earth in the middle like a ham sandwich. This was of enormous help to the Lutherans who spoke of the *ubiquity* of Christ, based upon the supernatural omnipresence of God, available everywhere but with us <u>in particular</u> as the *Presence of Christ* in the sacrament on the altar.

Much older than Copernicus, the ancient rabbis had interpreted that when God showed Moses how to bring forth water from the rock to save the people from dying of thirst, the rock then followed Israel through the desert to sustain them in their journey to the Promised Land. The rabbis saw the rock as *the wisdom of God*, and the water as the *Torah*.

Following on this, St. Paul declares *(I Corinthians 10:4)*:

> *All drank the same spiritual drink. For they drank from the spiritual rock that followed them, and the rock was Christ.*

If Christ could be present with Israel to nourish them with water in the desert, why cannot he be present on the altar to nourish us with his body and blood?

The Darkness Deepens

Right after his summons to adult ministry, Christ was driven into the darkness of the desert wasteland to be tempted by Satan. Why should we expect anything different following a significant turn in the road of our lives? *Remember*: the Holy Spirit was the power behind both his baptism by John and his temptation by Satan. It is the grace of God and his abiding protection that brings us the victory.

As our conversion deepens, our conflict with the world escalates. This has been true for me in all the conflicts of my life.

Jesus warned his disciples about this *(John 15:18)*:

> *If the world hates you, be aware that it hated me before it hated you.*

Jesus was a faithful Jew for all of his earthly ministry, and Jews know all about being the brunt of the hatred of this world.

Even Hitler's holocaust was not new. It is a *type* of the genocide planned by Haman in the Book of Esther and repeated by pogroms down through the centuries. The Nazis were more extreme because they had more modern methods of both technology and propaganda at their disposal.

Jesus goes on to make it clear *(John 15:19)*:

> *If you belonged to the world, the world would love you as its own. Because you do not belong to the world, but I have chosen you out of the world—therefore the world hates you.*

Hate is a violent and brutal word. One of the dark secrets about romantic religion is that, while it makes itself appear benign and welcoming on the surface with its sentimental desire to wrap everybody into its fold, if you do not conform to its unbending ideology it will rise up like a swarm of hornets against you when the nest is broken.

I know. I experienced hate in Chicago. I was weeping then, not vomiting.

Following my 1984 epiphany in the sanctuary at midnight, the furnace blazed more fiercely just as Nebuchadnezzar had provided for the three young men who had refused to bow down to the golden statue of his idol *(Daniel 3:19,21)*:

> *Nebuchadnezzar was so filled with rage against Shadrach, Meshach, and Abednego that his face was distorted. He ordered the furnace heated up seven times more than was customary ... and they were thrown into the furnace of blazing fire.*

Born in the Dark

When we are born of the flesh, we are born in the dark, literally. The seed of the father is implanted into the womb of the mother, and there we grow for nine months in a watery darkness.

Our spiritual birthing comes from the Holy Spirit, which is the seed of God the Father implanted into the womb of our soul. The soul is the feminine and receptive *anima* in each of us, whether we are male or female persons. Most men don't understand their receptive dimension, which is why men often resist spiritual rebirth. Check out Nicodemus *(John 3:4)*:

> *How can anyone be born after having grown old? Can one enter a second time into the mother's womb and be born?*

The masculine *animus*, common to both males and females, is the decision-making force of will within each of us. When it stands against the will of God we have sin.

Our procreation is based on God's original Creation *(Genesis 1:1–2a)*:

> *In the beginning when God created the heavens and the earth, the earth was a formless void and darkness covered the face of the deep.*

Here, the biblical language "the deep" means "watery" *(Genesis 1:2b)*. After nine months of gestation, we emerge into the light. But as we know, that is not the end of the story. It is just the beginning. It takes years of formation to bring us to adult maturity.

A child is like a lump of soft clay, to be given shape by the many forces that form us *(Genesis 2:7a)*:

> *The Lord God formed man (adam) from the dust of the ground.*

This process is described further by the prophets *(Isaiah 64:8)*:

O Lord, you are our Father; we are the clay, and you are our potter; we are all the work of your hand,

and *(Jeremiah 18:3 and Jeremiah 18:6b)*:

I went down to the potter's house, and there he was working at his wheel . . . Says the Lord: Just like the clay in the potter's hand, so are you in my hand, O house of Israel.

We all know how this process works in our own lives: First, life will pound us like a lump of soft clay to give us our initial shape. Then we are thrown onto the wheel and spun around like crazy until we are dizzy in the head. After the confusion of being spun in circles, we are thrown into the furnace and the heat is turned up until we are cooked. That is what happened to me in Chicago.

After 1984, my following two years were a dark and desperate time. By the close of 1986 my tenure in Chicago came to an end. Even so, despite all else, the people and I did celebrate the 150th Anniversary of the parish together in June 1986 in an upbeat and honorable manner. That was a blessing.

The Light at the End of the Tunnel

When the circumstances of life pitch you into a very dark place—and they do at one time or another for most of us—know that there is a Light at the end of the tunnel. It is the Light of Christ.

King David, from whom the Messiah comes, led a life plagued by the consequences of his own transgressions. He had to face armed rebellion led by his son Absalom, repeated attacks from other enemies, and numerous other threats. Yet he speaks of the Lord this way in *Psalm 23:4*:

Even though I walk through the valley of the shadow of death,
I fear no evil; for you are with me;
Your rod and your staff—they comfort me.

And Psalm 139:8 tells us:

If I ascend to heaven, you are there;
If I make my bed in Sheol (Hell), you are there.

By mistaken choices of my own, I had made my bed in Hell. But the Lord was with me, even so. When the tunnel still was dark, I found remorse and learned to repent.

When you seek the light, be sure that it is the Light of Christ. The Dark One always is there too, seeking to seduce us. Even he can masquerade as the Light, and he carries in his satchel many tools of deception to snag us. I am always saddened to see how many otherwise loyal and observant Christians still fall for fraudulent spiritualities, even in this modern and enlightened age. Among these treacherous scams are horoscopes, tea leaf reading, tarot cards, water divination, witchcraft, spells, curses, attempts to communicate with the dead, and especially false prophets and their cults. Holy scripture warns us against such things. See especially Deuteronomy 18:10–11 and Matthew 7:15, among many other places.

Remember, however, the deeper the darkness, the greater is the contrast with even the simplest of lights. Even one small candle will illumine your way through the darkest dungeon. How much more it is when you walk by the Light of Christ. I know. I have been there.

And Recovery

1987 found me in an entirely new calling as an Interim Pastor for three small village parishes in Maine. Interim ministry is a designated specialty to counsel a congregation in its time of transition from one settled pastor to another.

If the previous Pastor had died or retired or moved on following a long and peaceful settlement, then your task is to stir the pot and help them prepare for a new future as they search for a successor. If the previous Pastor had departed under a cloud, where there was conflict or trauma, then the Interim's task is to calm the waters and help heal the pain so that the search for new leadership can be fruitful.

An ironclad rule is that the Interim cannot apply for the vacant position. You provide your counsel and then move on.

At my Interim in Maine I followed a traumatic and failed pastorate. I knew all about pain. I was an expert in pain. Helping these folks to heal was healing for me. It was a gift of grace.

I remember a conversation during that time at a local pastors' meeting. Dorothy Spoerl was a retired pastor with a PhD in educational psychology. She had grown up in Brooklyn, New York, long before I was there. I sometimes think that half the world was born in Brooklyn.

Dorothy was sharp as a tack. I had known her for more than 20 years although I had not seen or spoken with her since her retirement. We were talking about congregations in conflict and I said, "*I've seen the movie.*" Quick as a whip she replied, "*Yes, you starred in the show.*" and then she immediately added, "*As a matter of fact, you got scarred in the show.*" She knew all about Chicago. Word gets around.

Moving from Chicago to rural Maine was like moving to a monastery. At 5 PM, all of the shops on the main street locked their doors and pulled down the shades and the sidewalks were rolled up like a Bedouin's bedroll when it's time to move on. You could fire a cannon down the middle of the main street and no one was there to get hurt. Even the journey to Portland, an hour away, seemed like a trip to Times Square. It was magnificent. It was a time of rest, and I needed a rest.

A New Chapter, 1988

Late in 1988 I received a call to return to regular settled ministry at an urban parish near Boston. By this time, I had enough sense to pay close attention to theological compatibility in the search and call process. In this case, this was a church cast in the same mold as the family church in which I had grown up. It was the right fit. It was like a homecoming.

It had some features that were even more elaborate than my childhood church. It was classic English gothic like my pro–cathedral building in Chicago. Unlike Chicago, this was built from a more warm and embracing stone, orange and light brown instead of grey.

Inside, the sanctuary walls were painted a deep maroon, but with the entire chancel in gold. There was a Presence Light over the center altar, a huge rood beam separating the chancel from the rest of the sanctuary, and kneeling benches in the pews. The rood beam was topped with a large cross and had an Ascension text inscribed across the beam in gold letters for all to see *(John 12:32, KJV)*:

And I, if I be lifted up from the earth, will draw all men unto me.

This architecture had been guided by a pastor at the turn of the 19th to the twentieth century who later became President of St. Lawrence University in upstate New York where my grandfather Perkin had attended seminary, and where I had later followed. The St. Lawrence University Chapel was designed by this Pastor in grand fashion like his church in Massachusetts, and is a majestic centerpiece on the campus.

Our church building in Enfield dated from the early 1900's, but the parish had first been gathered in the 1640's as part of the Massachusetts Puritan establishment.

The Puritans were a very plain people who disdained excessive decoration. They believed in clear glass windows, white-washed walls, with no cross on the steeple. They considered the cross to be idolatrous and pagan, and they did not celebrate Christmas because the date is not found in scripture.

I remember one pastor friend who was astounded when he first stepped into our sanctuary and saw the lavish decor. *"How is it,"* he asked, *that a parish gathered by the Puritans could now look like a Greek Orthodox Church?"* All I could say was, *"Things do change over the centuries."*

It was a prayerbook church, nurtured for decades by prayerbooks in the pews that had the liturgy for Morning and Evening Prayer and the Eucharist, with musical settings for the Psalms in Anglican plainchant for the entire congregation to sing, which many new by heart.

I very soon learned from Mabel Jackson, an older woman who had been in the church for years, about how the spiritual formation of a people interacts with the worship space they inhabit. She confided in me that her husband had died a horrible death from cancer and that her adult daughter had committed suicide. She said, *"When I step in here and ponder that text from the Gospel of John over my head, I find a deep consolation and peace that I find nowhere else."* She was one of the saints of the church.

The Inner and the Outer

This was a situation in which the inner spirit and the outer form of the worship space were congruent and concentric. I had known the exact opposite in Chicago. Most of the people there were committed to an Enlightenment Rationalism that heralded their own Herculean powers. This had thrown them into deep spiritual confusion because of the explicitly biblical themes expressed in stone that surrounded them. This was a conflict between the interior and the outer that must of them could never surmount

There is an ancient prayer attributed to Socrates that says, "*May the inner and the outer be at one.*" They had failed that test.

After Socrates, Jesus gives his perspective on the inner and the outer when he describes the spiritual condition of the Pharisees (*Matthew 23:27*):

> Woe to you, scribes and Pharisees, hypocrites! For you are like whitewashed tombs, which on the outside look beautiful, but inside they are full of the bones of the dead and all kinds of filth.

Our building in Toronto, by contrast, dated from the 1950's after a revered nineteenth century gothic church had been sold and demolished. That new post–war space resembled, most of all, something like a basketball court, a high school auditorium, or a labor union hall. It presented no conflict for the rationalists who liked things "crisp."

Space is *sacramental*. The Catechism in the Book of Common Prayer describes sacraments as "outward and visible signs of inward and spiritual grace." (*page 857*).

The kind of space in which you worship does make a difference. It will either sustain you or leave you cold, confuse you or harmonize you with a supernatural God who is both sovereign and intimate.

Seven

Forgiveness

And out of pity for him, the lord of that slave released him and forgave him the debit. But that same slave, as he went out, came upon one of his fellow slaves who owed him a hundred denarii, *and seizing him by the throat, he said, "pay what you owe."*

—MATTHEW 18:27-28

Forgive?

FORGIVENESS DOES NOT COME easily. We fight against it at every turn. The greater the offense and the deeper the wound, the more we resist forgiving the offender. When we have been deeply hurt, the act of forgiving seems nearly impossible. But forgiveness is the key to finding your blessing. Forgiveness unlocks the door to your new life in Christ. Pray to the Lord about it. He will give you the strength and the grace.

The Aftermath of Abuse

How could I possibly forgive all those people in Toronto and Chicago who had sought to do me harm? Well, I couldn't—on my own. Forgiveness is difficult work, and I needed the Lord's help to bring me restoration. And this takes time. It was not just a simple matter of wiping my brow the day after and saying: *Well, that was tough—but of course I forgive all those folks. It's over and done and that's that.* Perhaps there are those truly saintly few who can do this with a snap of the finger, a short prayer and then move on without missing a beat. If so, I am not in their company. Such a quick process of resolution was beyond possible for me, as I suspect it would have been for the majority of us mortals on this earth.

I remember sitting at home in Chicago when the end was near. I was in a stupor, numb. I spent time flipping through the "help wanted" section of the Sunday paper thinking that perhaps I could find a job selling shoes. That seemed like a benign and stress-free occupation. I was too far away from engineering school, 25 years before, to be able to restart that path without a lot of remedial catch-up. Besides, I had neither the energy, the motivation, nor the resources to pursue that direction. I felt lost and worthless. On top of all the rest, I had yet to face the fact that selling our property during a down housing market in order to move to Maine would bring me to the brink of financial ruin. The original trauma was bad enough. Resulting consequences would bring more dislocation and stress. The aftermath often does.

When an abused woman does finally make the break from a rotten marriage, there is rent to pay and groceries to buy . . . how? There is also the need to recover a sense of self-worth . . . how? I felt like that: bewildered, abandoned, overwhelmed, and hopeless. But the Lord was there, through it all. He always is. He companions us in our darkest hour.

Semitic Prayer

I had a rabbi friend in Chicago who had struggles with his congregation. He once told me that when he was feeling desperate, he went into his sanctuary late at night, opened the Tabernacle where the Torah scrolls are kept, then sat out in one of the pews and said: *Now look here, Lord: You got me into this. Now get me out of it* . . . In time, he did.

Christians need to learn more about semitic prayer, and practice it. Christian faith is a semitic religion. This means that you can argue with God. Abraham did. And Moses did. So did the prophets. They testify to the truth of *Emmanuel*—which means "*God with us.*" He always is.

Forgiveness is Complicated

Forgiveness is rarely a simple act of will: *Oh, Harry did me wrong, so I will just forgive him.* Forgiving a small slight may sound easy, but forgiving a large assault does not come so easily, as most of us know only too well. Following the attacks in Chicago, I first lost my confidence, then my property, then my self-worth. Thoughts of forgiveness were far from my mind. Brute survival was paramount.

But we do need to begin right away before the bitterness settles in and begins to fester within us. The way to begin is to speak the word of forgiveness and the reality of it will follow in due time. Beware, however—we carry within us severe impediments against doing this.

I did not want to forgive. A desire for revenge, a bout of self-pity to convince myself of how evil they were, and a pit of depression fueled by relentless sadness all beckoned to do me in.

Grief When the Bitterness Ebbs

I had grief for what was lost: a dream of what might have been, and grief for my lost dignity, direction and purpose in life. Grief is normal, natural, and necessary, so long as it is balanced in proportion to your loss. If you have no grief then *you had no relationship* with what was lost. Either it had no real value or you just didn't care.

When his friend Lazarus died, *John 11:35* tells us: *Jesus began to weep.* In the *Authorized Version of 1611*, commonly called the *King James Version*, this is translated simply as: *"Jesus Wept,"* making it "the shortest verse in the Bible" in that early translation.

Then there is grief that is out of balance, going way overboard, even of pathological proportions. I learned an important lesson about this when my parents died. They each died at about the same age in their mid-seventies and in much the same way—swiftly, without warning—from a massive and unexpected stroke. They died about four years apart since they were about four years apart in age.

When my father died, I blubbered and wept uncontrollably for days, even weeks. I could hardly contain myself or carry on with simple life responsibilities. When my mother died about four years later, I was deeply saddened. I grieved—but not in the near pathological way as when my father had died. When he died I had thought my response was "normal." So when my mother died, I quickly began to feel confused, with a great sense of shame. I began to ask myself: *Did I not love my mother? Why am I not weeping in the same out-of-control manner as when my father died?* My confusion and shame lasted longer than my grieving for her.

The answer to this dilemma dawned quickly many years later when I was in a casual conversation with another pastor. He was sharp, and had the sense to pick right up on it. He pointed out the one big factor in their deaths that was different for me. It was *relationship*.

In his final years, my father had made himself absent from us. In retirement, he took a part-time symphony position in Birmingham, Alabama, and spent the remaining part of each year touring around the country on a Greyhound bus. All I ever heard from him was the occasional post-card with no return address. He didn't stay in one spot long enough to receive a reply.

My mother and I, on the other hand, had remained close—even when I was far away from Philadelphia serving a church near Buffalo. She and I had said everything to one another that needed to be said, sometimes many times over. There was no <u>unfinished business</u> when she died. My father, on the other hand, knew nothing of my adult life since I had been a college sophomore. At his death, I not only was grieving his dying. I was more intensely grieving over the <u>unfinished business</u> between us, things that now could never be said, life events that now could never be known or shared.

Forgiveness is an Act of Will

True forgiveness is a grace of God, but we need to respond in order to receive it. God gives the grace. We exercise the will.

In the end, we must do the forgiving and mean it. Christian love is not a "feeling," but an act of will. Forgiveness is not a matter of developing a warm fuzzy feeling for those who wronged us. It is *an act of will* to forgive, as God has forgiven us. Jesus teaches us about this in the *Parable of the Unforgiving Servant*. He goes to extremes to make his point.

In this example, the slave in question owes the lord of the manor 10,000 talents. A talent was a large measure of weight used on a scales to reckon the value of gold or silver. It is near impossible to translate the value of 10,000 talents from those times until now, but the reference in the parable meant a fabulous sum—like millions of dollars—that would have been impossible for the slave ever to repay.

After his master forgives him this unthinkable debt, the forgiven slave goes out and accosts a fellow slave for a debt of 100 denarii, a trivial sum by comparison. When he cannot pay this small amount, he is thrown into debtors' prison by the one who had just been forgiven so greatly.

When his master learns what has gone on, he summons him and says *(Matthew 18:32–34)*:

> *"You wicked slave! I forgave you all that debt because you pleaded with me. Should you not have had mercy on your fellow slave, as I had mercy on you?" And in anger, his lord turned him over to be tortured until he would repay his entire debt.*

The point of this parable is that we cannot calculate the value of forgiveness. Furthermore, when we are unforgiving we think we are justified in our stubbornness. But unforgiveness is carnal thinking. It is a masque for revenge. Stubbornness is a soft form of vengeance. After stubbornness comes bitterness, then bitterness leads to the desire to strike back. If you do act out the revenge, you can find yourself in deep trouble. If we do not act it out, the desire for revenge settles within us as an abiding resentment that never goes away. It can become buried so deeply that we forget the resentment is there, but it grows like a malignant tumor undiagnosed.

A Deadly Poison

Maintaining bitterness of heart is like drinking a deadly poison and expecting the other person to die. The abiding spirit of unforgiveness is the source of torture for the unforgiving slave in this parable. The *torturers* to whom the slave is given over represent the inner poisons he still carries around of bitterness, grudge, and revenge. These are Satan's demons. They never leave until we forgive.

The Wrath of God

Much was made in earlier times about the *wrath of God*. Preachers don't talk a lot about this anymore because it has fallen out of fashion. We don't often preach hellfire these days, or ever say much about *the Wrath of God*. The currency today is to be optimistic, not punishing, in what we preach.

The sentimental religion that was in vogue in his day was portrayed in 1937 by theologian H. Richard Niebuhr. He described the conventional faith of his time as believing that:

> *A God without wrath brought men without sin into a Kingdom without judgment through the ministrations of a Christ without a Cross.*

Unfortunately, this kind of sentimental religion still is with us. The Wrath of God is real—in both the Old Testament and the New. It is not so often about direct punishment. It is more often about *the sorrow of God* for the wayward. On our side of this equation, the wrath of God is *the absence of God*. The horror of Hell is the *complete* absence of God.

The Sorrow of God

The wrath of God (*ira Dei*, in the Latin) does not mean the *rage* of God, but rather the *righteousness* of God in relation to human sin. The holiness of God does not admit darkness into his kingdom. The wrath of God is the *divine No* against sin. This is *a divine sorrow* for the unrepentant sinner. According to Martin Luther, beneath this *divine No* lies the *deeper Yes* of grace.

If *the Grace of God* is <u>intimacy</u> with him, then *the Wrath of God* is <u>distance</u> from him. We distance ourselves from him by what we do. Since God does not admit sin into his presence, if we are stubborn about what we cling to, he may then withdraw himself from us in sorrow.

We then are left to our own devices. When we are far from him and he is far from us, and the consequences of what we do catch up with us, the Wrath of God manifests itself in the form of our stewing in our own pot without help from the Lord. When we have made ourselves so isolated from his favor, we then come to know the wrath of his absence. When this happens, the wiles of this unruly world can buffet us about without mercy. Sow the wind and reap the whirlwind.

The will of God is not to punish us. The will of God is to save us. He went to the extreme to accomplish this. *He poured himself* into human flesh and went to the Cross himself to do it. The death of Christ is not a *defeat*. It is the *victory* of God over Satan, sin, and death. The *God who dies* is the scandal of all human thought and the bane of every other religion. The God who dies is *Christ, the power to save.*

How Have You Handled Your Pain?

As we move through the years of this mortal life, most of us have had our share of misfortune, calamity, dislocation or abuse in matters of health, family, relationships, employment, education, career, or other venues we inhabit. Too many of us have had more than our share of sickness, betrayal, abandonment, threat or hopelessness. Very few of us are born with a silver spoon in our mouth and, among those few who are, even fewer can report that the silver spoon was never taken away.

How do we handle such things? How have you handled the tribulations of this life or the shipwrecks that threatened to do you in?

The testimony of scripture repeatedly shows us that those whom Jesus healed sought after him *assertively* to obtain what they needed.

The paralytic man who could not reach Jesus because the crowd was too great had his friends remove roof tiles and let him down by ropes as he lay on a pallet in order to set him at Jesus' feet. That's assertive. (*Mark 2:4–5 and Luke 5:18–20*).

The woman suffering for twelve years from hemorrhages pushed her way through a crowd merely to touch the hem of Jesus' garment, and she was healed. That was assertive. (*Matthew 9:20–22*).

Jairus, the leader of a synagogue, fell at Jesus' feet and begged him to travel to his house to heal his daughter, near death. She died while they were on their way. Jesus restored her to life while the people laughed at him. Jairus was assertive. (*Matthew 9:18–26*).

While Jesus was resting away from the crowds he tried to avoid the Syrophoenician woman whose daughter was possessed by a demon. She pleaded with him, even saying that dogs eat the crumbs that fall from the children's table. Jesus relented and merely said the word, and her daughter was healed. This mother was truly assertive. (*Mark 7:24–30*).

Don't Blame God

When such dire circumstances befall us, we have a choice: We can be assertive and seek the remedy we need or we can acquiesce, suffer our burden, and say things like: *Oh well, I guess that's my lot in life*, or *Oh, that's God's will for me*, or even, *Oh, that's the cross I have to bear.*

You can suffer your lot or blame fate but it is dead wrong to blame God for hapless disaster. That is called *Insurance Policy theology*. It is not the faith of scripture, sacrament, and church teaching.

We all know about *Insurance Policy theology*. They call it "Acts of God" when they speak of unnamed fire, flood, tornado and storm. These are not *Acts of God*. They are the blind forces of chaotic nature in this fallen creation. God does not will poverty, sickness, disease, or misfortune. He wills life, health, prosperity and restoration for us. He set aside his divine prerogatives to take on human flesh and walk among us, so that he could share our burdens in order to achieve this.

Assert yourself against these debilitating things and you are harmonizing your will with the Will of God. Seek Christ and he will come to you. Declare that you are a child of the living God and he will restore you.

The *Once and Sufficient Sacrifice*

Insurance Policy theology derives its power from a twisted misinterpretation of Jesus' call to discipleship. In Matthew 10:38, Mark 8:34, and Luke 9:23, Jesus does not say, "*Take up my cross and follow me.*" He says, "*Take up your cross and follow me.*" Our cross is not sickness, suffering, and death. *Our Cross* is our Christian vocation, our Christian calling, our summons to witness the Lord for his saving work. When you witness Christ, this world may punish you for it.

The Letter to the Hebrews is shot through and through with a message about *the once and sufficient sacrifice*. After speaking about the long line of Levitical priests who offered sacrifices day after day and year after year for their own sins and for the sins of the people, *Hebrews 9:12* tells us:

> *Christ entered once for all into the Holy Place,*
> *not with the blood of goats and calves,*
> *but with his own blood, thus obtaining eternal redemption.*

This *Holy Place* is the Cross of Christ itself, which for him was not a place of death and defeat but the throne of <u>victory</u> over darkness for our sakes.

Our task is not to climb up on his cross and hang there with Christ. Our task is to fall at the foot of his cross with confession, thanksgiving, and praise for what he has done for us—a work we could never do for ourselves. He is the divine and blameless one who erases any blame of ours—if we turn to him and ask.

This *once and sufficient sacrifice* was a key rallying cry for the sixteenth century Reformation, a time in which Christians everywhere were consumed with trying to justify themselves before God with their own endless sacrificial works of charity, mercy, and prayer. All this was driven by an anxiety that we haven't done enough to please the Lord or merit his favor.

The Point of It All

I once had a conversation with a parishioner who was a psychiatric nurse at a State penitentiary. She described an interview with a prisoner who was sitting across from her as they spoke through a latticework grille that separated them. They weren't getting anywhere.

All the time they were talking, he was slashing his arm with a razor blade. After a while, he stopped of his own accord. She calmly asked, "Are you done now?" He said, "Yes." Then they made progress.

Even the most disturbed of us have a will that we can exercise. We cannot blame God for our misfortune. There always is help. And we need to ask for help if help is to be helpful.

John Calvin tells us: *The chief end of man is to glorify God and enjoy his presence forever (Geneva catechism, 1545, and later elaborated in the Westminster Shorter Catechism of 1647)*. This is not a God who punishes. He is a God who saves—to whom we return thanks.

We hold the keys to the wrath of God. The wrath of God is not a divine delight to do us harm. It is the result of our acting outside the economy of grace. If you willfully jump off the subway platform and deliberately place one foot on the main track and the other on the third rail, you will be electrocuted. Not good. And certainly not by "the will of God."

The Nature of Sin

Adam and Eve in the Garden of Eden were intimate with God. They talked with him as a caring Father. He sought to nurture them out of their infancy and train them into maturity, but they took matters into their own hands before it was time. They were cast out of the Garden to fend for themselves in order to prevent them from doing more damage there.

The result is our *isolation from God*. After Adam, instead of *intimacy* with God, we suffer an infinite *distance* from him. We cannot bridge this gap on our own. The yawning chasm is too great. We are mortal and temporal. God is immortal and eternal.

And *what is sin*, anyway? Before there are *sins* in the plural, which are human actions outside the will of God, there is *sin* in the singular, a *state of being*, a *condition of this mortal life*. Sin is *separation*. Sin means *isolation* and distance from God.

The sins (*in the plural*) we commit are rooted in the separation (*sin in the singular*) between us and God, between time and Eternity. Eternity does not mean *endless duration*. Time and eternity are entirely different categories. Only God can bridge the gap. He did this by *taking on human flesh* and being born in a barn amid the smell and noise of farm animals. *Incarnation* means carnal, and carnal means *flesh*. At the Incarnation, the immortal God became a mortal man.

This *Incarnation* of God in Jesus Christ *beatifies* our human nature by lifting us up toward the divine. This is a profound work of God that sanctifies all human life. In this way, the Incarnation is the foundational saving grace, even before we get to the Passion of the Cross.

An old theological conundrum asks, *Which is the greater sacrifice on God's part: The Incarnation, or the Passion?* The answer is a toss-up. But given the blanket effect the Incarnation provides for all humanity, it may have the edge in this equation of transforming grace. We each have to make a personal decision to go to the foot of the Cross—or not. But the fact is, the Incarnation is a work whose benefit has already been achieved for all of us.

We are isolated from God by a gulf we cannot cross by our own devices. I have known this terrible isolation in my own life. I have also come to know the intimate companionship of the God who saves. A lot of religion is based on the human effort to reach toward the divine, which in the end is a futile enterprise. The essence of Christian faith is that God reaches toward us when we cannot reach toward him.

Saving Grace and Futile Idolatry

We do not bring about our own beatification. This is a work of God, not a human achievement. God reaches down toward us because we cannot reach toward him on our own. That is a futile effort that leads only to idolatry.

Idolatry is the *First Sin* among all sins (*Exodus 20:3*):

You shall have no other gods before me.

Idolatry means the worship of false gods, the substitution of proximates for what is ultimate. The ancients carved idols of wood and stone. We carve idols of vain ambition and worthless pursuits.

Martin Luther describes the human mind as a perpetual factory of idols. Chief among these today is the sentimental piety about which H. R. Niebuhr wrote. It masks a devotion to a manufactured religion of moral striving, along with our fruitless search for the "secret divinity" of humankind within us. This religious quest for God begins with human curiosity and ends in idolatry. This quest is a modern obsession that prevents us from seeing God's true action of reaching toward us.

Different Kinds of Sin

Some sins are *acts* that we commit. Underlying these are *attitudes* or compulsions that drive us. Medieval writers had a lot to say about the *Seven Cardinal (or deadly) Sins*. These are predispositions more than specific actions. They fall into three general categories in a kind of hierarchy from the base to the highest: There are (1) *carnal* sins, (2) *ego* sins, and (3) *spiritual* sin.

The first three of these seven deadly sins are *carnal*: Gluttony, Rage, and Lust. The next three are *ego* sins: Envy, Avarice, and Arrogance. The final of the seven is *spiritual sin*: Sloth. Not all sins are crimes (transgressions of civil law) and not all sins are vices (violations of moral norms). Sin is that which *isolates* us from God.

The bedrock sin, beneath and upholding all others, is *idolatry*. Idolatry means running after strange gods and venerating fraudulent objects of devotion. I once saw a video clip of an African bishop giving an orientation to some visiting missionaries from the United States. He described a difficult issue in which African Christians attend mass and then run home to a fetish altar where they light candles and burn incense with magical incantations.

I thought to myself: *That's not so unusual. Almost every American home has a fetish altar, be it the TV (with its sportscast) or the computer.* And now we have mobile devices to command our devotion.

I have a friend who was slavishly devoted to his car. It was a model no longer being manufactured. He doted on it. One night a drunk driver demolished it while it was parked in front of his house.

He was in despair. I wanted to commiserate with him but he was not at home. I conveyed my sorrow to his wife—also a good friend—and she corrected me. *It is good that it happened*, she said. *It was idolatry. He needed to be delivered from it.*

The Sin of Eve

Note that the *Sin of Eve* is different from the *Sin of Adam*. As *Types* for all of humanity, this is important to understand because there are differences between the sexes despite the gender confusion of our time.

The *Sin of Eve* was to *let herself be deceived* by the snake, whereas the *Sin of Adam* was *direct disobedience*. If we follow the sequence of the text in *Genesis 2:7* and *2:18* we see that Eve was created *after Adam*, and that God commanded Adam not to eat from the tree in *Genesis 2:17* <u>before</u> the creation of Eve. Therefore Eve did not hear the command directly from God. She received it second-hand from Adam. Adam, however, was *given the command directly* and then *willfully did otherwise*.

We should observe that *once you have been deceived* and then come to see the truth, you likely will not let yourself be deceived again. On the other hand, if you are *willfully disobedient* on one occasion you will very likely be disobedient again, and again, and again. Trick me once, and you're to blame. Trick me twice, and I'm to blame. Eve was tricked. Adam was disobedient.

This plays out down through scripture. It is mostly men who are disobedient or fail to heed the message throughout the Old Testament and on to the disciples of Jesus. It is the women, on the other hand, who tend to be quick to see the truth and adhere to it. We see this in the Old Testament, but especially among the women disciples of Jesus in the New. Peter, James, John and the others are thick-headed and stumble around repeatedly, while the women hang on Jesus' word, sit at his feet, evangelize others, and even remain at the cross while the men run away, not to be heard from again until it is all over.

It was Mary Magdalene, Joanna, Mary the mother of James, and the other women with them who were *the first evangelists of the resurrection*, but when they ran to give *the Good News* to the men, they dismissed it as the frivolous talk of women *(Luke 24:11)*:

> *But these words seemed to them an idle tale, and they did not believe them.*

How It Works

The most blessed thing in this world is to know that you are a sinner who has been forgiven—not by the judgments of men but by the counsels of God. St. Paul tells us that God *reckons us to be righteous* apart from our own misdeeds—even when they vividly demonstrate how unrighteous we are. Paul says (*Romans 4:7–8*):

> *Blessed are those whose iniquities are forgiven, and whose sins are covered. Blessed is the one against whom the Lord will not reckon sin.*

There are some who know that they are sinners, but cannot believe they could ever be forgiven. I know a lot of folks like this and I pray for them.

Then there are some who believe that they have no sin—that perhaps they have mistakes or failures or shortsightedness or other venial shortcomings, but not *sin*. I pray even more for them.

The first group here suffers from *diminished self-worth*. They need to know that nobody is beyond redemption who turns to the Lord and asks. The second group misunderstands the nature of sin.

The term *ontology* refers to *being*, not doing. It refers *first of all* to what we are, before it refers to what we do. What we are is mortal flesh. Sin is not primarily a moral category—of deeds done or not done. Sin is *ontological* before it is *moral*. Sin is first of all a matter of *what we are by nature*—which is *creature*, not Creator, and fallen creatures at that.

The ontological nature of sin is simple: it is *distance* from God. The sins we commit are rooted in this *separation* between God and ourselves.

The Sinless Ones

The secular mind has no notion of sin. Most secular-minded folks are smart enough to see that there is evil in the world, that moral codes are needed for society to function, that crimes are inevitable and need to be punished, that personal relationships can be disrupted or destroyed by transgressions and betrayals that are not even criminal.

But evil action, moral violation, crime, transgression and betrayal do not define sin. As we have said, sin is *distance from God*. Since the secular mind has no God, it therefore cannot have distance from something it believes does not exist. So the unbelieving person who does behave, and who does live an upright life, has no notion of sin. When death comes, his light goes out and that's that. Done. Or so he thinks—until the Lord in heaven greets him and shows him something more.

Just as sin is i*solation from God*, grace is *intimacy with God*. When God reaches toward us or breaks through into our awareness, we can ignore him and run the other way, or we can respond and draw closer to his invitation. Yet the closer we draw toward God through prayer and praise, the more *convicted of sin* we become as we begin to apprehend the *distance* between his holiness and our mortality.

Holy Dread

When we sense our distance from God, that is when true despair and darkness descend. They take hold of us with a holy dread. We begin to understand that there is nothing we can do to please him because our limited and finite lives are nothing before his infinite majesty. We are like the slowest turtle who eventually tires of trying to outrun a marathon champion. We then are hopeless until we take hold of our only hope: The *work of the Cross* on which Christ defeated Satan, sin, and death for our benefit.

It is no wonder that the secular mind chooses to ignore or deny the advances of God. We commit the sin of nonchalance before the holy because we cannot bear the heat of the divine furnace that purifies the soul by burning away the dross of self-reliance.

It seems an attractive alternative to live without sin because we see no God who defines our distance from him. Attractive, that is, until the allure of our achievements dissolves before some shattering circumstance. Then we are at the bottom of a dark well where the walls are too slimy for a foothold to get ourselves out, and we face either death or grace.

Pascal's Wager

If you're not sure about what you believe, or whether you believe anything at all, why not try *Pascal's wager*? It goes something like this: *If there is no God*, yet you confidently believe in him, you will live with comfort, love, and hope. True, a life of faith might also cost you the wages of greed, envy, vanity and aimless ambition. But on the balance, these are works of self-satisfaction with no good purpose. To sacrifice them in favor of

Christlike graces is a winning trade in itself. Then when you die, and there is nothing but "lights out," you will have lost nothing in this life.

On the other hand, *if God is real*, but you do not believe in him, your life on this earth will be a contest between transient charms and the hopeless futility of lost dreams. Then when you die and face the judgment seat of Christ, you risk the forfeit of an eternal heaven. You lose both ways.

Actually, I don't recommend it. To me, it borders on mocking God with a cynical reasoning. But if that is the best you can do, try it. You have nothing important to lose in this life, and everything to gain in the next.

Blaise Pascal lived 1623–1662, on the cusp of the modern age. In his day, medieval certainties were passing away and skepticism was the reigning fashion. Now, four centuries later, we think differently. Today, classical skepticism seems hollow and brittle. Today, we live with the empty dread of "make it up for yourself as you go along . . ." and, if it doesn't work out, too bad for you . . .

A New Environment

My new parish in Enfield, Massachusetts, was sweet comfort after the abuse of Chicago. I was to spend 13 years in this new place, longer than any previous settlement. We had some great adventures, including a citywide celebration of the 350th anniversary of the parish, which in the original constitution of the Massachusetts Bay Colony of the 1600's also meant the anniversary of the town.

In the original Puritan system of Massachusetts, the colonial legislature (known as *The Great and General Court*) authorized the establishment of parishes whose boundaries defined the town. The General Court also authorized the appointment of the Pastor as a "public teacher of piety, religion, and morality."

The term "parish" derives from the ancient Roman Empire, where it meant a geographical administrative district for a territory or province. In each Massachusetts town, the parish register was the voters' list, and the parish meetinghouse was the place of worship for the church as well as the place of government for the Town Meeting.

This church system was known as the *Standing Order*. "Denominations" as we know them today were unknown until the 1800's. They are largely an American invention to accommodate the differences that came with population shifts in the new Republic and waves of immigrants from various parts of Europe. In our case, we were the only church in Enfield for more than 150 years, from 1648 to about 1805 when the Baptists first arrived.

When churches of the Standing Order like ours were eventually taken off the tax rolls in the 1830's, many had to buy back their Meetinghouse from the town in order to have a place for worship.

An Example Close to Home

In our case, the first pastor in Enfield came under criticism from some parishioners in 1651 when they complained to the magistrates that his preaching included "weak and inconvenient expressions." They petitioned the General Court for redress and accused him of a "miscarriage of justice." As a result, his sermon manuscripts were read and debated on the floor of the legislature and the magistrates fined him 10 pounds. They also fined the parish 50 pounds for misconduct in their improper settlement of the pastor in the first place. The pastor's fine was soon remitted because he had no property but his books, while the elders of the parish had their estates assessed to pay their due, which took ten years to collect. Meanwhile the pastor departed and returned to his home in England.

Things do change over the centuries. In our case, population shifts in the communities around Boston following World War II, along with the loss of traditional shoe and textile manufacturing that had flourished in the nineteenth century, brought tough economic times to the town. This brought a decline in the size of the parish, although some members could not comprehend the relentless force of the dead hand of demographics.

The Troublesome Deacon

One person who did not comprehend what demographics can do was Edgar Baxter, a deacon and a long-standing church member. One year Edgar came to be elected President of the Parish Board. At every monthly meeting, he made it his business to take me to task for being the cause for the shrinkage of the church. At every meeting from September through through May his harshness escalated until he so dominated the conversation that he drove all other business off the agenda and intimidated the other trustees into not speaking up.

I tried to be patient with him because you cannot debate with darkness. Finally, in exasperation, I confronted him during one regular monthly meeting. I told him that he was dead wrong. I pointed out that we had a steady stream of new members with small children who brought new vitality to the church, but they soon departed in waves shortly after they came in order to find cheaper real estate farther north. I called our parish a stopping place on "the express train to New Hampshire."

Edgar blustered and sputtered briefly but remained silent for the rest of the meeting. He resigned from the Board shortly after although he remained loyal to the church, for which I was grateful.

When the meeting was over, everyone else from the Board gathered outside in the parking lot. They congratulated me with relief that after months I had finally spoken up. (I wanted to say, "*Well, why didn't some of you speak up?*" but I decided to leave well enough alone). We were at peace.

The Test

That summer we held joint worship during July and August with the Methodist Church down the street—with one month in our building and one month in theirs.

One Sunday at the Methodist Church, Edgar was at worship. To distribute the Communion we followed the customary Methodist practice for serving, with the congregation kneeling at the altar rail to receive the sacrament. As appropriate, the Methodist Pastor, as host, led with the bread and I followed with the cup. As he came to each person kneeling, he said, "*The Body of Christ, broken for you.*" I then followed, saying, "*The Blood of Christ, shed for you.*" I instinctively would emphasize slightly the word, "*for you.*"

All of a sudden, I caught sight of my troublesome deacon kneeling at the altar rail about ten persons ahead of me. Internally, I panicked. All I could hear cranking inside my own head as I approached him were the words, "*but not for you.*"

The Lord has a great sense of humor. I was put to the test. Here I was, the sacramental minister offering the Blood of our Lord to this hapless soul, and I wanted to refuse him. I was convicted on the spot by my own deeply buried vanity, arrogance, and resentment. I repented. I moved right along and served Edgar the cup with good cheer and the right word of blessing.

I was humbled by this revelation. In a flash I had forgiven him. More than fifty years ago, one seminary professor had said to us: *You don't have to like them all, but you do have to love them.* I was too young then to understand what he meant, but I understand him now.

The Tenacious Legacy of Abuse

Who of us has never been abused in this life? Abuse comes to every one of us at some time or another, in large or small doses. Relentless abuse festers in the wounds of the previous. These abiding resentments produce debilitating injury unless we find ways to renounce their effect by forgiving the abuser. They dull the spirit and darken the soul unless we find remedy.

Forgiveness does not come naturally. We are carnal creatures by nature and vengeance is our natural inclination. Our carnal nature wants "justice," by which we mean "payback"—retaliation, retribution, satisfaction—by meting out an equal share of punishment to match the injury or damage we have received.

Unfortunately, this usually results in a downward spiral of destruction as victim becomes abuser and abuser becomes victim. And if the victim cannot locate the original abuser, then we find substitute stand-ins who vicariously take his place as new receivers of abuse from us.

Forgiveness issues from a grateful heart, and gratitude is rooted in grace. The categories of *Nature* and *Grace* are entirely different. Nature is the shape of our carnal mortality, while grace is a gift of God.

Blanket Forgiveness

The signal example of forgiveness is the first of the *Seven Last Words* of Jesus from the cross *(Luke 23:34)*:

> *"Father, forgive them; for they do not know what they are doing."*

In this prayer to God the Father, Christ asks his Father to forgive countless named and unnamed perpetrators in his arrest, trial, and conviction—the high and the mighty, the lowly and the clueless, the Roman officials and the religious authorities, Pontius Pilate and King Herod, the Temple Police and the soldiers who pounded the nails, his disciple Judas who betrayed him and the chaotic crowd who called for his death. In the end, he is asking forgiveness for each and every one of us. The meaning of the Passion is that each and every one of us was there, each and every one of us took part in his trial and condemnation, each and every one of us is a coconspirator.

We would like to avoid this truth. Remember the Easter Sunday back in Toronto when one seasoned member of the congregation accosted me in Coffee Hour, shouting in a voice loud enough for everyone to hear, *What do you mean, "I am responsible for the Crucifixion?" I wasn't there. That was long ago and far away. This is here and now.*

On one level, that was a claim to personal innocence and holiness. On a much deeper level, it represented our inheritance from the Enlightenment. Rationalism and romantic religion want to historicize and therefore relativize the message of biblical faith. Once you do that, you lose the foundational truth that biblical testimony is essentially *emblematic*—it is typological. It represents the character of all humanity. Scripture is the Word of God *for us*, speaking to us. More specifically, the living Word of God is not the written text of scripture. The living Word of God is Jesus Christ himself. The written text is a vehicle.

The Person of Jesus and the events in scripture are not *"long ago and far away."* The Word of God speaks directly to us, now. When you understand this, you learn never to speak of Jesus in the past tense.

The Choices We Make

The grace of God is freely given and always available, but we have to accept it to receive it. We can always say *No*.

There were *three* crosses at the crucifixion, not just one. Two thieves were crucified along with Jesus, one on each side, with him in the middle. They are emblematic for the entire human race. Hear the text directly on its own terms *(Luke 23:39–43)*:

> *One of the criminals who were hanged there kept deriding him and saying, "Are you not the Messiah? Save yourself and us!" But the other rebuked him, saying, "Do you not fear God, since you are under the same sentence of condemnation? And we indeed have been condemned justly, for we are getting what we deserve for our deeds, but this man has done nothing wrong." Then he said, "Jesus, remember me when you come into your kingdom." And he replied, "Truly I tell you, today you will be with me in Paradise."*

These two thieves represent all of humanity. Moreover, they represent each one of us. We can either turn toward Christ or turn away. We can choose to ignore him and mock him, or we can turn toward him and ask for help. Christ offers Paradise to anyone who asks. Each one of us is a child of Adam and subject to all the snares of this world. Any one of us, no matter how equivocal or miserable our circumstances, can turn to receive the grace he offers and the Lord will deliver. And each of us can always go our own way, to rely on our own resources—whatever we think they are.

Make the Effort

Make the effort to forgive, even when you don't feel like it. Even a modest act of forgiveness will unleash a tidal wave of grace.

Grace means pure and undeserved gift. It also means allowing our motivation and action to overlap the intention of God.

Our human harmony with the will of God underlies all of Jesus' instructions in the *Sermon on the Mount (Matthew chapters 5, 6 & 7)*. His Word is not a moral code of rules we must follow to be saved. The entire *Sermon on the Mount* is "kingdom talk"—a picture of life in the kingdom of God. This comes to us as gift, pure gift. This gift is the initiative of Christ to reach toward us. But like any gift, *we have to accept it* in order to receive it.

Imagine that someone leaves a brand new Mercedes–Benz in your driveway, and the keys on the kitchen table with a note, "this is for you . . ." Yet day after day you ignore it and leave the keys right where they are.

The Source

Our ability to forgive others is based on love your enemies (*Matthew 5:43–44*) from the *Sermon on the Mount*. This in turn is based on *Leviticus 19:18*. This is Jesus the Jew speaking here, which he is, and does, throughout the Gospels.

The original Hebrew in *Leviticus 19:18*, which is translated as "love," can also be rendered as "esteem." Esteem your neighbor (or your enemy) as yourself takes us back to self–esteem. How can we esteem anyone else as ourselves if we have no self–esteem?

Our self-esteem is attacked when we are abused. We lose our self-esteem when the attack is relentless. I lost mine in Chicago. But the Lord restored it to me.

Christ is in the Restoration business. This world punishes. The Lord restores. Loss of self-esteem is what makes forgiving so difficult. Pray to know the image of God in which you were made (*Genesis 1:27*):

> *God created humankind in his image,*
> *in the image of God he created them,*
> *male and female he created them.*

There is no more solid self-esteem than this—to know that you are a precious child of God.

Moreover, the *Sermon on the Mount* is not addressed to "the world" but to the disciples who have taken up the call to follow Jesus. Matthew 5 follows the calling of the first disciples in chapter 4. Then we hear in *Matthew 5:1-2* that when the crowds had gathered, Jesus assembled his disciples apart to teach them:

> *When Jesus saw the crowds, he went up the mountain; and after*
> *he sat down, his disciples came to him. Then he began to speak,*
> *and taught them . . .*

"Sitting down" was the customary position of a rabbi to teach his followers. This was "classroom time" for his disciples. The crowds were allowed to listen in and hear, of course, in case any more of them wanted to join Jesus in his "Way."

At the conclusion of the *Sermon on the Mount*, we do not hear how well the disciples received this, but we do learn that the crows were "*astounded*" at his teaching (*Matthew 7:28*). This indicates that they still were "of the world." Some of them, perhaps, were in process toward becoming disciples, while others simply remained confused and perplexed.

"Feelings" Won't Save Us

Never confuse "feelings" with faith. Following our emotions is the stuff of sentimental religion. We do not find salvation by going up to the mountain top to hold hands and hum. Neither do we find salvation by going to the seashore for a "rock party" where we all sit in a circle on the beach and pass around a stone worn smooth by the surf, each to feel it in our hand and say, "*Oh, Wow . . .*"

In the end, we all die the same mortal death. The work of salvation has already been done for us by Christ in his victory at the Cross. This is the "once and sufficient sacrifice" of *Hebrews 9:12*. We are saved by the grace of his atoning work, a work no mortal effort can achieve. It is ours to receive.

See This Visually

The famous painting by Warner Sallman of Christ knocking at the door of a rustic stone cottage is familiar to many, but it is easy to miss some important spiritual clues it contains. It is based on this text from *Revelation 3:20*:

> *Listen! I am standing at the door, knocking; if you hear my voice and open the door, I will come in to you and eat with you, and you with me.*

The painting has strong contrasts between shadows and light. This contrast between darkness and light is reflected in this opening Call and Response to begin *Vespers*, or *Evening Prayer*:

> *Jesus Christ is the Light of the world:*
> **the light no darkness can overcome.**

These lines are followed by the *Phos hilaron*, an ancient apostolic hymn to the glory of God and the light of Christ. The Greek word *Phos* means light, and is the basis for our word *phosphorescence*, an enduring luminescence or glow.

This title is customarily translated as *O Gladsome Light, O Gracious Light*, or *Joyous Light of Glory*, although in common usage we get the English word *hilarious* from the ancient Greek *hilaron*. The apostolic Greeks may have known something that most of us have lost about the laughter of God at the futile strivings of Satan. He is no match against the victory of Christ. The literal sense of *hilaron* is *exhilaration of spirits*.

The major message in Sallman's painting lies in one detail that is very easy to overlook: the cottage door has no knob or handle on the outside. It can only be opened from within.

The door is ours to open.

The power of God operates by persuasion, not coercion. Christ knocks. He does not smash down the door with a battering ram. We are the ones who can decide to open the door or leave it closed.

Make the effort. Open the door. Make the right choice.

Impossible?

The word "impossible" appears only 19 times in all of scripture. This is not a lot. And most of the references speak about things that are impossible for us, but not for God. Indeed, in *Luke 18:27* Jesus tell us, *"What is impossible for mortals is possible for God."* Matthew's Gospel renders this comment as *"for God all things are possible." (Matthew 19:26).*

One of the most terrifying texts in all of scripture is this passage from The Letter to the Hebrews (Hebrews 6:4–6):

> *It is impossible to restore again to repentance those who have once been enlightened, and have tasted the heavenly gift, and have shared in the Holy Spirit, and have tasted the goodness of the word of God and the powers of the age to come, and then have fallen away, since on their own they are crucifying again the Son of God and are holding him up to contempt.*

This forbidding statement comes like a slap in the face with a cold wet towel compared to much more comforting and familiar lines from the Gospels, which tell us that for God all things are possible. A bone chilling threat is perhaps a better description than a cold wet towel because the sting of a slap passes away quickly.

What makes this *falling away* from grace such a threat? Essentially *the falling away* it describes is much more serious than backsliding. This text refers not to *backsliders*, those who have merely lost their faith. It refers to *apostates*, those who deliberately *denounce* Christ and disown him after once knowing him. As the text says in the closing portion of verse six:

> *... on their own they are crucifying again the Son of God and are holding him up to contempt.*

This shifts the conversation away from the action of God to the actions of the apostate. Then it becomes a *threat*, not a warning. The Lord issues warnings. The consequences of our own bad behavior become a threat. And the language of verse six is all in the present tense: It is not what the apostate has done. It is what he is doing now and is continuing to do.

What this text means is that neither God nor the praying community can "restore to repentance" those who continue to exercise their own stubborn will against Christ. Only the remorseful can repent. And this is an act that comes from within. Take heed.

From Unexpected Mouths

Mark Richardson showed up in church one Sunday morning. I had never seen him before and no one else in the congregation knew anything about him either. He was a stranger with no history or previous connection with us. He stayed for the Coffee Hour afterward and I chatted with him as a newcomer. He casually said, *"I usually spend Sunday mornings propped up in bed, reading the Sunday paper. The Lord spoke to me this morning and said, 'You need to be in church'*—so here I am." It was amazing, but I received it as casually as he offered it. As an aside, I have learned over the years that some of the most important pastoral work happens in Coffee Hour—if you take the time to listen and to hear.

He became a regular. Most Sundays his 13 year old daughter Brenda came with him. As time went on, he grew in his faith and understanding and we talked about a lot of significant spiritual and theological things in Coffee Hour. Soon I noticed that his daughter Brenda would sit with him in the pew at the edge of her seat, in rapt attention to every word of the sermon. Then she would query me in Coffee Hour about things that I had said. Her feedback was perceptive, precise, and confirming—more than most adults I can remember.

Some of my critics began to engage him, complaining that I was preaching too much about Jesus and not providing "more intellectual substance" such as doing book reviews from the New York Times bestseller list or cheerleading for denominational social justice programs.

Mark's wife Sujata also came with him almost every week. She had been born in India from Sikh parents, but had converted to Hinduism when she was young. She went devotedly to the Hindu Temple every Sunday evening and came to church with Mark almost every Sunday morning. She too got caught up in conversation with some of my critics. One Sunday morning she could not contain herself any longer and blurted out to me, weeping, *"They're crucifying Christ all over again."*—almost a direct quote from *Hebrews 6:6* above. As a Hindu she had minimal understanding of Christian faith and no familiarity at all with scripture. But the Lord chooses through whom to speak his Word.

Renounce, to be Renewed

The most difficult person I have ever had to learn to forgive is myself. I know me better than I know anyone else. I know my sins better than I know the sins of anyone else. Looking back, I confess that I spent much of my first 20 years preaching stupidness and calling it wisdom.

While teaching his disciples, Jesus lists a whole series of sins that proceed from the human heart (*Mark 7:21–23*):

> *It is from within, from the human heart, that evil intentions come: fornication, theft, murder, adultery, avarice, wickedness, deceit, licentiousness, envy, slander, pride, folly. All these evil things come from within, and they defile a person.*

It is no comfort to read such a list, and then try to excuse myself on the basis of "lesser sins" he names, just because I am not guilty of theft and murder. It takes only a few items from this comprehensive list to convict us of his basic point, which is found in verse 23: *"they defile a person."*

Notice that Jesus defines this list from the beginning as *"intentions,"* not even as actions or deeds. Each one of us needs forgiveness here, starting with forgiving ourselves, knowing with confidence that God has already forgiven us from the Word and work of Christ on the cross.

The hardest part of self–forgiveness is to confess that we each are to a certain extent coconspirators in our own victimization, even if we simply were naive or overly trusting. Yet our Lord's blanket forgiveness covers even this.

Over the years, when Christ was knocking at my door, I failed to hear the knock. Instead, I was drinking from the well of futile fantasies and vain imaginations. I had been culture–trained by the human speculating that trusts in its own concoctions as sufficient to save us. But eventually the well water tasted sour. That is when I began to see that we have choices—deep choices within—of what to follow and what to reject. To reject is to renounce. To renounce is to repent. To repent is to forgive. To forgive is to be renewed by the power of the Holy Spirit.

Compound Abuse

The abuse I received later in life compounded the injury I first received from the wrong forces of spiritual formation and misguided prophets of romantic hope. Wounds take time to heal and sometimes the scars remain for a lifetime. Jesus had wounds and scars that did not disappear with the resurrection.

On that first Easter evening, Jesus appeared to his disciples and *"showed them his hands and his side" (John 20:22)*. Thomas was absent at the time and missed out on this encounter with the Risen Lord. He joined them a week later when Jesus appeared to them again. This time he said to Thomas *(John 20:27–28)*,

> *"Put your finger here and see my hands. Reach out your hand and put it into my side. Do not doubt, but believe." Thomas answered him, "My Lord and my God."*

In this exchange, Thomas becomes the patron saint of all believers. He does not deserve the bum rap of being called the *doubter*. And Jesus' scars still were there, even after the resurrection.

Broken

Chicago broke my will, my spirit, my hope, my purpose in life. I realize now that *I had to be broken* in order to listen for the Lord and to learn how to depend upon him.

I had to be broken in order to become whole. This world does the breaking. The Lord does the restoration. Even so, signs from our brokenness remain in the aftermath—signs like Jacob's limp or the scars on the resurrected body of Jesus following that first Easter morning.

At times of quiet when my mind wanders, I sometimes muse over all of the ugly things that have happened to me through the years—from when I was a child to the battering of the adult world.

I know that I am not alone. As a pastor, I have listened to far too many stories of neglect and abuse, of dislocation and terror, not to know how violent this life can be—even for those who do not live in a designated combat zone.

Aside from social, political, and cultural strife, the blind forces of nature are not exempt from inflicting mindless and senseless mayhem on unsuspecting human prey. I have seen too many stunning video clips on the television evening news of people's homes on the Massachusetts coast sliding into the sea during a relentless ocean storm. To see this and not to know the unconsolable grief of losing everything without reason takes a truly dull spirit. Nature is full of glory on a quiet April sunrise over a tranquil ocean. But when the sky turns dark at noon and the waves pound the beach in fury, nothing can stand.

Hate?

All the much more are the vagaries of human interaction. When I look back on my life, I can easily think of all the punishing circumstances that have come my way and all the people who have done me wrong. All this could—maybe *should*—invoke the hatred of my heart.

Are we not entitled to hate? We live in an *entitlement culture* in which everything is geared to *the service of Self*—so do I not have a right to hate those who have violated me? Our entitlement culture is based on identity politics and the giving of labels to every possible category of class, race, sex, age, and position in society—and then identifying which of these are either the oppressed or the oppressor. Then in the end, each of us can claim to be a victim.

Once we name our own form of victimization and consequently name our oppressors, we gain *the right to hate* in the course of seeking redress, or as a motivation for taking revenge. It all seems so legitimate and justified.

Except—there is one simple problem with this whole structure of vengeance and reaction. It turns in on itself in a relentless cycle of unsatisfied retribution like a snake devouring its own tail until it cannot consume any more of itself.

Abiding Bitterness

I have met some people who have continued to harbor unforgiveness and bitterness of heart against family members or social forces for real or imagined grievances for fifty years after, until death removes them from this mortal life with no resolution for their ills.

I served one parish in my career where the abuse was intense. It would have been so very easy for me to have festered this injustice in my heart for decades afterwards—forever condemning the perpetrators for what they did to me. All this is carnal thinking.

Thanks be to God that the Lord has led me on a better path. I have learned to forgive every person who has ever done me wrong, should their memory reappear in my consciousness. The more deliberate among us should make the effort to take an inventory to be sure that no one is left out of our forgiving. Keep this in mind:

*Forgive us our trespasses, as we forgive those
who trespass against us. And lead us not
into temptation, but deliver us from evil . . .*

The Lord led the way for everyone to forgive when he showed us a blanket and sweeping forgiveness to his crucifiers and their conspirators in the first of his Seven Last Words from the cross. Some folks will dismiss this as pious claptrap. But consider the alternative. The alternative is an abiding circle of retribution, retaliation, and reprisal.

This was not *a selective forgiveness* directed toward Pontius Pilate or the High Priest of the Sanhedrin or the soldiers who pounded the nails. It was broadcast to all the world, that we might follow.

See, learn, and do likewise. I have seen the darkness and heard the owl.

Eight

Blessing

> *Jacob was left alone; and a man wrestled with him until daybreak. When the man saw that he did not prevail against Jacob, he struck him on the hip socket; and Jacob's hip was put out of joint as he wrestled with him. Then he said, "Let me go, for the day is breaking." But Jacob said, "I will not let you go, unless you bless me."*
>
> —GENESIS 32:24-26

Wrestling with Jacob

EARLY ON IN MY career I was seriously impressed by this text from Genesis about Jacob's wrestling and blessing. So much so, in fact, that it quickly became a signature piece for me.

When I arrived at my first church in Brooklyn after seminary I was given the opportunity to write my own weekly Associate Pastor's column for the parish newsletter. A lot of pastors do this and choose cute or catchy names like *Parson's Pickings*, or *Mystical Musings*. In my case, it was an easy call. I quickly chose *Wrestling with Jacob* as the title for my column.

In fact, for me it became more than just the title for a newsletter column. I invested a lot of energy in its design. I spent hours looking for just the right graphic to go with the title, and hit upon an abstract black and white line drawing that vaguely resembled a muscular fellow in a pose something between a dance step and a jump off a cliff. It was not high level art but it seemed just right for my column. I made a number of photocopies of the mockup to be sure I would not lose it when we sent our copy to the church printer, and kept them in my file.

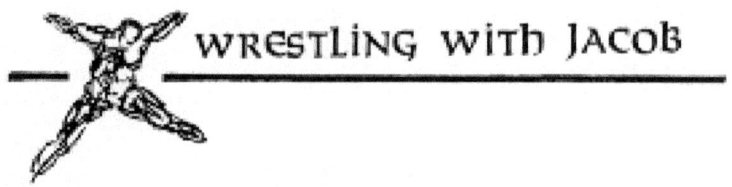

1965 Newsletter column graphic

It certainly seemed appropriate for the 1960's when everything was in turmoil. Both church and society were wrestling with large and demanding issues. More than that, it seemed especially to apply to me because I had a dark and indistinct sense that I was wrestling with deep spiritual issues that I was hardly able to identify. They seemed like a murky mixture of chaos and promise that would step unexpectedly out of the shadows at unpredictable times, offering small flashes of light and truth, then vanish as quickly as they came.

A Slippery Character

Jacob was a tough customer. God had issued a remarkable summons to his grandfather Abraham, who was an otherwise unremarkable person. By his own merit alone Abraham would have disappeared into the mists of time unnoticed and unknown. But God intervened into Abraham's life. He summoned him to depart from Ur (an ancient Sumerian city south of present day Baghdad, near the conjunction of the Tigris and Euphrates Rivers) and to follow him to uncertain places.

As *Genesis 12* relates, Abraham simply dropped everything and followed the bidding of a God he had never heard of and did not know. He went, operating on pure and innocent trust. He simply bundled up his family and whatever possessions he could carry, and left behind his pagan community, tribal heritage, and everything familiar to follow this uncommon summons. That alone is remarkable. Who of us would do such a thing? For this, St. Paul calls him *the Father of Faith*. For his unquestioning fidelity, God gave Abraham a promise that he would become *the Father of Nations* whose descendants would be *(Genesis 22:17)*:

> *as numerous as the stars of heaven and the sand that is on the seashore.*

His *blessing child* Isaac, the seed of the promise, was faithful and trusting like his father Abraham. Isaac's son Jacob was an entirely different kind of character. When he was born, his twin brother Esau came out first, but Jacob grabbed his brother's heel as he came out of the womb *(Genesis 25:26)*. This was a sign of more cunning things to come.

Jacob's very name means "supplanter" or "devious." He later tricked his first-born brother out of his birthright. After that he tricked his blind and elderly father Isaac into blessing him instead of his elder brother Esau, for whom the blessing was intended.

What's in a Name?

Be careful what you name your children. When I was in my small church outside Buffalo, one "alternative lifestyle" couple named their child *Amanita*. She was a charming and delightful little girl, but the name Amanita refers to a species of poisonous mushroom so toxic that death usually follows quickly after eating. This mushroom is also known as *the Destroying Angel*. I shudder to think of what became of this child as she grew into a young woman, and what inner darkness she had to struggle with in order to overcome the curse her parents had given her.

After Jacob's vision at Bethel of angels ascending and descending on a ladder from heaven, he set up the stone he had used for a pillow as an altar. Then he tried to *bargain with God* that he would honor him as Lord *on condition* that God would bless him, feed him, protect him, and keep him.

It is one thing for Abraham to have bargained with God over the fate of Sodom and Gomorrah, if any few righteous people were to be found there. It is quite another matter to challenge God with an offer *to worship him as Lord* in return for his blessing *(Genesis 28:20–22)*. Jacob was fulfilling his devious name.

Learn to Surrender

As we said, Jacob was a cunning and complicated character. One of his impediments was that he found it difficult to surrender himself to the guidance of the Lord. He was stubborn. He wanted to do what **he** wanted to do, even when it meant deceiving his brother, deceiving his father, deceiving his uncle.

We cannot fully receive the Lord's blessing unless we surrender to him. *Surrender* is just like in the old cowboy movies: *Hands up!*

If it is the Sheriff who says *hands up*, you had better obey or you might land in jail. If it is a gang of bandits who say *hands up*, you had better obey or you might even more likely be shot dead. However, when it is the Lord who invites you to offer your *hands up*, you ought to obey or you will miss the Lord's blessing. *Spiritual surrender* is not a matter of going to prison. It is the gateway to grace.

Jacob's Blessing

God eventually did bless Jacob, but not without an unusual struggle. Jacob was running away from his uncle Laban, whom he had deceived after Laban had deceived him. I suppose he thought it was time for payback. He camped for the night on the riverbank at the Jabbok creek and sent his family and flocks across the stream for protection because he knew that his brother Esau was now after him.

He spent the night alone, and there he had a wrestling match with an unknown assailant who blessed him at the end *(Genesis 32:24–26)*. More than that, he received a new name. His assailant asked him *(Genesis 32:27–29)*:

> *What is your name? And he said, "Jacob." Then the man said, "You shall no longer be called Jacob, but Israel, for you have striven with God and with humans, and have prevailed." Then Jacob asked him, "Please tell me your name." But he said, "Why is it that you ask my name?" And there he blessed him.*

When daybreak dawned, the truth also dawned: Jacob called the place Peniel, saying *(Genesis 32:30–31)*,

> *"For I have seen God face to face, and yet my life is preserved." The sun rose upon him as he passed Penuel, limping because of his hip.*

The name *Peniel*, and its variant *Penuel*, means "*The face of God.*"

A change of name is a classic sign of conversion. We see this most evidently in the change of Saul's name to *Paul* after his encounter with the Lord on the Road to Damascus (*Acts 9:1–19*). This also is the basis for the ancient Christian practice of granting a new name, a *baptismal name*, at the time of baptism. It signals the inauguration of our new and covenantal relationship with God.

Surprise: It Happened Without Notice

Life in Brooklyn had been rewarding and enriching. Then it came time to move on. As the years unfolded past the decade of the 1960's and I departed for upstate New York, then Toronto, then Chicago, I carried my graphic and its title with me and used it at each new place to head my pastor's column. After all, it was *me*.

It was only after I arrived in Massachusetts to take up what would be the longest settlement in my career that, after a few years had passed, I woke up to the fact that I was no longer using my signature graphic or its title. Neither did I have any desire still to use it. Somewhere in the intervening years it had passed away without notice. As a matter of fact, I cannot even remember when I stopped using it. I realized then that it had represented an important chapter in my life and that chapter was now over.

Each of us has chapters in our lives that define our experience. When one chapter closes and the next one opens, we move on. We get ourselves into real trouble when we cling to a previous chapter in our lives when it no longer applies. When it is done, it is done.

Looking Back

Never confuse faith with nostalgia, or nostalgia with the *teaching Tradition* of the faith. Faith is not based on looking back. Lot's wife looked back and she was turned into a pillar of salt (*Genesis 19:26*).

Faith always looks forward. It is based on the *promise of God* that stretches out before us. No matter how old we are, or what we have been through, the Lord continues to prepare us for something new even when we do not see it. Receive it with joy.

There is nothing wrong with looking back if your purpose is to comprehend where you have been, assess the reality of the present, and prepare for the future. This is what we do when we take a pause and go on a retreat to pray and be refreshed. Looking back is necessary for self-reflection, repentance, and renewal. Just be sure that it does not turn into an occasion for wallowing in things past that will never return, or for wistfully venerating lost rhapsodies.

I hear folks today who talk as if they are still living in the 1960's because it was such a formative time in their lives. They obviously cannot let go of old categories and perspectives. That was a monumental decade but the issues are different now. 2019 is not 1969 redux.

Ideology is a relentless jailer with no provision for posting a bond or remitting the sentence. The only way out is total repentance and renunciation.

I once new a pastor who was truly frozen in time. He preached a sermon about *the yellow running dog lackeys of the international corporate capitalist conspiracy*. He thought he was being radically progressive. In truth he was a prisoner of 1937 thinking and its then fashionable Marxist–Leninist ideology. He had not grown an inch in forty years.

Jacob's Limp

Anyone who has had a challenging encounter with the Lord walks away from it with Jacob's limp. It is given to us as a reminder of the awesomeness of God and of his majesty, but more importantly as a *warning* against the temptation to spiritual pride.

St. Paul tells us about this *(II Corinthians 12:7b–9)*:

> . . . *a thorn was given me in the flesh, a messenger of Satan to keep me from being too elated. Three times I appealed to the Lord about this, that it would leave me, but he said to me, "My grace is sufficient for you, for my power is made perfect in weakness." So, I will boast all the more gladly of my weaknesses, so that the power of Christ may dwell in me.*

We are never told who or what this "thorn" is. In one breath he speaks of it as a "messenger," suggesting a troublesome person. In the next line he calls it an "it" when he asks the Lord to take it away. Assailants and accusers usually pass along in their time, but afflictions can abide, so it sounds like a torment rather than a tormentor, but that is not the point.

The point is that Jacob's limp can last for a lifetime, and scars come in many forms. Most of us walk with a spiritual limp. Some of us walk with a spiritual club foot. Keep on walking. The Lord will give you strength. And if you pray about it, you will discover that your scars reveal a deeper blessing.

Sarah's Prayer

If we are not careful, Jacob's limp can leave us with an aftermath of sorrow, grief, and bitterness. Do not let these things hold sway over your self-worth. One scripture that spoke to me vividly when I was in a very dark place was Sarah and her prayer in *Tobit 3:7–17*. The Lord answered her prayer, but not in the manner she expected.

Sarah had married seven husbands, but each had died before the marriage even was consummated. She was falsely accused of killing them, and bore the reproach of her community. She was so despondent that she prayed for death. The Lord answered her prayer, but not by taking her life. Instead, the Lord sent the Archangel Raphael to comfort her, and then granted her a blessed and lasting marriage with Tobias, son of Tobit.

Sarah's prayer is remarkable and memorable *(Tobit 3:11b–13,15e)*:

> *Blessed are you, merciful God! Blessed is your Name forever; let all your works praise you forever. And now, Lord, I turn my face to you, and raise my eyes toward you. Command that I be released from the earth . . . Why should I still live? But if it is not pleasing to you, O Lord, to take my life, hear me in my disgrace.*

I was Sarah. Every pastor is Sarah, espoused to congregations that die on us like Sarah's husbands. Yet she triumphed. And so have I.

Humor Heals

My life has been profoundly blessed. I have been blessed by every church I have served, even the difficult ones with difficult people—*angular personalities*, we might call them.

I have been blessed by the music I have known—especially the opportunity for live performances: the Philadelphia Orchestra, the Chicago Symphony, the Boston Symphony and many lesser ensembles. I have also been blessed to hear many of the jazz greats of our time, on stage or in smaller venues like restaurants and clubs. I cherish live performances by

Cannonball Adderley, Ahmad Jamal, Miles Davis, Charles Mingus, Dave Brubeck, Herbie Hancock, Moe Koffman. and others.

I remember a wonderful evening years ago with the jazz pianist George Shearing at Ontario Place, a summer pavilion on the lakeshore in Toronto. He was blind, and had a personal assistant who guided him onstage to his seat at the piano.

He bantered with the audience before the music got under way. He described his trip in from the airport. It quickly became obvious to him that the taxi driver was going in circles and was lost. So he said to him, "*Why don't you let me drive?*" He brought down the house with laughter.

Not many of us are so easy about our own particular form of Jacob's limp as to joke about it, especially in public in front of a whole crowd of theatre goers.

Humor heals. Laughter is a gift of God. It will keep you whole. Beware, however, that it is one thing to laugh at your own limp, but it is quite another matter to laugh at others'. When you make someone else the butt of your joke you can inflict sad damage.

39 lashes

When I retired the first time around in 2001, a good friend and colleague preached the sermon for the occasion from the following text, in which St. Paul is recalling his career *(II Corinthians 11:24–28)*:

> *Five times I have received from the Jews the forty lashes minus one. Three times I was beaten with rods. Once I received a stoning. Three times I was shipwrecked; for a night and a day I was adrift at sea; on frequent journeys, in danger from rivers, danger from bandits, danger from my own people, danger from Gentiles, danger in the city, danger in the wilderness, danger at sea, danger from false brothers and sisters; in toil and hardship, through many a sleepless night, hungry and thirsty, often without food, cold and naked. And, besides other things, I am under constant pressure because of my anxiety for all the churches . . .*

That sums up my career quite well. It is an accurate chronicle of my first 36 years. In Toronto I received the 39 lashes. In Chicago I was shipwrecked, then adrift at sea. My detractors along the way were many—spiritual bandits who tried to steal my faith, false brothers and sisters, my own people, who were polite to my face but plotting when out of sight.

There were sleepless nights, perilous pathways through the wilderness, anxiety for the churches.

The text begins with a reference to an item in the Law *(Deuteronomy 25:3)*:

> *Forty lashes may be given but not more; if more lashes than these are given, your neighbor will be degraded in your sight.*

In his sermon, my friend described the 39 lashes as *"one step short of total disgrace."* I take great comfort in that. Yes, I bore the burdens of St. Paul. But I never had to face total disgrace. I thank the Lord for sparing me.

Without the Jews We are Nothing

Remember that Paul was a Jew speaking about his fellow Jews more than about Gentiles (Gentiles were *foreigners*, not part of the *Covenant bond* that ties together the people of God). His perils ring true for me because my abusers, like Paul's, were not strangers. They were the people of the church with whom I am in Covenant partnership.

Remember too that Jesus was a Jew. He told the Samaritan woman at Jacob's well *(John 4:22)*:

> *You worship what you do not know; we worship what we know, for salvation is from the Jews.*

Christian faith is a semitic religion. Christian faith is the narrative of God keeping Covenant with his people. Those who call Christian faith "a philosophy" are sadly misguided. Christian faith is not a moralistic agenda and its scriptures are not a philosophical essay. Christian faith is a *personal relationship* with Jesus Christ.

Christians forget this at our peril. Without the Jews, we are nothing. Without the Jews, we would still be worshipping Jupiter and Zeus and their coterie of heroic gods and goddesses. Or, if we were a bit less high–minded, we would be following after Isis and Osiris, Orpheus and Eurydice, Dionysus and Demeter, Attis and Cybele, the Magna Mater, Mithras, or other secret and less savory figures in the Oriental mystery cults.

The cults of Magna Mater (*the Great Mother*) and Mithras (*a Persian sun god*) were favorites among Roman soldiers. We should note that the cult of Magna Mater did nothing to elevate the status of women in the Roman Empire.

Keep in mind that no matter how *sincere* your worship, you are *sincerely wrong* when you are running after strange gods.

What Is Faith?

Faith is a gift of God. It is not a human achievement. Faith is not a matter of intellectual attainment or of correct doctrinal belief or of zealous devotion of heart. Faith is not an exalted wisdom from our own inspiration. Faith is not insight welling up from within our own human experience.

The source of faith is *totally Other*. Faith comes from *the Word of God the Father* implanted into us. Faith is the *external seed* of God introduced into the *internal womb* of the human soul by the power of the Holy Spirit.

Women understand this more naturally than do men. Men do not so easily understand that spiritually the human soul is *feminine* and *receptive* in character. Whether we are male or female of flesh, we each have a soul and we each have an ego.

Our ego is assertive and willful—again, whether we are male or female of flesh. Being receptive at times and being assertive at times are necessary characteristics of mature persons, both male and female. Whoever we are—either male or female—there are times for an open hand and there are times for a closed fist. But to be *receptive* to the Word of God we need to be in touch with our soul—the feminine and receptive component that is the common property of both males and females.

When the external seed of the Father is placed into the internal womb of our soul, our part is to nourish it properly so that it may grow into its destined maturity. Or we can ignore it and starve it until it is stillborn. Or we can abort it by our own rebellious will and fickle nature. I know about my own rebellious will and fickle nature. It took me some time, being battered about by the tempests of this world, before I began to comprehend the depths of the Gospel. Once I did, there was no turning back.

Extrinsic Truth

We speak of God as Father because his truth is <u>extrinsic</u> to this world. The *Word of God* is <u>Revelation</u>. Revelation derives from *outside* the things of this earth. It is not an *intrinsic* human wisdom mined like nuggets of gold from the depths of our own imagination.

The *Word of God* is the seed of the Father externally implanted at Creation *(Genesis 1:2)* into the womb of the *dark waters of Chaos*.

The *Word of God* is the seed of the Holy Spirit externally implanted into the heart of the believer.

The *Word of God* is the seed of truth externally implanted into Lady Wisdom, the *Receptive One* in the book of Proverbs, who then serves as the Evangelist for all who would hear her (*Proverbs 1:20–21*):

> *Wisdom cries out in the street; in the squares she raises her voice. At the busiest corner she cries out; at the entrance of the city gates she speaks.*

The *Word of God* is the seed of the Holy Spirit externally implanted into Mary, the mother of our Lord, to bring forth the human Jesus on earth.

The *Word of God* is the seed of the Holy Spirit externally implanted into the heart of each believer, so that we can do *the work of Mary*, which is to *bring Jesus to birth* in this world.

John the Baptist tells us how we receive this seed (*Matthew 3:11*):

> *I baptize you with water for repentance, but one who is more powerful than I is coming after me; I am not worthy to carry his sandals. He will baptize you with the Holy Spirit and fire.*

The truth of Christ is fire, because it burns away the dross of this world. But beware: when you receive this gift, the world may extract its price from you for it.

The Consolation of My Closet

It has taken me too many of my 50+ years as a pastor to learn that I would rather be *biblically correct* than politically correct. Even the church has succumbed to the fashion of the times. If you step out of line from current custom by using biblical terminology, you court abuse by those who seek to update our language according to the manner of the day, even calling it God's Word when it is not. So I have learned to pick my battles and shun the rest. When the sunny romantics hold sway, I rely on the consolation of my closet. Your own prayer closet is where you and the Lord can meet in safety.

The prophet Isaiah tells us (*Isaiah 9:2*):

> *The people who walked in darkness have seen a great light; those who lived in a land of deep darkness—on them light has shined.*

I was once among those who walked in darkness—for far too long—but I have seen the Light of Christ. When his light shines on what we have done to our language I am deeply saddened. We now have decades of new hymnals published, for example, where the texts have been scrubbed to remove any possible offense to categories targeted by identity politics. We can no longer say *Lord* because it is feudal, *King* because it is monarchical, *Father* because it is patriarchal, *high* and *low* because it is hierarchical, *Him* or *Himself* because these are sexist, *darkness* and *light* because these are racist, and we must even call Jesus *Jessica* in order to be "inclusive." What else is left?

Even the ancient pagans knew better. They spoke of *Father Sky and Mother Earth*. Oriental religions speak of *Yin and Yang*. Reality is incomplete without both, interacting.

Those like myself who uphold the canonical language of scripture against these eccentric revisions are now an endangered species. We are now the only remaining category who needs protection.

These "inclusive" categories do not include me. So I retreat to the consolation of my closet for safety, prayer, and solace when the revisers are in control. They are oblivious to the fact that their ideology of being non-offensive deeply offends those who hold to the canons of faith. Their desire to be "welcoming" slams the door against those of us who do not bow down to their novelties and decrees.

I used to become angry over these things, but that response was part of my own walk in the dark. I am now filled with sorrow over such matters and, instead of anger, I am moved to pray for their benighted advocates.

A New Adventure

When I retired the first time and finished my career as a settled parish pastor, I thought I was *finished*. After some months of cooling off, I looked for part time work and found a job where I spent a year driving rental cars around Logan Airport. That was a trip.

I would rise up before 5 AM, take an early train into Boston, then transfer to the subway to take me to my destination, where I was to check in before 7 AM. It was a small contracting company with two transport vans that held 12-15 drivers each. The owner of the company (who was the hands—on general manager) would parcel out the assignment orders for the day, and at precisely 7 o'clock we would pile into our assigned van and the driver/crew captain would tell us where we were to go and what we would be doing. One of our two crew captains was a young woman who always seemed more pleasant to work for than the other guy, whose sarcastic nature often got the better of him.

Most of us would pray for a day in which we would have a number of longer trips, like taking a fleet of cars to an auction yard in Framingham or Brockton to be sold when their mileage was too high for continued use in the rental market. Some days we would take a fleet to the airport in Manchester, New Hampshire. This provided a long and relaxing drive taking our assigned vehicle to its destination and another quiet trip when would return in the van. Some days we would go to an enormous gathering yard the size of several football fields underneath the Tobin Bridge, where we would pick up new cars that had just been off—loaded from a ship docked in Boston Harbor, then drive them back to the airport to start their new life in the rental market.

The truly tedious days were those full of short trips from one airport lot to another or across the bridge to an overflow lot in Chelsea. On one occasion our small crew moved 180 cars from one lot to another, which averaged 15 trips per person for the day. That was stupefying.

I met one driver who had walked the entire *Camino de Santiago*, the medieval pilgrimage trail of St. James in Spain. We had a lot of good conversation. Several other interesting folks were new immigrants from Russia and the Ukraine, learning English and making their way into American society. Some drivers were sloppy and foolish, denting cars in the parking lot or losing their way from the pickup spot to our destination. Some few were downright vulgar. They called themselves the "F Troop," and the rest of us tried politely to avoid them. They were an interesting cast of characters.

Cars going for auction had no license plates, so we each would be given a company fleet plate on thick rubber tabs that we would fasten in place for the trip by anchoring the tabs under the closed trunk lid. One hapless fellow failed to secure his plate properly and lost it somewhere on the Massachusetts Turnpike between Boston and Framingham. He had to explain the loss, of course, when the trip was over.

"*I don't know what happened.*" he said, and he had no way of knowing just where it had fallen off. The owner of the firm had to deal with the State Police, the Registry of Motor Vehicles, the insurance company, and other potential liabilities. After this driver left for the day, we never saw him again.

The Next Summons

After I flunked retirement the first time around, the Lord gave me a new summons to become an Interim Pastor. This is a form of consulting ministry that helps congregations move between one settled pastor and the next. Tough experience has shown that when one pastor dies, retires, or moves on, it is courting the disaster of a failed pastorate to have the next person try to start up the following week.

In years gone by this practice sometimes worked, when ministerial placements were handled by an "old boy network" (or "old girl network," as the case may be). In this process, neighboring pastors would recommend a replacement by word of mouth from a short list of friends.

This no longer works today. It takes time for a properly constituted Search Committee to do the work of assessing the congregation's needs and to review candidate profiles for the next potential pastor.

A *Settled Pastor* is a *Covenant Partner* with the people of the congregation—a *relationship of espousa*l something similar to a marriage.

An *Interim Pastor* is *not in Covenant* with the people of the congregation and has the role of a *transition consultant*, roughly similar to a marriage counselor.

This Interim/transition process typically takes a year at minimum, more typically two years and sometimes three. If the previous incumbent left under a cloud or there was severe trauma in his or her departure, the interim process can take a lot longer. I have had several interim appointments that lasted for three years, necessary to help bring people through extenuating circumstances. The time of transition in a parish can be highly complex, with dynamics of grieving, remembering, evaluating, and rejoicing. These resemble the events of death, a funeral, divorce, new courtship, and a wedding.

Beforehand, I could never have imagined myself doing such a kind of work as a calling. Now, over the course of 15 years, I have served eight Interim appointments at various parishes in Massachusetts and New Hampshire. In hindsight, this has been an enriching time of new learning and adventure. *These have been my best years* and a source of true blessing. The Lord is full of surprises.

Ongoing Conversion

Salvation is a process, not a single event. St. Paul in his Letters speaks of salvation in *past, present,* and *future* tenses. I *was saved* by the work of Christ on the Cross—what the Letter to the Hebrews calls the *"once and sufficient sacrifice."* Right now, I *am being saved* by the ongoing work of the Holy Spirit in my life (*I Corinthians 1:18*). And at the End of Time, I *shall be saved* by the final victory of the lamb over the beast when Christ calls his faithful to himself (*Revelation 17:14*).

There are stages in this process. Three major ones are sometimes called (1) *justification*, (2) *sanctification*, and (3) *glorification*. These correspond to the *was*, the *going on now*, and the *End of Time*. I *was* justified by the cross. I *am being* sanctified now by the Holy Spirit. I *shall be* glorified at that Final Day.

We have an awesome God. He ministers to every stage of our lives through his Trinitarian majesty, which he designed in order to be with us at every turn, and to bring us to himself.

I spent my childhood in Lutheran Sunday School and am now a pastor in the Reformed family of churches. I have spent joyful renewing time in Anglican and Roman Catholic monasteries, and careful reflection over the years with Jesuit spiritual directors. The full Church of Christ is far greater than any one denominational family or historic tradition.

I sometimes feel that my whole life has been a walking ecumenical encounter, and I am much the richer for it.

Holy are We?

A conflict often develops between what is called *forensic justification* over against an unbridled *desire for sanctification*. The sad fact is that seeking sanctification can too easily become an oppressive program of trying to live a holy life in a way that is damaging more than edifying.

I confess that I have always been attracted to the notion of forensic justification as the more realistic of these two choices. But I also admit that we ought to look for some measure of sanctification in our own lives or else we fall into a lazy acceptance of the unacceptable. This can easily indulge an amoral tolerance of what is profligate.

Forensic Justification

Here is how *forensic justification* works: At the *End of Time*, I stand before the Judge in the heavenly courtroom. God the Father sits on the bench. The Holy Spirit is my defense attorney (*the "Advocate"—John 14:26*). In the jury box sits the "great cloud of witnesses" (*Hebrews 12:1*)—the saints, prophets, and apostles of the church. The prosecuting attorney is Satan, the *Accuser (Job 1:11 and 2:5; Revelation 12:10).*

Satan steps forward to start the proceedings. *Now let me present before the court this Duke Gray*, he begins. And he proceeds to recite my yellow rap sheet, a chronicle of all the sins of my life. The list is long. It goes on and on. I break out in a cold sweat. What he presents is accurate and true. And he has a parade of witnesses against me to prove it. I am doomed.

When he finally is finished, The Lord Holy Spirit steps up to address the court. His defense is short and takes hardly a minute. He calls only one witness to the stand: Christ himself. Jesus simply says, *His sins have already been acquitted. I paid for them at the Cross*, and he sits down.

The Father turns to the jury and asks, *What is your verdict?* They turn to one another knowingly, and without hesitation respond: *Not guilty*. The court is rigged, of course. God is in charge. He knows the outcome before it begins, just as in the Book of Job.

I take comfort in all of this because I know that my sins are many, like the woman who washed Jesus' feet with her hair in *Luke 7:47*. I also know that God has forgiven me through the redeeming work of Christ.

Sanctification Gone Bad

My own Reformed tradition has many examples of the mischief that happens when sanctification takes on a life of its own and subverts the Gospel itself by trying to enforce rules of holiness.

Some religious progressives ridicule conservative Christians who issue policies of no liquor, no dancing, no lipstick, no movies, no theatre, no sports, no frivolous music, no raucous entertainment, and the list can go on.

Yet many progressive Christians blindly follow their own holiness rules and see no contradiction between this and their criticism of conservatives. They insist that we recycle our trash, go for vegetarian diets, solar panels, identity politics, justice initiatives where everybody has "rights" because everybody is a victim of something or other, and the list goes on. When these issues are all you talk about, the Gospel disappears.

Both extremes are examples of an overzealous implementation of what is called the *Third Application of the Law*. The Third Application of the Law is *sanctification*.

My first date in high school was at the end of my senior year when I found someone who seemed to appreciate music as I did, although I did not know her very well. We went to a number of summer concerts at the Robin Hood Dell in Fairmount Park, a series of casual evenings in an open air environment with wooden park benches nestled in a large hollow of grass. The musicians who played were drawn from the Philadelphia Orchestra and the music was first rate. She seemed to enjoy it all, as I did.

The summer music series ended in July with nothing more to follow, so in August I invited her to go to a movie. She politely and quietly said *No*, without any explanation. I could not afford a restaurant date so I forayed about for other things to do, but she continued to say *No*. Had I done something wrong? Had I offended her in some unknown way? It was a mystery. I never heard from her again.

It was only years later when someone else from our high school class told me that she had been enrolled in a small college for that September, and that one of the conditions for her to be accepted was to sign a contract that included her personal agreement to adhere to a list of forbidden things on religious grounds, even before she arrived on campus. Going to the movies was among the forbidden things, but apparently the symphony was not. She had never said a word.

Fear and Trembling

For many years I have been troubled by St. Paul's word to the church at Philippi *(Philippians 2:12b)*:

> *Work out your own salvation with fear and trembling.*

I worry about this because—despite Paul's constant declaration throughout his many Letters that we are *saved by grace* and not by works—this sounds too much like an invitation to *works righteousness*. That is where we try to demonstrate to God how holy we are, and to others how diligent we are in observing his commands. The Pharisees were experts at this, and we know what Jesus thought of them.

Paul himself answers the potential misunderstanding of his own text by the very next line *(Philippians 2:13)*:

> *. . .for it is God who is at work in you, enabling you both to will and to work for his good pleasure.*

Even so, this text can lead us astray if we lift up the value of our own noble deeds and acts of mercy in such a way that they surpass in importance our relationship with Christ. Then we backslide into *Pharisee religion*: endless charities, endless programs, endless prayers, endless obligations, endless church.

Efforts to save ourselves through righteous works, or to display to others that we are saved by our own holy living, are manifestations of spiritual pride. Spiritual pride is *sanctification* gone sour. On the other hand, we need to seek some measure of sanctification in our lives or else we are left in spiritual infancy. Then we become casualties of arrested development by relying on forensic justification alone.

Acquitted?

Back in Toronto I remember reading a news item in the paper that described an accused arsonist in Vancouver and his fate. He had been arrested by the RCMP (The *Royal Canadian Mounted Police*—the "World's Greatest Police Force" of Nelson Eddy fame). They knew he had burned down a particular building but they had no hard evidence to go on. So they placed a secret video camera into his jail cell.

There, they obtained a tape of him kneeling in the middle of his cell, weeping and crying out, "*Oh God . . . Oh God . . . Help me . . . Let me get away with this just this once.*"

When the police presented this tape in court as a confession, it was the only real evidence they had against him. The judge denied the RCMP permission to use the tape in the trial, saying that "prayer was a privileged communication" just like speaking to your attorney or making a confession to a priest. The accused arsonist was acquitted.

Pushed to the limit, forensic justification can be like that. We are acquitted in the Lord's heavenly courtroom. But is that enough?

Forensic Justification is Not Enough

We need *sanctification* if our new life in Christ is to bear fruit. But spiritual growth takes time. As infants we learn to crawl before we can walk, and we learn to walk before we can run. Why should it be any different with our spiritual rebirth and growing up? St. Paul told the church at Corinth *(I Corinthians 3::2–3a)*:

> *I fed you with milk, not solid food, for you were not ready for solid food. Even now you are still not ready, for you are still of the flesh . . .*

Forensic justification by itself can leave us in an unrighteous state where we wallow in our catalog of sins and do not see anything worthy in ourselves. Even though we are acquitted by the divine court, if nothing within us has changed, we merely continue along just as we were. If God has declared us justified when in fact we are not, we are left either with a guilty satisfaction that "I got away with it," or with a secret sense of shame that we somehow tricked fate by being delivered from Satan's grip when we should have been condemned. Either way, we are left with an inward darkness that does not disappear. Even when we do accept that our sins have been remitted by the work of Christ on the Cross, we need to receive *the influx of grace* that awaits us through the anointing of the Holy Spirit. The spiritual masters of the early church called this process *amendment of life*, or *conversion of manners*. It is a hollow conversion if you claim to be blessed by God but nothing changes in your way of living.

Of Course We Need Laws, and *the Law*

Our need for laws is a uniquely human attribute because every human society has some moral sense of right and wrong. Nature is violent but not evil. The lioness takes down an antelope to feed her family. The lion may devour cubs he perceives to be a future threat to his dominion. Neither makes a moral judgment.

Evil is a human perception. Animals do not have it. Our perception of evil is also a gift of God. It is part of the *imago Dei* that shapes our creation. However, it usually is clearer for us to discern evil in hindsight than to confront it when it is current and timely, as the 1930's buildup to WW II sadly shows. Unlike us, God operates by foresight, not hindsight. That is why he is the author of Law.

Promise too is a human attribute. The lion lives by the day. We live according to a destiny. If we are to receive the promise of God, our destiny, we need the Truth of God to secure it and the Law of God to guide us.

St. Paul tells us (*Ephesians 4:25–26,30a,31*):

> *Putting away falsehood, speak the truth to our neighbors . . . Be angry but do not sin. Do not let the sun go down on your anger. Do not grieve the Holy Spirit . . . Put away all bitterness and wrath and anger and wrangling and slander . . .*

Then he says (*Ephesians 5:1–2a*):

> *Be imitators of God, as beloved children, and live in love, as Christ loved us.*

How can we possibly live lives that imitate God if we are sinners?

Here we see the resolution to the conundrum of Law and Grace. Trying to keep the Law to make ourselves holy is impossible. The Law does not lead us to grace. But the Grace of God enables us to keep the Law.

We usually get it backwards. The Law does not bring us to grace. But grace leads us to keeping the Law. Grace, which comes from the holiness of God, grants us the power to live holy lives. But turning the *Gospel* back into *Law* leads first to futility and finally to damnation.

Law and Gospel

St. Paul tells us that the Law of God is our <u>schoolmaster in sin</u> (*Galatians 3:23–26*):

> *Now before faith came, we were imprisoned and guarded under the Law until faith would be revealed. Therefore the Law was our disciplinarian until Christ came, so that we might be justified by faith. But now that faith has come, we are no longer subject to a disciplinarian, for in Christ Jesus you are all children of God through faith.*

The principle is simple: if nobody knew that murder was wrong, we would kill, as animals do, without any sense of sin or shame. Some very primitive societies operated this way in regard to, for example, child sacrifice to appease bloodthirsty, arbitrary, and tyrannical gods.

Even advanced societies like the ancient Aztecs and Greeks had ritualized forms of sacrifice. The Greek custom of infanticide for unwanted newborns was to leave the child on a mountaintop to die of exposure.

The Aztecs had a more elaborate system in which adult sacrificial designees would be housed, fed, specially dressed and trained for a year in advance. For some, it was an honor to be chosen. When the appointed time came, a long and elaborate ritual killing would be done by the priests at the top of a huge pyramid temple. They would cut out the beating heart of the victim while still alive, and then throw the body down into a deep pit at the center of the temple's pinnacle. Archeological evidence has uncovered depositories of countless bones of the sacrificed.

Three Uses of the Law

The *Law of God* was not given to *save* us. It was given to *train us* in the basic differences between right and wrong. In its classic formulation, there are Three Applications of the Law. These are as follows:

The *First Application* of the Law is *civil*. The Ten Commandments that God gave to Moses on Mount Sinai (*Exodus 20:1–17 and Deuteronomy 5:6–21*) list basic requirements that are needed to bring order to any civilized society, whether it be Jewish or Christian or neither. A well-ordered society needs laws against murder, theft, fraud, and corruption.

The *Second Application* of the Law is *tutorial*—it is our *schoolmaster in sin*, as St. Paul develops it. It teaches us the *holiness of God* and the impossibility for any human holiness even to approach his. The Pharisees sought to keep 613 daily rules of the Law derived from the Book of Leviticus to establish their holiness. Jesus shows us how futile this effort is.

The *Third Application* of the Law is *sanctifying*. It is a *school of grace* that lays out a norm or guideline for the sanctification of the Christian believer. What this can mean is where the mischief lies. At best, it means a life of gratitude to God for our salvation in Jesus Christ. At worst, it becomes a mean—spirited return to Pharisee behavior.

In short, the Law of God (1) *coerces*, (2) *terrifies*, then (3) *invites* our obedience and gratitude for a transformed life.

Running Off the Rails

When we ignore this Third Application and concentrate only on the first two, we use the Law to expose our *bondage to sin*, and then move directly on to the *proclamation of the Gospel* as the remedy for an unregenerate and remorseful life. Critics point out that this can lack any serious attention to social ills and public reform.

By contrast, when our preaching moves right through the first two applications of the Law and then concentrates on the Third to demonstrate the marks of living a sanctified life, we can then spend all of our energy trying to reform the whole of society into a Christian world order. John Calvin did a lot of this to clean up the city of Geneva, which was a corrupt and rotten place when he came to it.

Somewhere there is a proper balance between these two emphases. I usually find myself wanting to shy away from a too vigorous attention to the Third Application, because I have seen the damage done by zealots who end up ignoring the Gospel altogether and degrade the Christian life into keeping a set of holiness rules. Certain later forms of what some folks call "Calvinism" include a lot of things that Calvin himself would not have recognized.

Moralistic Deism

When all I hear is endless talk about social justice initiatives, the Gospel is lost. If your passionate concern is to change the world, then take an active part in your political party or local community organization. They are often equipped to do the job better than the church.

Nineteenth century moralism taught us *to seek salvation* by works of justice and charity, upright living and visionary movements for reform—earlier versions of missing the boat. There is nothing wrong with doing good works, but good works do not bring us salvation. We cannot save ourselves or justify ourselves by anything we do, because the best we can do is never good enough.

I see this all the time. Often this becomes nothing more than *moralistic deism*, which is no substitute for Christian faith.

I recently attended an ecclesiastical council where a young woman gave a simple example of this in her Ordination Paper. (In a congregational church system, an *ecclesiastical council* is a gathering of delegates—some clergy, mostly lay—from neighboring churches to examine and vote upon a Candidate for Ordination to the ministry).

In this case, the Candidate's area of specialty was Christian Education. She described a meeting she had held with parents of small children in which she asked them the question: *If you had to make a choice, which would you rather see? That your child grow up to be a good citizen or a good Christian?* The vast majority of the parents present answered, without much thought or hesitation, a *good citizen*. She was appalled. So was I.

What these parents represented was a theology that is *a mile wide and an inch deep*, too common in too many of our churches. But this young woman represents a new generation. There is hope.

Sources

For a long time, I had assumed that this formulation of the Third Application of the Law came from Calvinist sources. More recently I was surprised to learn that it came from Philip Melanchthon, the attorney and theologian who was Martin Luther's right hand man. As much as anyone, Melanchthon was the architect of the Reformation.

John Calvin picked up this *Third Use* from Melanchthon and elaborated it greatly. In time, Calvin's later followers reversed the order of the First and the Second, beginning with *the schoolmaster in sin* and then moving on to the *civil*, which blended directly into the Third Application to reform society.

Nineteenth century American culture reflected this in spades, especially in the many movements for social reform in child labor laws, antislavery protests, censorship demands and temperance movements, leading finally to Prohibition in the early twentieth century.

Society today is moving in an entirely new direction. Today, everything falls under the *Authority of the Self* as King. Psychiatric diagnosis calls this *narcissism*.

This means that if we have 300 million people, we have 300 million kings and queens—each in charge of their own lives, with everything else subservient to the Self. All that we have and all that we are must bow down to personal preference and individual taste. Pushed to the extreme, the center does not hold.

A culture where <u>Self</u> rules is an ominous forewarning of the failures of *romantic religion*—the hallmark of Perkin Warbeck—which we shall revisit later in Chapter 9.

When Bill Barclay Died

Back in Toronto I had to suffer a congregation that was completely unhinged from the sources that originally had given it shape. It was functioning more as an intellectual debating society or a moral improvement club than as a Christian community of devotion and praise. Some of these folks thought their mission was to reform the whole world—according to their own agenda, of course.

Bill Barclay was a Sunday morning regular. We spoke often. He was a calm and cheerful fellow, and not one of the hard line rationalists that dominated the place. His short white hair flowed into a short white beard to create a circle that framed his round and ruddy face almost like a halo. It highlighted his angelic demeanor.

His wife Erin called me one day in a panic. "*Bill has had a seizure*," she said. "*The ambulance is arriving shortly to take him to the hospital.*" I told her that I would be there right away.

I arrived quickly at the hospital. They had put her with Bill in a plain and unadorned holding room. "*He died on the way*," she said. "*I told them not to take away his body. I cannot let him go.*"

We talked for a few minutes. Then I asked, *Does prayer mean anything to you?* She paused and said, hesitatingly, "*Well, I never thought very much about it.*"

I placed my hands on Bill's chest and asked Erin to do the same, which she did. "*Gracious God, the author of all creation*," I said, "*we thank you for the life of Bill Barclay. We cherish his time among us. Receive him now into your everlasting care, and bless Erin with your abiding peace, through Jesus Christ our Lord. Amen.*"

She leaned forward and kissed him on the cheek. She breathed a sigh of relief and said, *They can take away his body now.*

Ask not what you have lost. Ask what blessings you have received. And give thanks to God for all his gifts. The abundance of the Lord is boundless.

This was a converting moment for Erin. She would need many more before she could really come to the Lord. Each converting event builds on the previous, like an infant taking her or his first steps. Soon we learn to walk without holding on. We start by walking our own path. In time, we may come to walk with the Lord on his path if we have the grace to follow. Then, he can truly disciple us if we open ourselves to his leading.

Followers? Or Disciples?

Jesus had lots of followers but not so many disciples. Following his *Bread of Life discourse*, many followers of Jesus were offended by his teaching. So we hear him ask (*John 6:66–69*):

> *Because of this many of his disciples turned back and no longer went about with him. So Jesus asked the twelve, "Do you also wish to go away?" Simon Peter answered him, "Lord, to whom can we go? You have the words of eternal life. We have come to believe and know that you are the Holy One of God . . ."*

There are many who want Jesus as Savior but not as Lord.

Do an Inventory

As my own conversion has deepened over the years, the Lord has revealed more and more things I need to repent for. As our faith deepens, he shows us ever more occasions of *how far we fall short* of the holiness he invites.

Inventory your scars. Scars can be reminders of devious deeds done (*like those of "scarface"*) or they can be trophies of victory over darkness like Jacob's limp. Whoever you are, whatever your stage on life's way, whether you are 19 years old or 90, do an inventory of your scars and you will learn from them.

Chronological age and spiritual age are not the same. Some folks become hardened adults too early in life as a result of overcoming trauma in matters of health or family or the assaults of this world. You can be a child but be in spiritual grad school if your distress was great and the Lord showed you how to deal with it constructively. On the other hand, some remain in spiritual kindergarten, living in confusion and doubt even into their 80's and 90's.

Take the time to make an inventory of your "turning points," the turns in the road that were moments of pain/conversion/epiphany.

Look for Your Models

Take time to review those significant figures in scripture with whom you can identify. These include *Call Narratives* that describe the summons of God that led particular persons to do what they did. Your inventory may also include portrayals of those who are *Types* for your own life, persons whose character or circumstances speak directly to you in edifying ways. Name your own. The following speak vividly to me (*your list will no doubt be different*):

- ***Jacob***—His conversion brought him pain as well as blessing.—*Genesis 32:24-26*.
- ***Joseph***—He forgives his brothers for all they did to him when he had the power over them to take revenge.—*Genesis 45*.
- ***Rahab***—She was a pagan prostitute who guided Israel to safety.—Joshua 2:1-24. She also features in the genealogy of Jesus as the mother of Boaz, making her an ancestor of king David.—*Matthew 1:5,6*.
- ***Ruth***—An accursed Moabite who becomes the great grandmother of David.—*Ruth 4:21,22* and *Matthew 1:5,6*.
- ***Deborah***—She was the Judge who was strong when Barak, the commander under her, was weak.—*Judges 4-5*.
- ***David***—He was an adulterer and murderer from whose Covenant Jesus came.—*II Samuel 7:1-17* and *11:1-26*.
- ***Isaiah***—He is known as the priest who become God's prophet when his sins were forgiven.—*Isaiah 6:1-8*.
- ***Jeremiah***—He was the "weeping prophet" who could not speak properly and complained that God had deceived him.—*Jeremiah 1:4-10* and *15:18*.
- ***Amos***—He was the prophet who complained that he was only an untutored nurseryman, a dresser of sycamore trees.—*Amos 7:14*.
- ***Jonah***—He was the reluctant prophet who was a Type of Christ, according to Jesus himself.—*Jonah 1:17* and *Matthew 12:39-41*.
- ***The unnamed woman*** who washed Jesus' feet with her hair.—Her sins were many, like mine, and they were forgiven.—*Luke 7:47*.
- ***Nicodemus***—He was the lost and confused teacher who came around in the end.—*John 3:4* and *19:39*.
- ***The unnamed woman*** at Jacob's well—She evangelized her entire city, despite three strikes against her.—*John 4:39-41*.

Pray the Scriptures

When you find a passage of scripture that speaks to you, first read it over silently and slowly. Then read it again, out loud, even more slowly. Pause at each line, even at each word, and listen to the sound of your own voice. Let it sink in. Then keep quiet for a while. The Lord will speak to you through it. Scripture is his word. You can then talk with him about it. In time, your conversation with the Lord will become an enriching habit.

Be Self-Critical

Examination of conscience is an ancient practice by spiritual directors and other faithful Christians. It leads to self-awareness, confession of sins, and restoration to health and wholeness.

A critical spirit applied to oneself can be very liberating, but it can also lead to the danger of diminished self-esteem when not rooted in spiritual discipline.

Our true self-worth is not found in what we do or fail to do. Self-worth is given to us as a *birthright* in Creation *(Genesis 1:27)*. Recover this, and you will be made whole.

Each and every one of us is a person of *infinite worth* in the eyes of God. When the Lord looks upon us, he sees himself. We are cast in his image, not in the image of a centipede. But if we allow Satan to muddy the mirror and corrupt our divine image, we are lost. God can restore us if we accept his grace. When we stumble—and we will stumble—the Lord will pick us up if we ask.

A critical spirit applied to others is quite a different matter. That is to fall into the blame game, turning ourselves into perpetual victims and letting every offense turn someone else into an oppressor.

Get Help

When I was just starting out in Brooklyn, I ran across a short article written for social workers. Its theme was, *When is help helpful?* The short answer is, *When we ask for it.* The message of the paper was that *help is not helpful* unless those who need help admit that they do and seek it. Without this, persons and programs that try to fix the problems of others are an exercise in futility.

When it comes to spiritual matters, we all need help. Essential issues of life and death, direction and purpose, are not innate or self-evident. If we think they are, we are deluded. They are beyond our ken because they come from an outside source. That is the essential structure of Creation: the soil does not bring forth fruit from itself. The seed of Revelation is *implanted from without* before it can grow within.

Christian faith is based upon the *Word of God*, which is *external seed* from without, implanted into the soul within. Anything else is to seek saving help by some form of spiritual parthenogenesis. Mary did not become pregnant on her own. The Lord Holy Spirit impregnated her with the seed of God the Father. She then gave birth to Jesus, the *living Word of God*.

And God is *personal*. He is neither the "great undifferentiated whoosh" nor the "unmoved mover" of Aristotle. He is the *moved mover* who debates with Abraham over the fate of Sodom and Gomorrah, who argues with Jeremiah about the value of his prophetic call, and who cries out from the Cross, *"forgive them, for they don't know what they are doing."* He laughs with us when we are glad, weeps with us when we grieve, rejoices with us in our victories, consoles us in our sorrow.

Most of all, he invites us to join him as *Covenant Partners* in his saving enterprise.

Find help by reading his Word for nourishment. Find help through prayer—a daily conversation with him about things both important and trivial. He is eager to listen.

Find help by receiving the sacrament of his Body and Blood at his banquet table. Find help by keeping company with faithful Christians who will listen to you and, if necessary, admonish you toward a better place.

How to Pray

For most people, swearing comes naturally, but praying does not. When you hit your thumb with a hammer while trying to pound a nail, most of us do not need a seminar on what to say when we cry out a curse. Or, the same is true when we slice a finger while chopping vegetables. Prayer doe not come so naturally.

There are exceptions.

Years ago I had a young friend, full of bravado, who would loudly boast of being an atheist.

He was eager to try skydiving. He later reported that the only thing he could remember from the event was the sound of his own voice, as they pushed him out the door of the airplane, crying out loudly in a long, slow, descending plea: *Oh . . . God . . .*

For him, this was a converting moment, the first of many.

Noise

Put yourself in a proper environment for true quiet time. We live in a culture of *incessant noise*, including mindless racket that masquerades as music.

I once had dinner at the home of a young woman parishioner who had recently married and who wanted to show off her new habitat. After visiting for a while in the living room, we moved to the table. Part way through the meal, I began to notice a low level drumming sound that resembled radio static and never paused or went away. It seemed to be coming from the open door of the bedroom.

Finally I asked, *"Jennifer, what is that noise?"* *"Oh,"* she replied, *"that's a white noise machine. It's wonderful. I can't live without it and I can't sleep without it."* I did not have the courage to ask her husband what he thought of it. He was a meek sort of fellow and she clearly was the dominant figure in the family.

Savor the Silence

Find quiet space in your home, if you can. Visit a monastic chapel or guest house when you are able. You will learn much from the rhythm of community prayer and the singing of the Psalms against a backdrop of extended and deliberate silence.

I am often dismayed by the fidgeting uneasiness in the average parish church when you schedule more than 15 seconds of silence during worship—not to mention the unrelenting social chatter that goes on before worship from the moment you enter the door. Who can pray with that going on?

Obtain a spiritual director if possible. This does not always need to be a trained professional but it does mean a seasoned and faithful Christian who can listen. There is a long tradition of having a *spiritual friend*, someone you trust with intimate details of your own prayer life and relationship with the Lord, including your confusions, doubts, and struggles.

When I first was at seminary in upstate New York, the Dean arranged a special teaching time with a psychiatrist from a neighboring hospital. I do not forget his arresting comment when he told us that one of the best therapists he had ever met was *a sleeping car porter* on the train between New York and Chicago. He also added that some of the most healing therapy goes on between friends. The same applies to your spiritual nurture.

Guard Your Tongue

During some of my darker years, I got into a routine habit that aggravated my wife no end. She was right to be upset. Whenever we were out walking or driving and I saw an especially decrepit, shabby, or wasted old man shuffling by, I would automatically say, "*He looks how I feel.*" My wife would go ballistic and I would respond, "*I was only joking.*"

But it is no joke constantly to deprecate yourself. It took me time to come to grips with the fact that *the words we speak* are shapers of reality. When you constantly tear yourself down you are sending yourself into the prison of diminished self-esteem. When you constantly demean, debase, or humiliate yourself, you are offending God and his Creation.

Words are a uniquely human gift. Other creatures make noises, grunts, barks, or cries that they understand. These can communicate pleasure, comfort, or invitation; pain, warning, alarm, or attack. They *reflect* realities, but they do not *give shape* to reality. They do not convey memory or history, promise or destiny. Human words do. Words do this because our gift for words derives from the Word of God.

In the beginning, God *spoke*, and things <u>became</u> *(Genesis 1:3)*:

God said, "Let there be light; and there was light."

The Letter of James tells us *(James 3:3-6a,9)*:

If we put bits into the mouths of horses to make them obey us, we guide their whole bodies. Or look at ships: they are so large that it takes strong winds to drive them, yet they are guided by a very small rudder wherever the will of the pilot directs. So also the tongue is a small member, yet it boasts of great exploits.

> *How great a forest is set ablaze by a small fire! And the tongue is a fire! . . . With it we bless the Lord and Father, and with it we curse those who are made in the likeness of God.*

The old children's ditty says, "*Sticks and stones can hurt my bones, but words will never hurt me.*" This is not true. Words have the power to destroy, as well as to create.

This is true for public rhetoric as well as for private talk. The speeches of Adolf Hitler enthralled masses and gave shape to a national program of evil even before he was elected to any public office.

Beware what you say. Make the right choice (Deuteronomy 30:19):

> *I call heaven and earth to witness against you today*
> *that I have set before you life and death, blessings and curses.*
> *Choose life, that you and your descendants may live.*

Gratitude

Whatever else, be grateful. Be grateful for your scars. You will learn from them. Be grateful for whatever form of Jacob's limp afflicts you. It is a sign of God's blessing. It will bring you closer to Christ.

Progress in prayer rests on three particular points of practice: (1) *Forgiveness*, (2) *Gratitude*, and (3) *Surrender*. Forgiveness is key. It opens the door to the others. Forgiveness leads to *gratefulness of heart* and gratitude leads to our ability to *surrender* to the authority of God.

Gratitude is the heart of prayer. Thank God every day for your station in life. Your gratefulness will lead you toward more grace.

Some years ago, the church I then was serving sponsored several A. A. groups. Almost every week I would see an old man with a cane slowly negotiating the stairs. For all I knew he was younger than I, but he seemed to have carried a weight of remorse over burdens I did not know. He appeared to have once carried baggage that had aged him beyond his years.

He was not a member of the parish and I never knew his name. But each time I saw him I would ask, "*How are you?*" He would always reply with much the same message: "*I am doing wonderfully well. Every morning when I wake up and open my eyes, I give thanks for another new day. And when the day comes that I don't open my eyes, then I'll have nothing more to worry about.*"

He obviously had made peace with the Lord.

Nine

Perkin Revisited

*O Lord, you brought up my soul from Sheol, restored
me to life from among those gone down to the Pit. You
have turned my mourning into dancing; you have
taken off my sackcloth and clothed me with joy, so
that my soul may praise you and not be silent.*

—PSALM 30:3, 11–12A

Impressionable Images

Small children can be highly impressionable, far more than we often are as adults. The messages and images we receive when we are young can exert their influence on us for a lifetime.

This can be a liability or it might be a gift. If what we receive is valuable and edifying, it can serve us well. If what we receive is deceptive and corrupt, it can cost us decades of struggle to survive the damage and reset the compass of our lives.

One of the gifts I received from my father, aside from a love for great music, was a taste for the appreciation of fine art.

When I was young, Dad would take me to the Philadelphia Museum of Art. There he would introduce me to various paintings and sculptures that had spoken to him in special ways. He would often give historical or aesthetic background comments not found on the small cards posted on the gallery walls. I came to marvel at how much he knew about medieval, renaissance, and modern impressionist painters for someone who had never graduated from the 8th grade. He would speak in detail, for example, about the beams of sunshine and light that Vermeer would introduce on the left into an otherwise dark Dutch room, or the elongated figures El Greco would use to portray verticality. I thank him for that gift.

The museum in Philadelphia is a magnificent and sprawling structure at the head of Benjamin Franklin Parkway. Its majestic stairway at the front entrance was popularized for all to see in the film *Rocky*, as Sylvester Stallone ran up its steps. It is a prelude to the treasures within.

Diana the Huntress

Inside the main hall is a grand staircase equally impressive with the one outside. On the balcony landing there is a giant statue by Augustus Saint-Gaudens of *Diana the Huntress*, graceful and commanding with her arched bow and arrow seeking her prey.

I recalled this many years later when a close colleague referred in a sermon to the *Hound of Heaven* by Francis Thompson. He used the image of Diana to portray the quest of the Holy Spirit to bring us to Christ. Diana, with her pack of hunting dogs, relentlessly pursues her target, her arrows continually hitting the heels of her intended and she never gives up until the victory is won. Likewise, the Hound of Heaven pursues us until we are his. I am his.

Prometheus Bound

One of the most vivid images for me on these trips to the museum was a huge painting of Prometheus by Peter Paul Rubens. The painting, entitled *Prometheus Bound* and finished in 1618, shows Prometheus chained to a rock with an enormous eagle eating out his liver.

The *Myth of Prometheus* is one of the classic tales of ancient Greece. Prometheus is one of the race of Titans, unique creatures one step beneath the dominant rule of Zeus and the other Olympian gods. The key action in this drama is that Prometheus steals *the fire of the gods* from Mount Olympus and gives it over to humans for our benefit.

This *fire* represents divine wisdom, knowledge, and power. For this seditious act, Prometheus is condemned to eternal punishment by Zeus, the chief of the gods. His fate is to be chained to a mountain in the Caucasus where every day an eagle feasts on his liver. Overnight, since Prometheus is immortal, his liver is regenerated only to be devoured by the eagle again the next day. In time, Hercules slays the eagle and Prometheus is delivered from his torment.

Prometheus Unbound

Once Hercules had slain the tormenting eagle and had broken the chain, Prometheus was free to run amok once again.

The figure of *Prometheus Unbound* became an emblem for the *eighteenth century Enlightenment*, where Rationalism began to overtake biblical Revelation as the touchstone for truth. Now that we humans have received the purloined fire of divine wisdom and consequently have become the masters of our own destiny, who needs God? Or so the passionate followers of Prometheus believe. They have had a hard time, however, convincing any vast majority of this today in the wake of the twentieth century horrors of two World Wars, armies of the unemployed selling apples on the street corner during the Great Depression, and the abject depravity of the Holocaust. Where is the glory Prometheus once promised?

By this twenty-first century, it seems that no one is the master of anything except for brutal tyrants and terrorists who survive by stealth and deceit.

Even so, the wistful hope of Promethean heroism lives on in small pockets of romantic piety and moralistic deism where endless talk multiplies the visions of a new world order of harmony and tranquility.

Back in Toronto, I remember those who were convinced that *proper communication* was the key to world peace. They believed that if we were all to renounce our familiar languages—not to mention national sovereignty—and everyone were to learn to speak *Esperanto*, the world would be saved and all would be well.

Believing that *communication will save us* is where magical thinking takes over. Then, sentimental notions about human nature leave us truly lost in the woods, a dark place where we cannot find our way out. Romantic promise leads to the tunnel at the end of the light.

Magical thinking about *communication* sounds like Neville Chamberlain and his Munich Agreement with Adolph Hitler in 1938. You don't debate with darkness.

Prometheus at the Tower of Babel

The spirit of Prometheus was not confined to ancient Greek lore. The Book of Genesis tells us *(Genesis 11:4)*:

Then they said, "Come, let us build ourselves a city, and a tower with its top in the heavens, and let us make a name for ourselves.

So who are *"they"* in this passage? This narrative begins in *Genesis 11:1* by referencing: *Now the whole earth . . ."*They" is us. Following the original rebellion against God by Adam, this was mass rebellion by all humanity. In response to this, the Lord declares *(Genesis 11:6)*:

. . . this is only the beginning of what they will do; nothing that they propose to do will now be impossible for them.

Prometheus was a single Titanic figure who stole the wisdom and knowledge of God by ascending the heavenly mountain to bring God's power to earth. But in Genesis, the whole earth was building itself a tower to reach for the powers of heaven. The whole people of earth were imbued with a Promethean spirit to steal not only the Lord's gifts, but also his authority, much like a small child plundering the birthday cake before breakfast to spoil the afternoon party. The Lord does not want a disorderly house.

So Who *Was* Perkin Warbeck?

The original Perkin Warbeck was a fifteenth century Pretender to the English throne who failed in his attempts to dislodge Henry VII from power. It is not entirely clear the extent to which Perkin was the author of his own ambitions, or was merely a hapless tool used by the enemies of Henry to try to get him out of his seat.

As part of his schemes, Perkin took the name *Richard of Shrewsbury, Duke of York*—announcing himself to be the younger son of King Edward IV. Henry's supporters claimed that Perkin was an impostor and not even

English, but Flemish by birth. But Perkin had many followers—always a possibility when those loitering at the edges don't like the ruling order.

After a series of misadventures in France, Ireland, Scotland, and Cornwall, Perkin was captured in 1497, held prisoner in the Tower of London, and executed for treason in 1499.

My grandfather Perkin took this name for his own editing, writing, and lecturing career. In a promotional pamphlet from the J. B. Pond Lyceum Bureau in New York from 1906, he offers this explanation:

> You know Perkin the elder was a Pretender to the British throne (it was the English throne) and got hanged for it; and as I never was a pretender I thought I ought to do something to even things up for the Warbeck family. It's so chilling to be always looking back on an ancestor who never did anything worth remembering except to get himself hanged for putting up a bluff and failing to make good.

For his ill-fated admixture of bravado and blundering adventure, the original Perkin comes down to us through history as a half-tragic, half-comic figure, notable for his vainglorious expectations and grandiose estimations of his prospects for success.

In his own peculiar way, Perkin appears as a *Type of Prometheus*, a prophetic figure for the wild hopes of the nineteenth century and their smoldering debris in the 20th. My grandfather's choice of his name seems almost like a dark prophecy for his own demise.

The 5th Commandment

The 5th Commandment in the *Decalogue* that God gave to Moses on Mount Sinai tells us *(Exodus 20:12* and *Deuteronomy 5:6)*:

> Honor your father and your mother, so that your days may be long in the land that the Lord your God is giving you.

I am using here the familiar numbering system common to Anglican, Greek, and Reformed churches. Lutherans and Roman Catholics number them differently, combining #1 and #2 (the one true God, and false gods and idols) and dividing #10 about coveting into two (your neighbor's house, then his family and possessions). In this way both lists come out to ten. In the Lutheran/Roman numbering, the command to honor parents would be #4.

Honoring parents certainly implies honoring grandparents as well. I intend no dishonor to my grandfather when I make a critical assessment of his life and work. He is what he was. And no one is perfect.

He was a creature of his time, as all of us are. I have read his original manuscripts in the family archives that have come down to me, and carefully keep them in a storage container under my desk. As I examine them, it is clear to me that he possessed a skilled facility with words, colorful and blunt in his expressions in ways that quickly engage any reader. He was a talented craftsman with language who set a high standard that I struggle to emulate.

A lot of what he says, however, reflects the visionary romanticism and Promethean heroism of the nineteenth century that came crashing down in the 20th. He named his magazine the *Areopagitica*, after the Areopagus in Athens where St. Paul debated the Epicurean and Stoic philosophers, and he cites that text (*Acts 17:18–19*) in his choice of naming. He also cites John Milton's choice of this same name for a scathing pamphlet he wrote in 1644, addressed to the English Parliament to defend freedom of speech.

However, after reading my grandfather's papers, it seems clear to me that he was following in the footsteps of the Epicurean and Stoic philosophers more than the footsteps of St. Paul *(Acts 17:21)*:

> *Now all the Athenians and the foreigners living there would spend their time in nothing but telling or hearing something new.*

That love of novelty sounds to me more like idle talk than prophetic truth.

Faith Unravelled

It has taken a long time for the disintegration of faith to manifest itself. Running parallel to three centuries of Rationalism, Moralism, and Individualism since the Enlightenment, there is a predicable sequence of steps in some forms of Calvinism that lead directly to atheism. It is easy to recognize these stages once you look at the clues.

It begins with some Reformed folks who overemphasize the *Sovereignty of God* to the detriment of his tender care, mercy, and especially his Incarnation in Christ. John Calvin would have been dismayed by this, but later generations that claim his name have, over time, developed things he would not condone.

Once you unduly stress the overarching Sovereignty of God, his Majesty soon becomes his *remoteness*, leaving behind the God who wrestles with Jacob, speaks to Moses in the burning bush, comes to Elijah in the "sound of sheer silence," debates with Jeremiah over his childhood stammering, instructs Jonah to go to Nineveh and then admonishes him at the end for being angry over his great success.

The remote God then becomes the *inaccessible* God, and this leads directly to *Deism*, the great eighteenth century movement that dominated both church and society. In Deism God becomes a kind of *Divinity Emeritus* who started things up at the beginning and then went into retirement to leave everything to our own human devices.

It takes not very long for Deism to become *agnosticism*, the studied doubt over whether God is even necessary since we are left to handle everything ourselves. Agnosticism then becomes *atheism* for those who are convinced about their doubts, and the genealogy of God from Calvinism to atheism is complete.

Jim Knowles, a Lutheran Pastor friend, and I were attending a large ecumenical gathering where the Reformed preacher in his keynote sermon went on and on about *how we are saved* by the Sovereignty of God. When it was over, I turned and looked at Jim who solemnly knitted his brow and said, "*No, I don't think so; the Sovereignty of God does not save us. We are saved by the Cross.*"

It was a quintessential commentary on the Lutheran/Reformed great divide.

Progress?

We rejoice in progress, and America celebrates progress as a hallmark of our place in history. There is progress in science. There is progress in medicine. There is progress in technology. There is progress in culture. There is progress in art, music and literature. There may even be progress in religion. But there is no such thing as *progress in faith*.

Faith must be born afresh in every new generation, in every believer, in the heart of every person who loves Christ, or it is not faith.

Many who have lost faith in an intervening God now believe in an intervening government. The difference is that God intervenes to enrich our lives with grace, while government intervenes to manage our lives with regulation and control. This is not progress.

The German American theologian Paul Tillich reflected late in his life about an encounter he had when he came to the United States in 1933. He had spoken to a meeting of theological students and expected strong disagreements to arise. He had criticized various prevailing ideas about God, Christ, the Holy Spirit, the church, sin and salvation—but the response was cordial, even ho-hum in its agreement, until he criticized the idea of progress. His listeners were dismayed and thrown askew. They said, *"In what then can we believe?"*

He had touched the raw nerve of a deeply held dogma in the American consciousness. This dogma, embedded in the culture, had in turn become a corruption of belief within the church. *Faith in Christ* had been replaced by a *faith in progress*. At a subconscious level, this means that Christ had been replaced by Prometheus.

How about a Donut?

Linda Bradley was a layperson from California who was a church administrator, active in her own parish and had served for years in many leadership positions. I was on a committee with her and she made one of the most perceptive theological comments I have ever heard. She remarked that most of the churches she knew were providing a *donut religion*: Attractive around the edges, but *nobody home* at the center. *We have a donut hole religion*, she said. She was dead-on brilliant in her judgment.

It is alluring to be involved with the busyness of churchianity—programs, events, administration, community, sociability, even worship done "just right." This is so easy because it involves things visible. But God is invisible. St. John reminds us *(John 1:18a)*:

> No one has ever seen God.

It is all too easy to center ourselves on *nothing* if we do not have a vivid life of faith and an active life of prayer eager to listen for the Lord. He always is there, calling and knocking on our door.

The prophet Isaiah spoke about this Donut Hole Church hundreds of years before there even was a church *(Isaiah 29:13)*:

> *These people . . . honor me with their lips, while their hearts are far from me . . .*

Jesus quotes this Isaiah text approvingly in both *Matthew 15:8* and *Mark 7:6*.

The Donut Hole Church is a busy place. It maintains the appearance of church, while its real agenda is striving to reform the world according to one or another political ideology. Sadly, I have seen many such places. Even more sadly, too many otherwise good people in the pews cannot tell the difference between a true loyalty to Christ and what is, at worst, a fraudulent spirituality. In the true church, the Gospel is preached, the sacraments are celebrated, and faithful hearts know very well that the Lord is home at the center.

The Culture Captivity of the Church

The irony in all this is that the Donut Hole Church reigns supreme in New England in those very churches that were established by those first religious refugees who settled the Plymouth Colony in 1620 and the Massachusetts Bay colony in 1629/1630. I know. I have served among them as pastor and have seen many more as a guest visitor. I have seen first hand the results of *the world* evangelizing the church instead of *the church* evangelizing the world.

This did not happen overnight, but rather in incremental stages like slow—growing toxic mold. Preaching the Gospel in New England is a tough call. It frequently is like sowing seeds on inhospitable ground, just as Jesus said in the *Parable of the sower (Luke 8:5–7)*.

This is the land where the great evangelist George Whitefield once preached. The church I served in Enfield, Massachusetts, hosted Whitefield in the 1740's. So many people came that the church had to remove its windows so that the overflow crowds outside could hear him. Later, when I served a number of congregations in New Hampshire as an Interim/Transition pastor, parishioners often lamented that their membership was so small. They were shocked when I mentioned that Vermont ranks #50 in the United States with the lowest percentage of people participating in church, with New Hampshire right behind as #49.

The dead hand of demographics is one factor. On the other hand, empty people living aimless lives are spiritually hungry. When a church has spent decades preaching romantic ideologies instead of the Gospel, people are not being fed.

As a measure of how far we have fallen, at most of the eight Interim pastor appointments during my second career, I regularly scheduled the *Battle Hymn of the Republic* for the closing hymn on Memorial Day weekend. At more of these parishes than I care to remember, I would have people come up to me afterward with tears in their eyes, saying, "*Oh thank you. We haven't been able to sing that for years because it was forbidden by our previous pastor for being not 'politically correct.'*"

And this hymn was written by Julia Ward Howe of Massachusetts, after meeting Abraham Lincoln at the start of the civil war! Moreover, the *Cambridge Platform* of 1649 defines the church on earth as the "church militant," in conflict with its enemies.

The prophet Ezekiel says this (*Ezekiel 34:2b,3b*):

> *Thus says the Lord God: Ah, you shepherds of Israel who have been feeding yourselves! . . . you do not feed the sheep.*

Christ and Culture

The church today in much of secularized Europe seems eviscerated. By contrast, the church in the United States seems like a patchwork quilt torn in the middle by schism between traditional denominations on the one side, and newly energized evangelical voices on the other. These new alternatives offer hope and promise where familiar churches have failed.

In my own career, too many of the churches I have served display an insidious corruption in which the Gospel is given lip service as Isaiah said, but where the driving message is one or another social or political ideology. Among those who have succumbed to this infection, there is a prevailing blindness to their compromised state which makes their enfeebled condition almost impossible to challenge or reverse. The voice of Christ is lost in the culture—compromised church.

The truth of the ages applies especially today: *Christian faith is a deviant voice in a pagan culture.* When we lose that perspective, all is lost.

The fact is that American society today is moving toward becoming once again like the culture of pagan Rome, where Christians were thrown before wild beasts to be torn apart for sport in front of cheering crowds. In this kind of environment the only "safe" Christians will be those whose churches are so compromised by the world that they pose no threat.

The Forbidden "E" Word

In too many churches today the word *evangelism* is so feared that it is forbidden to be mentioned in polite company, and especially from the pulpit.

I was attending the retirement party for Sr. Margo, a friend at a neighboring Roman Catholic parish. She had spent her entire adult lifetime in Religious Education for children and young adults. We were sitting together at a large banquet table in her parish hall and she quietly conveyed a telling perspective. She said, *"The trouble with us is that we sacramentalize before we catechize, and we catechize before we evangelize."*

She was speaking about the familiar pattern where too many children go through elaborate First Communion ceremonies and are never seen in church again except for a wedding or a funeral (often their own). She had accurately belled the cat.

She may also have been conveying a wistful but hidden envy about how Protestants do such a great job of bringing their people to Christ. I quickly said to her, *Margo, I hope you don't think that this is a uniquely Roman Catholic problem. I have seen endless scores of people in Reformed churches who cannot tell the difference between being a good citizen or being a Christian, and where the "E word" is never spoken.* It is an almost intractable problem for all of us.

Organize Something New?

If reforming the church into a place that truly *changes lives* is so intractable, why not start up a new one? A conventional wisdom in church circles says, *It is easier to start a new church than to reform an old one.* The quick conclusion to want to start something new is popular today, but it avoids the ancient dilemma of *schism*. The long challenge here is the question of sin: *Which is the greater offense? Schism or heresy?*

The difficult answer points to *schism* as the *worse sin*: Schism freezes the situation into unrelated channels that can go on for centuries, with neither party ever speaking again to the other. Heresy, on the other hand, however flagrant or stupid, always admits the possibility of repentance or reconciliation because the conversation continues.

More than that, schismatic communities that base their identity on a *No* to someone else's *Yes* are more likely to fade away in time because their foundation is negative.

Replacements for Scripture

When I was in Brooklyn in the 1960's, there was a "progressive" parish in Manhattan that tried to break new ground with "relevant worship" to fit the day. It was part of a long-standing mainline denomination and should have known better. But this was New York.

Along with the Pastor dancing in leotards to illustrate his sermons, he introduced the practice of including three Lessons to be read as part of the liturgy: The *Old Testament*, The *New Testament*, and the *Now Testament*. The latter was either a piece of poetry or a snippet from a philosophical essay, an item from secular literature, lines from a Broadway play, a news item or an editorial from the New York Times or the Village Voice.

It was cute but blasphemous. Once you elevate a secular source to the same status as holy scripture, you entirely undermine the authority of the canon that defines the church. The practice caught on and spread to other denominations where local taste seemed impelled to prove itself as "with it."

Quite some years later I was at a clergy meeting where the banter led someone to suggest that we publish a compendium of "readings" as an alternative to the Bible. As the conversation went on, someone proposed that we replace the Old Testament with *The Prophet* by Kahlil Gibran and the New Testament with *Jonathan Livingston Seagull*. Then if we wanted to publish a deluxe version, we could join them together in a leather-bound edition with gilt-edged pages and the words of Jonathan in red.

An immediate moment of telling silence took hold, and was instantly followed by muffled snickering around the circle as the serious nature of what we were joking about became embarrassedly evident. We quickly moved on to other things. Humor can masque, and then reveal, truth.

Scripture Misused

A much more widespread practice commonly goes on that amounts to the same undoing of canonical authority, even by otherwise serious Christians who seem blind to what they are doing.

This is the use of scripture as *illustration* instead of as *source*. It goes something like this: Old Pastor Jack sits back in his study, drawing on his pipe and ruminating over what *Great Thought* he wants to preach about on Sunday. This is the typical basis for what commonly is called "topical preaching"—for example, a sermon on *Making Modern Marriage More Meaningful*.

After he hits upon his topic and perhaps a catchy title, he sets about working on a manuscript or making notes for what he wants to say. Somewhere near the end of this process he flips through the Bible to find passages that illustrate his point.

The *source* here is not scripture, but the Pastor's own imagination. Many preachers do this constantly, while their congregations entirely miss seeing the difference between this and authentic biblical preaching. If that is what you do, you might just as well illustrate your points with poetry as with scripture—because in either case *the source* is your own speculation instead of the Word of God.

Lectionary preaching reverses these functions of *source* and *illustration*. The Lectionary provides *the source* for the day. Once *you are given the text*, you have to wrestle with it whether you like it or not—and some events in scripture are not easy to deal with. Otherwise, how many times a year are we going to preach on *the Beatitudes* because the people like it and their eyes can glaze over in bliss.

Insipid Worship

One of the big buzz words today is the notion of "creative worship." I suppose this means that whoever uses time-tested forms and patterns is guilty of "uncreative worship" or at worst, of being boring.

This often means substituting liturgical twaddle for the Psalms, alternate poetry to replace the Gospels, rewriting familiar hymns to fit the language conventions of the day, writing new texts that are either cheerleading for fashionable social issues or psychological testimonies to narcissism, new music that has the quality of advertising jingles, new "art forms" that are either infantile or tacky, and praise bands where nobody sings but the bandleader, since nobody in the pews can read music or wants to sing because they are accustomed by the culture to being entertained by the TV or by a mobile device.

The *culture captivity of the church* comes in many forms, some amusing, some offensive. We sometimes hear newly "creative" words like *Godself* and other language oddities, or hymns that border on blasphemy because they stray so far from the theology of scripture.

For Example

Try this for a scrubbed-up rendering of *Genesis 22:8*, where Abraham is being tested:

> Abraham said, "God Godself will provide the lamb
> for a burnt offering, my son."

Such fig-leaf covering is not only laughable; it wrecks our language, cripples our prayer, and leaves our spiritual life impoverished.

More subtle than this are new texts that shift the focus of attention from the Lord to self-absorbed people singing about their own needs and accomplishments. For example, one of the most time-honored hymns of praise, by Thomas Ken (*1637–1711*), begins:

> *Praise God from whom all blessings flow . . .*

In the mood of our times, the language for this hymn—if it were being being written today—would more likely resemble:

> *O look how we are praising God . . .*

Who is the real center of attention here?

Form is the Foundation

Form is the foundation of all reality. Form is like the structural steel framework of a building around which the concrete is poured. Form was the means that the ancient Romans relied on when they figured out how to pile stones and bricks in such a way that would create an arch to support an aqueduct and therefore transport water for miles to nourish a city. Many of these still stand today after more than 2000 years.

In grade school we had a year long course in Pennsylvania history. The point was stressed that we were known as the *Keystone State* because, like the keystone at the center of a Roman arch, it stood in the center of the 13 colonies and held together the nascent nation about to be born.

The Form of God is Order

The Book of Genesis begins with *form* as the order of God (*Genesis 1:2*):

> *In the beginning . . . the earth was a formless void . . .*

This formless void was then given shape and form by the power of God, by means of his breath, which *"swept over the face of the waters."*

The two operative words here, from the Greek, are *cosmos* and *chaos*. Chaos is formless disorder. Cosmos is harmony and order. *Cosmos* is God's order for this disorderly world.

These two primary terms reveal the intimate connection between mathematics and music since music (or sound of any kind) is created by vibration, and musical scales and harmony are based on mathematical multiples. An octave (meaning eight notes) is created when the frequency of the lower note is doubled to create the same note, higher in pitch, an octave above. It all proceeds from there.

God is, among his many other attributes, the Master Mathematician. His desire for Cosmos and harmony creates all things and brings us the music of the spheres.

Christ as the Form of God

At Christmas we celebrate the *Incarnation* of God in Christ Jesus. Christmas makes Easter possible, because the Incarnation makes the Passion possible. Here is how St. Paul speaks about *the form of Christ* in the Incarnation *(Philippians 2:6–7)*:

> *Who, though he was in the form of God,*
> *did not regard equality with God as something to be exploited,*
> *but emptied himself, taking the form of a slave,*
> *being born in human likeness.*

We see Jesus, born of Mary, in human form. He relinquished his divine form in order to take on our humanity, but in doing so, he did not relinquish his divine essence. This caused the multiplication of endless heresies in the early church, until the truth was sorted out at the Council of Chalcedon *(451)*.

Chalcedon defined the two natures of Christ *(fully human, fully divine)* in one single Person *(Jesus of Nazareth, known as the Christ, or Messiah)*. This understanding is what we have today in the classic creeds of the church *(Apostles' Creed, Nicene Creed, Athanasian Creed)*. *Fully human, fully divine* is entirely contrary to the pagan Greek notion that many of their deities were *half* human and *half* divine. This difference is huge.

Without this understanding, we get lost in dysfunctional confusions about the work and Person of Jesus. If he is merely human, then the

Passion is a sacrificial martyrdom that any zealous leader could (*maybe should?*) follow, a heroic model that perhaps inspires but does not have the power to save. If he is only divine, then the Passion is a sham without human suffering. If he is "two persons" in one body, then we enter the morbid absurdity of *multiple personality disorder*—a psychiatric affliction all too common in our day.

The possibility that these ancient heresies might be reintroduced is why the magisterial reformers (*Martin Luther, John Calvin, and others*) insisted on the orthodoxy of the first seven great ecumenical Councils, in addition to scripture, as the touchstone for faith.

The Lord Holy Spirit

We see the harmony of God in the perfect equilibrium of the Holy Trinity. The Trinity displays the community of the godhead, both in the distinctiveness of the three Persons and in their mutual indwelling. All earthly relationships either derive from this pattern with richness and grace or devolve from the Lord's model into corruption and cupidity.

Once during a break between speakers at a Social Justice conference I remember overhearing a side aisle conversation between an ardent Reformed pastor and a Greek Orthodox priest. The Reformed pastor asked the priest if his church had a social action program. "*Yes, of course we do.*" the Greek priest replied, "*It's called the Holy Trinity.*"

The Lord Holy Spirit is the entry point into this divine circle. Too many Christians miss this point. Some have commented that those first Puritans who ventured across the Atlantic in the early 1600's to settle the Massachusetts Bay Colony came with two and a half Persons of the Trinity, at most.

In an entirely different venue, I was attending a summer conference at the Franciscan University in Steubenville, Ohio, where one of the keynote speakers was the Rev. Tom Forrest. He was in his 80's at the time, still jet-setting around the world from one charismatic event to another.

He described a casual dinner table conversation he had the evening before with a fellow priest. He had been given home hospitality at a local rectory for the conference we were attending. He reported that he and his host got into a dialogue about charismatics. His host said, "*Well, you folks do a lot of good work, but I'm not sure about all that Holy Spirit stuff.*

It seems off the chart to me." Fr. Forrest replied, *"Well then, I guess you believe in the Holy Duet."*

A Person, or an "It?"

It is sad to note that many otherwise faithful Christians today still do not comprehend the simple truth that *the Holy Spirit is a person*, not an "it."

In his *Farewell Discourse* the night before he died, Jesus is explicit about the work of the Holy Spirit. He also makes it clear that the Holy Spirit is a person, not "the great undifferentiated whoosh." (John 14:16–18):

> *I will ask the Father, and he will give you another Advocate, to be with you forever. This is the Spirit of truth, whom the world cannot receive, because it neither sees him nor knows him. You know him, because he abides with you, and he will be in you. I will not leave you orphaned . . .*

And (John 16:7,13–15):

> *I tell you the truth: it is to your advantage that I go away, for if I do not go away, the Advocate will not come to you . . . When the Spirit of truth comes, he will guide you into all the truth: for he will not speak on his own, but will speak whatever he hears, and he will declare to you the things that are to come. He will glorify me, because he will take what is mine and declare it to you . . .*

"Advocate" means both helper and defender. In 1984 in Chicago, when my spirit was broken and my life was at the bottom of the barrel, the Lord Holy Spirit was my Evangelist without any human intervention. It took me years to digest the truth that this was my primary conversion.

Years later, when he trusted me more, I saw the Lord Holy Spirit in a dream. He appeared as a humble and ordinary looking fellow, attired in a plain white alb (*the baptismal garment of the apostolic church*). He simply said to me, with a slow and welcoming sweep of his hand, *"Come; I'll show you The Way . . ."*

The Way, of course, is Christ. He is *the way* to the Father. Before all this, I had read a lot about Jesus and said a lot about Jesus, but I did not really <u>know</u> Jesus. It is the Lord Holy Spirit who opens that door. Then, when you come to know Jesus, the Son will introduce you to the Father. Thanks be to God.

Form Does Matter

Everything in this mortal universe has a form that contains its essence, or a shape that conveys its character. We commonly hear, "*Oh, form doesn't matter. It is only the substance that counts.*" That is only half true. When something is half true, the other half is a lie.

Form does matter. For example, none of us can survive without sufficient water to keep our systems hydrated. But if we have no container, it is very difficult to drink our necessary water for the day only by cupping our hands under the tap. Most of it slips through our fingers. The cup is the *form* that holds the *substance* (in this case, *water*).

A particular substance demands the proper form to give it power and significance. It would be difficult if not impossible to serve hot coffee in one of those small thin triangular paper cups you find at the office water cooler.

You could drink a fine vintage wine from a styrofoam cup, but it would be an oddity at best and an offense at worst. A swig of sneaky pete worthy of a brown paper bag underneath the Third Street Bridge, but served in an elegant crystal chalice is a shock to the system.

The finest preparation by a gourmet chef served on a dirty plate that never made it through the dishwasher is totally unacceptable. These things are all the more true for the worship of the church.

The architecture of the space in which you worship matters. You can gather for worship in a pool hall or a cluttered garage if that is all you can find to keep out of the rain, but that is entirely different from space specifically designed for the adoration of the one true God.

Unusual Worship Space

Some years ago I was asked to do a funeral for a young man who had died in a boating accident. His family were not church members but they were closely related to another family in my parish. Had I refused their request I would have done damage to the pastoral relationship between me, the church, and the family who were my parishioners.

The service was to be held on a Saturday about noon at the yacht club where the deceased had docked his boat and where he had spent many devoted hours of his life. When I arrived, I discovered that we were to meet in the club's tavern. His friends had already gathered and were raucous and mildly drunk from having already spent the morning clustered around the bar reminiscing about their friend, his boating adventures and theirs, in an informally assembled makeshift wake.

The lounge area surrounding the bar was narrow and cramped, with small square tables casually scattered about. An undecorated grey colored box with the ashes of the deceased was sitting on one of these tables in the corner. With help from a few others we moved some of the lounge tables to clear an open space, shifted one table forward as a centerpiece, placed the box of cremains on it and covered it with a white table napkin. The guys moving the tables were friendly and cooperative but seemed clueless and confused about what we were doing. I had never met any of them before and I presumed that most or all of them were completely unchurched.

In a corner of the lounge I put on my alb and stole and then stepped forward into the open space by the table where the cremains had been placed. Most of the folks were still chattering on in a party atmosphere, crowded around the bar or sitting at tables, oblivious to my presence.

I opened my prayerbook and raised one hand in an open gesture of welcome and said, fairly loudly over the din of the crowd, *The Lord be with you*. About half the folks who had seen me move to the table quickly mumbled, *And also with you*, indicating that they did have some residual memory of church practice. Then I said, *Let us pray*, and everyone finally stopped their chatter and stood up, figuring that something else was now going on besides their party time. So we moved along and did what was required to honor the dead with the grace of the Lord.

The Shape of Worship Itself Matters

We had introduced the shape of worship into an alien space. The *form of worship* itself convenes the presence of God. Even the unchurched knew that something different from the ordinary was happening and even a distant memory of a familiar pattern brought a ring of truth.

Familiarity may breed contempt but it also is the wellspring of comfort. Familiarity can breed contempt when you take unfair advantage of things to which familiarity offers access. We call that pornography.

Familiarity and habit are necessary to life. To give a trivial example: What would it be like if you had to learn anew every morning how to tie your shoelaces? Or to learn all over again how to drive a car every time you stepped behind the wheel?

Novelty

The *power of the liturgy* rests on the bedrock of familiarity. Familiarity is the lifeblood of intimacy, tranquility, comfort and consolation. What would it be like to come home every evening and find all the furniture in the house rearranged?

Something like that happens when you arrive for worship each week and are confronted yet again by another novelty. If you constantly try to reword or replace the Lord's Prayer, its meaning and power soon are lost and no new version or replacement means much of anything either. How about something different to replace the communion elements every time we celebrate the Eucharist? Beer and potato chips, maybe? Then what—next time? After all, we are told it should be "creative" and "relevant."

The Power of the Familiar

We know the truth about the power of the familiar at the ball park when Harry Caray leads a packed crowd in singing *Take Me Out to the Ball Game* for the Chicago Cubs at Wrigley Field. Or when the Boston Pops concert at the Hatch Shell on the 4th of July ends with *Stars and Stripes Forever*. Why should it be any different at church for anchor points in the liturgy?

Familiar worship forms are *sacramental*. They are outward and visible signs of an inward and invisible grace. The human Jesus himself is *the sacrament of God*. He is the visible <u>form</u> of God on earth. In *John 14:9* he tells his disciple Philip:

> *Whoever has seen me has seen the Father.*

Familiarity is also *the gateway to revelation* when new truth bursts out from familiar sources. Everyone who reads scripture knows this. You can read—or hear read—a particular passage of scripture 127 times, but all of a sudden when you come upon it for the 128th time it releases a thunderclap that changes your life when God speaks directly to you through it.

When those enthralled with novelty are driven to tinker constantly with either the content or the sequence of the liturgy, everyone loses. And when the church fails to feed its people, it is a lot easier to stay at home and sit up in bed with your morning coffee and read the Sunday paper.

Recover Your Anchor Points

Become familiar with scripture and the Lord will speak to you through it. The only way to do this is actually <u>to read it</u>. *Surprise*! And use a real Bible. Don't try to read scripture on a mobile device. You need to be able to turn a real page and turn it back again when something grabs you. You will find yourself drawn back again and again to those passages and events that have spoken to you with power. These in turn will lead you to new riches in other texts that you have yet to uncover.

But you have to *make friends with scripture* if you want it to lead you through life's struggles and companion you through life's complexities.

I am continually dismayed when I see faithful members who have been around the church for years and yet do not know who the significant players are from Jacob to Jeremiah, or Joshua to James. Or who have no grasp of the whole sweep of Salvation History from Genesis to Revelation.

The point of these benchmarks is to guide us through the process of receiving our own salvation in life-changing ways.

Also become familiar with the basic patterns of the liturgy. This will edify beyond measure both your private prayer and your part in public worship.

Jack Hayford has been a major Pentecostal leader for decades. Pentecostals are known for having a free-flowing style of worship that seemingly has no structure to it. I remember a comment that Pastor Jack made during a conference I once attended. He said, *Don't say that you have no liturgy. Every church has a liturgy, whether you acknowledge it or not* . . . He then went on to detail the pattern he follows at his own church in California.

Unfortunately I have seen too many churches where the basic patterns of the liturgy handed down to us through the ages are either missing altogether or so confused and conflated that our spiritual lives are lost in the wilderness, and the life-giving connections we have with Christians in all places and times are severed.

For example, a Roman Catholic or a Lutheran or an Eastern Orthodox Christian who goes to a church in another country where worship is in a foreign language is not lost when the pattern of the liturgy is familiar. But if preaching is all there is, you won't get much out of it when the language is in an unfamiliar tongue.

Two Forms of Worship

The bedrock outlines of the liturgy are not complicated at all, despite the many variations that have evolved over the centuries. Essentially, the Christian liturgy has developed along *two separate tracks*, and both are wellsprings of grace that should not be mistaken one for the other.

The one is called the *Daily Office* and the other is the *Eucharist*. Both derive from centuries of Jewish practice, as do all things pertinent to Christian faith. The Daily Office of the Church derives from the Daily Prayer of the synagogue, while the Eucharist derives from the sacrificial offerings at the Temple in Jerusalem.

A small sign of this distinction is the common practice over the centuries of *standing* for the singing of the Psalms at Morning Prayer while remaining *seated* for the scripture lessons, but remaining *seated* for the Psalm at the Eucharist while *standing* for the reading of the Gospel.

In Chicago we lived in a modern four story condominium building made up of stacked townhouses, two stories each. All the units were connected by an outdoor elevated catwalk in an enclosed garden area, so it was easy to see the comings and goings of your neighbors across the interior courtyard since all the front doors faced inward (*This also meant lower condominium fees by not having to heat any inside hallways*).

One of our neighbors was a local rabbi, and I would often see him leaving home in the morning just before 8 AM and then leaving home again around 5 PM. We talked about this, and he said that he was stepping out regularly for Morning and Evening Prayer at his synagogue a block down the street. He also explained that weekly Sabbath prayer was not unique in itself, but is essentially an extension of Daily Prayer.

The same is true for the *Morning Prayer* of the Church, in cases where an elaboration of the Daily Office is used as the basis for Sunday worship. It all derives from the synagogue.

The Eucharist, on the other hand, derives from the Last Supper of Christ with his disciples the night before he died, which the early church quickly developed into *a Resurrection Feast*, not a funeral/memorial for remembering a dead Jesus.

Traditionally, small pieces of lamb from the Passover sacrifice at the Temple were given to pilgrims who gathered in Jerusalem for their own Passover meals in small quarters. This lamb would have been available in the Upper Room. John the Baptist speaks of his cousin Jesus as (*John 1:29*):

the lamb of God who takes away the sin of the world.

Sacred Space

Back in Toronto, a rabbi in our local clergy group gave us a tour of his sanctuary during our regular monthly meeting. The building was strikingly modern but was based on the design of the medieval Spanish synagogue. He pointed out the strong parallels between the arrangement of his worship space and that of a traditional Oratory in a Benedictine monastery.

The seating in his synagogue did not face forward as it does in so many churches, but was arranged in two equal but separate banks of rows facing directly toward each other across a large centre aisle as do the pews at a monastery. This is to enhance the responsive singing of the Psalms. The tabernacle for the Eucharistic elements is based on the tabernacle for the Torah scrolls at the synagogue.

In his practice, the Torah scrolls are taken from the tabernacle at one end to be opened and read from a lectern at the other end. They are carried down the centre aisle in a festive procession between the two banks of facing seats. This resembles the procession of the Communion elements down the centre aisle between the facing pews in a monastic setting. The elements are taken from the Offertory table at one end to the altar at the other end for the celebration of the Eucharist. The church did not invent something new. We follow the pattern God gave to Israel.

The Two Outlines

The bare bones outline for the Daily Office is simple, although it usually is elaborated greatly for Sunday morning worship. The same is true for the Eucharist.

The basic structure of the Daily Office is threefold, and consists of (1) *Psalms*, (2) scripture *Lessons*, and (3) closing *prayer*.

Follow this simple pattern at home for your own daily prayer and you will be on solid ground. Moreover, this will bring you solidarity with millions of other Christians around the world and down through the ages.

The basic structure of the Eucharist has two major parts: (1) the Service of the *Word*, and (2) the Celebration of the *Sacrament*. This second section itself includes four separate steps, often called *the four–fold action* of the Eucharist: (A) *taking*, (B) *blessing*, (C) *breaking*, and (D) *giving*. This is based on the ancient rabbinical practice of using a piece of bread from the table to bless any meal.

Jesus demonstrates this at the Last Supper in *Matthew 26:26*. He is, after all, our Chief Rabbi ("rabbi" means *teacher*). In the Upper Room, he (1) takes the bread, (2) blesses it, (3) breaks it, and (4) gives it to the disciples to eat.

This rabbinical pattern is modeled by Jesus a number of times in all four Gospels, such as in the feeding of the five thousand, the four thousand, and the revealing of his Risen self to Cleopas and his companion on the Road to Emmaus (*Luke 24:30*) on Easter evening.

Step number one—the *taking*—is the basis for the *Offertory*. The offering is not "a collection" like passing the hat to share the cost of pizza while watching the game on TV. The *Offertory of the Church* is not money. It is the Communion elements to be blessed at the altar.

Step number two—the *blessing*—is a longer section at the Lord's Table. It is designed to be a brief narrative of Salvation History, including the Words of Institution (*This is my Body . . . This is my Blood . . .*).

Step number three is the *breaking*, which follows the blessing. This classically is called the *Fraction*, and is enhanced in the Book of Common Prayer by the declaration of St. Paul *(I Corinthians 5:7,8)*:

> *Christ our Passover is sacrificed for us. Therefore let us keep the feast.*

Step number four—the *giving*—is the distribution of Communion.

Keep these simple patterns in mind and they will edify both your own private prayer and your participation in the assembly of God's people for public worship. They will enrich your faith and reconnect you with Christ.

A Spiritual Clock

The Daily Office has three major occasions: Morning Prayer or *Matins*, Evening Prayer or *Vespers*, and Night Prayer or *Compline*. In a monastic community, these are expanded to six or seven times of prayer to punctuate the day, according to the traditional Benedictine pattern.

Each of these prayer times served as a "holy coffee break" in the chapel to provide relief from farm work in the field or from tending the sheep or from caring for the sick in the monastery infirmary. They structured the day like a spiritual clock.

The rhythm of the Christian day follows the Hebrew pattern in which the day begins at sunset. So the first Office of the day would be

Vespers, about 5:00 or 5:30 PM, before the evening meal. Compline would be around 8:00 or 8:30 P.M. before bedtime, and Matins would be at sunrise before breakfast.

Our Daily Dying

In Christian spirituality, the occasion of sleep is *a daily dying* that signifies the death and burial of Christ, and Matins is a sign of the Resurrection to new life. In the Book of Common Prayer, Compline begins with this one line prayer:

The Lord Almighty grant us a peaceful night and a perfect end.
Amen.

Read "*a perfect end*" to mean a perfect death, and a perfect reception into the everlasting care of God. Following Compline, in a monastic setting a Rule of Silence is kept until these responsive opening lines at Matins from Psalm 51:15:

Lord, open our lips.
And our mouth shall proclaim your praise.

A Pastor friend many years ago told me that several times a year he would arrange to take a small group from his parish on a three day retreat at a nearby Benedictine monastery. They would arrive before Vespers, share an evening meal, and then have a brief orientation session before Compline.

After Compline they would retire for the night, and each person would find a pencil and blank writing tablet in their room. The instruction for this first spiritual exercise of the retreat was to write out your own obituary. Many would find this too intimidating to undertake.

Death is the prelude to new life. St. Paul tells us, speaking of our salvation in Christ Jesus (*II Timothy 2:11*):

The saying is sure:
If we have died with him, we will also live with him.

If we die daily with Christ, then each new morning is a fresh beginning and a pristine adventure. If you do not let the Old Self go and let it die, the New Self cannot be born.

Prometheus Failed

Prometheus Bound became a robust *Prometheus Unbound* by the end of the nineteenth century, as the result of three hundred years of the Enlightenment. Once liberated by Hercules, *Prometheus Unbound* became a heroic emblem to banish religion as superstition and deliver us into a new world order based on the *Rule of Reason* in place of Christian faith.

By his stealing the fire of heaven, the wisdom of God is transformed into the *Wisdom of Man*. Universal peace and harmony, based on communication, education, democracy and prosperity for all, replaces Christian hope—with Prometheus replacing Christ as the object of devotion.

Then Prometheus died. He was asphyxiated by the mustard gas of World War I, dismembered by the Great Depression, and buried in the potter's field of the Nazi holocaust.

Prometheus Unbound became *Prometheus Failed*. After this, bewildered people cast about looking for other strange gods and New Age enticements or relied on nothing but themselves.

Prometheus Failed is the *Perkin Warbeck* of our time, a figure driven by futile fantasies and empty aspirations. Pray to be delivered from such things.

Mary Shelley's Frankenstein

As a youngster, the horrors of the Frankenstein movies both thrilled and terrified my generation. We would mock scare one another by imitating the monster's awkward and animated gait. We would compare notes on the Boris Karloff and Lon Chaney versions. By play–acting we would masque the underlying darkness and render it tamed and domesticated.

Then in high school and college literature we met the elegant poetry of Percy Bysshe Shelley, but nobody ever mentioned his wife Mary.

It was only later in life that I chased down her novel about Dr. Frankenstein and discovered a spiritual treasure beyond compare. The first and obvious learning, naturally, was to discover that as children we had confused the name of the flawed and fickle scientist who created this monster with the monster itself, who had no name. Or maybe Hollywood had confused the matter for us.

Percy had written *Prometheus Unbound*, and was part of a lofty circle of intellectual Humanists who believed that the dawn of a new humanity had come, where thoughts of God were rendered unnecessary because we humans had acquired divine wisdom through advances in science, rationalism, and poetic imagination. With such new powers, who needed God?

The full title of Mary's novel is *Frankenstein, Or, the Modern Prometheus*. She nailed it. In her own original 1817 preface to the novel she eschews "any philosophical doctrine of whatever kind," a soft and polite demurral, certainly seeking to maintain harmony with her husband and his friends. Percy in fact enthusiastically encouraged her writing project. That said, the fact remains that her book is a stunning rebuke to Percy's wild hopes and vain imaginations of Promethean romantic thought.

The antihero of her story is Victor Frankenstein, the uncanny scientist who becomes the modern Prometheus by creating a human–like creature in his laboratory and bringing it to life. The monster is Dr. Frankenstein's Adam, but without a name. The monster never receives a name, though along the way, despite the hideous deformity of his wretched features, the monster demonstrates a wisdom and eloquence beyond any that his creator ever displays. At this early point in the story, the monster is the hero, whose sagacious wisdom puts to shame the flamboyant and foolish motivations of his maker.

The crux of the tale is that the monster desires a female companion of his own, because human rejection has driven him from society into an anguished isolation. He bargains with his creator to make him a mate. Victor Frankenstein agrees, reluctantly, and then reneges on his promise. The monster descends into inconsolable grief and despair, and out of his tortured loneliness he seeks a murderous revenge on Victor's family and friends. It all goes downhill from there.

Victor Frankenstein is the failed would–be god who creates his own Adam without an Eve, and then rejects him out of fear for what he has created. Mary Shelley fatally punctures the deadly ambitions of Promethean piety. Who better than a female author to portray the foundational distinction between birthing a human offspring and manufacturing a faux human in a laboratory, with all of the ominous consequences that playing God can bring? What if the monster did receive a consort? What if they had then procreated a whole race of monsters to rival humankind? Victor's darkest fear was also his moment of truth.

Whether she intended to or not, what Mary Shelley wrote is a magnificent Christian witness by way of portraying its darkest alternative: *trying to replace God* by thinking we can imitate him.

After Prometheus, Then What?

Prometheus represents the heroic striving of humanity to define itself. As Western culture became more secularized, Christ was banished from public discourse and Prometheus reigned for a time as the triumph of humanity without God. However, in a secular society all gods are suspect. Prometheus has now died the discredited death of failed promises. So what now remains?

With nothing left to claim our devotion, we devolve into the worship of our own pursuits. Modern culture is filled with those who live for nothing but Self. This is an ominous echo from the closing line of the Book of Judges *(Judges 21:25)*:

> *In those days there was no king in Israel; all the people did what was right in their own eyes.*

With nothing to worship but our own ambition, we no longer know light from darkness. Society becomes more and more coarse, carnal, vulgar and narcissistic.

Today, the question on many peoples' lips is not *"What must I do to be saved."* It is *"What must I do to be satisfied."*

Remember that Donut Hole Church? Now, so goes the culture. No longer can we say, "the center does not hold . . ." because there is no center. Even the dissident is lost. With nobody home at the center, there is no one to kick against. When anarchy takes hold, society fragments like splintered glass.

American culture did once have a defining center. Long before this new land became a nation, the Pilgrim founders at Plymouth (*1620*) and the Puritans at Massachusetts Bay (*1629/30*) had a vision for this land as a new Israel in Covenant with God. The Lord was at the center of all they did. This carried over to the founding fathers who signed the Declaration of Independence in 1776, blessing this nation in his holy Name.

This did not mean that everybody was a professing Christian. A free and open society always permits a variety of loyalties, so long as this does not include terrorism by some against those with whom they disagree. A defining center does not contradict peaceful alternatives. It provides a necessary order against anarchy.

We stand in need of revival. Revival begins in the deep recesses of the converted heart. That is how the apostolic church converted pagan Rome 2000 years ago. Revival comes when the Lord moves.

There Always is Hope

In the economy of God's grace, the Lord always finds a saving remnant, no matter how far the church has fallen and the culture has strayed. St. Paul tells us this (*Romans 9:27,29*):

> *And Isaiah cries out concerning Israel, "Though the number of the children of Israel were like the sand of the sea, only a remnant of them will be saved . . .*
>
> *And as Isaiah predicted,*
> *"If the Lord of hosts had not left survivors to us,*
> *we would have fared like Sodom*
> *and been made like Gomorrah."*

The Lord changes everything. He uses the most unlikely sources to bring forth Christ. I have learned not to disparage the small church. It can be part of the "saving remnant," so long as the Gospel is preached, the sacraments are served, and the faith is kept.

Authority

Authority is the bedrock question that undergirds faith. The question is not new. When the Roman centurion sought healing for his paralyzed servant, he approached Jesus and said (*Matthew 8:8b,9a,10,13*):

> *Only speak the word, and my servant will be healed. For I also am a man under authority, with soldiers under me . . .*
> *When Jesus heard him, he was amazed and said to those who followed him,"Truly I tell you, in no one in Israel have I found such faith."*
> *And to the centurion Jesus said, "Go; let it be done for you according to your faith." And the servant was healed in that hour.*

We live in a time when Prometheus has died and Christ has been banished from the public square. In addition, the voice of Christ is now curtailed even in the culture-captive church, so in whom do we trust? In whom or in what do we have faith? What about you? What ballast sustains your life?

When Moses had died and after Israel had successfully settled in the Promised Land, Joshua led them in a recovenanting ceremony. He challenged them directly (*Joshua 24:15,24–25*):

> "Now if you are unwilling to serve the Lord, choose this day whom you will serve, whether the gods your ancestors served in the region beyond the river or the gods of the Amorites in whose land you are living; but as for me and my household, we will serve the Lord."
>
> The people said to Joshua, "The Lord our God we will serve, and him we will obey." So Joshua made a covenant with the people that day, and made statutes and ordinances for them at Shechem.

Our Covenant with God stands always in need of renewal, as a nation and as a church and in the heart of every believer. This is because we humans stray—like cats. But some do find their way home again, in due time.

The Peace of Christ

St. Augustine in his *Confessions* says, *Our hearts are restless until they find their rest in you.*

The night before Jesus died, as part of his *Farewell Discourse*, our Lord tells us *(John 14:27)*:

> Peace I leave with you; my peace I give to you. I do not give to you
> as the world gives.

As I look back on my adult career and calling, I spent the first 25 years wrestling with Jacob. Then I spent 10 years in rehab. After that I spent 15 more years getting my bearings.

When my life was dark, the Lord gave me this Psalm. I commend it to you *(Psalm 34:4–8)*:

> I sought the Lord, and he answered me,
> and delivered me from all my fears.
> Look to him, and be radiant;
> so your faces shall never be ashamed.
> This poor soul cried, and was heard by the Lord,
> and was saved from every trouble.
> The angel of the Lord encamps around those who fear him,
> and delivers them.
> O taste and see that the Lord is good;
> happy are those who take refuge in him.

We live in an impatient age. We put the ATM card into the teller machine and out comes the money—*now*. Life is not like that. Conversion and blessing and new life take time to gestate. Whoever you are, whatever your circumstance, there is a promise of glory in store for you.

The Lord is the Promise Keeper. His Covenant love abides. Rely on that.

Postscript

I pray that no one is offended by what I have written. My intent is to explore and hopefully to edify.

From time to time over the years both enemies and friends have called me "Mr. Blunt." Where I am blunt it is for the sake of clarity. Pray for me.

A good friend and Franciscan priest in Toronto once said to me:

I'd rather offend the people than offend God.

I concur.

—*Duke T. Gray*

About the Author

DUKE T. GRAY HAS been a settled parish pastor in Brooklyn, New York; upstate New York; Toronto, Ontario; Chicago, Illinois; and exurban Boston, Massachusetts. In addition, he has served as an interim (*consulting*) pastor for ten other congregations in crisis or transition. He currently serves the Community Church of Hudson, New Hampshire.

His wife Gloria was born in Guyana, South America, and is active in the Roman Catholic Charismatic Renewal. She has served as a lay evangelist in Africa and Eastern Europe, and also leads a home Bible study.

www.ingramcontent.com/pod-product-compliance
Lightning Source LLC
Chambersburg PA
CBHW070246230426

43664CB00014B/2423